# PUBLIC RELATIONS MANAGEMENT IN MEDIA AND JOURNALISM

# PUBLIC RELATIONS MANAGEMENT IN MEDIA AND JOURNALISM

Jagdish Vachani

KANISHKA PUBLISHERS, DISTRIBUTORS
NEW DELHI-110 002

**KANISHKA PUBLISHERS, DISTRIBUTORS**
4697/5-21A, Ansari Road, Daryaganj
New Delhi -110 002
Phones : 2327 0497, 2328 8285
Fax : 011-2328 8285
E-mail : kanishka_publishing@yahoo.co.in

*Public Relations Management in Media and Journalism*
First Published-2007
Edition-**2017**

ISBN: 978-81-7391-903-8

PRINTED IN INDIA

Published by Madan Sachdeva for Kanishka Publishers, Distributors, 4697/5-21A, Ansari Road, Daryaganj, New Delhi-110 002, Typeset by Sunshine Graphics, Delhi, and Printed at Rajdhani Printers, Delhi.

# Preface

This book entitled "Public Relations Management in Media and Journalism" deals with the subject in its totality. Understanding of PR management in media and journalism helps the media agencies to adapt mutually with it publics and readers. Today, public relations has emerged as a planned and sustained effort to establish and maintain goodwill and mutual understanding between a media organization and its publics. Primarily, the publics are target audiences which include employees, members, customers, local communities, shareholders, national/state/local government officials with society at large. PR strategy for media and journalism focuses mainly on a recipe for developing a successful action plan to reach the objective of creating a better understanding and more awareness of the said company. It needs to be reiterated here that like any good business plan, key components of this PR strategy include research, identification of defined target audiences, key messages, measurable objectives, tactics and evaluation. Also, it should be clear that to get the best results, media PR agencies must create strategies that are measurable so that they can be properly evaluated. Besides, PR agencies in media and journalism should also conduct proper marketing research including communication audits, surveys of customers and industry competitors, private interviews with key customers and other audiences, focus groups with a cross-section of related key audiences and via the internet or world-wide web with online marketing research tools. Such marketing research will help define the key messages and help identify the best method for reaching out the key audiences.

This book provides readers with a detailed introductory account of role of public relations in media and journalism and its integral synthesis in long run. It also deals briefly with the origin and growth of public relations in media and journalism. Various case studies have been provided, including those of public relations specialists and managements companies. An overview of trends and practices involved in public and media relations management is presented. The focus here lies on the various management functions and the role of PR in improving it. Recent trends on public relations management in India, including its relationship with advertising, is discussed in detail. Methods of organizing a corporate public relations department is provided herein in detail. Similarly, all about media interviews is reflected upon in considerable length. Principles and ethics of professionalism in media and journalism has been given an indepth analysis, so has been the job/career prospects in public relations. Major guidelines and approaches of PR in media and journalism has been done along with case studies on related web-designing for maximizing press relations. Guidelines derived from usability studies with journalists have been dealt.

In sum, this book will suffice the modern day requirements as far as creating good public relation in the sector of media and journalism is concerned. It stresses on the importance of smooth and continuous two-way communication in growth and maturity of public relation in media and journals. Such integrational approaches need to be understood in proper perspective. The book is user-friendly and would definitely help develop a balanced perspective on the said subject.

**Jagdish Vachani**

# Contents

# Glossary of PR Terms

**ACE PR Value**

Unpaid for EDITORIAL has enhanced value as the reader/viewer sees it as being endorsed by the media in which it appears. The consumer views the piece through choice, and their attention to, and recall of the message is therefore considered to be greater than that paid to advertising. The industry agreed view, which reflects that difference, is that PR value is approximately 2.5 times greater than that achieved by ADVERTISING.

**Advertising**

The placing of a company's message, within various media on a paid-for basis, with the intention of widely 'advertising' that company's products or services.

Advertising is bringing a product (or service) to the attention of potential and current customers. Advertising is typically done with signs, brochures, commercials, direct mailings or e-mail messages, personal contact, etc.

The process of gaining the public's attention through paid media announcements.

**Advertising Cost Equivalent (ACE)**

The measurement of a piece of EDITORIAL and the comparison of those dimensions against published advertising rates. Puts a £'s value to PR.

**Advertorial**

A paid for feature that has the 'look and feel' of an EDITORIAL.

Some publications may write the copy, others may let you provide it.

The words 'promotion' or 'advertorial' on the article clearly identify it for the reader.

**Analyst**

An individual representing a trade or professional association who reviews and comments publicly on products, services and companies.

**Audit Bureau of Circulation (ABC)**

The Audit Bureau of Circulations provides an independent verification of CIRCULATION and data figures to facilitate the buying and selling of advertising space within National newspapers.

**Backgrounder**

An in-depth document that explains a product, service or company in the context of its need, place in the industry and place in history; often supports and explains an accompanying press release.

**Bio**

Biography (usually a brief synopsis of a person's credentials).

**Boilerplate**

Standard wording about a company that usually appears near the bottom of all company-issued press releases.

**Brad**

A data source on over 13,000 media entries across all sectors used for planning, buying and researching. Circulation and audience reach figures in each entry enable a comparison with other titles in the market. Also providing technical data about audited publications.

**Broadcasters Audience Research Board (BARB)**

A measurement service providing television audience data on a minute-by-minute basis for channels received within the UK. This data is available for reporting ITV and BBC nationally and regionally.

**B-roll**

Film or television footage that plays while an announcer speaks over it.

**Buzz**

Media and public attention given to a company, its products or services.

**Byline**

Name of the journalist or author of a piece of EDITORIAL, placed under the headline.

**Call Tree**

A list of names and contact information that should be notified immediately in a crisis.

**Circulation**

Circulation refers to the number of copies distributed by a Publication. Audited circulation figures are available for all major publications. Circulation should be clearly distinguished from readership (see IMPRESSIONS/IMPACTS, OTS and READERSHIP).

**Client List**

A list of a company's key clients; sometimes includes contact information.

**Collateral**

Secondary documents that accompany or support deliverables.

**Collateral PR**

The secondary effect whereby PR advantage is gained in other media by its coincidental relationship with the primary source.

**Column Inches**

An often-used measurement of PR success. A simple multiplication of the length of a piece of EDITORIAL times the number of columns.

**Communications Audit**

A systematic survey of members of a target audience (often members of the media or potential customers) to determine awareness of or reaction to a product, service or company.

**Competitor Analysis**

A measure of the success of a company's PR strategy in relation to their competitors', against a number of different measures.

**Composition**

The different components, in terms of the audience, that makes up/ composes a media's UNIVERSE. For example, 30.36 per cent of all of

'A Magazines' readers are within (compose) my TARGET AUDIENCE.

**Content**

Information.

**Copy**

Words printed in the press.

**Core Message**

More fundamental than a key message. Core messages are positioning words and phrases. They carry the subliminal thrust of an organisations intentions. For example, *...a quality product, well designed and widely available...* is a core message. PRESS RELEASES will contain the core message.

**Cost Per Thousand (CPT) (sometimes 'CPM', the 'M' being the Roman numeral for 1,000)**

A measure of value. It describes the cost of 1,000 advertising impressions.

For example, a campaign that achieves 750,000 impacts, with a £150,000 ACE value has a CPT of £5 (750,000 divided by £150,000).

**Coverage**

The coverage of a campaign is the total number of people within your TARGET AUDIENCE that may see your message. Sometimes referred to as 'REACH'. Most often expressed as a percentage, and the actual number together. For example, "this campaign will reach 10.71 per cent of my target audience which equates to 258,000 people."

**Crisis Management**

The crisis management is the handling of extraordinary events that best reflect a company's view while retaining politically correct relationships with the media.

**Demographics**

Data about the size and characteristics of a population or audience such as gender age, and income.

Often defined as socio-economic groups such as ABC1, generally upmarket, or C2DE, generally down market.

**Direct Mail**

Communication sent by post or e-mail to a targeted audience.

**Double Page Spread (DPS)**

Two pages of the same article running across the spine to create the visual impression of one continuous article.

**Duplication**

Where a person consumes more than one media. Someone who reads the Daily Mail may also read Hello! and Elle, for example. When calculating REACH and FREQUENCY, if the data is available, duplication is taken into account (see OVERLAP).

**Editorial**

An expression of opinion using text and images in a publication to make an article, feature, story or short 'piece'.

**Evaluation**

After you have implemented the tactics, review the results of your project. Ask yourself these four questions:

1. Did you meet your measurable objectives?
2. Did the story placed in the magazine emphasize your key messages?
3. Did the story appear in a magazine your audience reads?
4. Do your key target audiences have a better understanding of your company?

After you have reviewed the results of your programme, make adjustments to your strategy and objectives and continue implementing your revised strategy.

**Executive Summary**

A concise document, normally on one side of an A4, highlighting key research findings for busy people.

**E-zine**

Online newsletter or magazine.

**Fact Sheet**

A short (generally one-page) document that provides a "snapshot" look at a company, product or service.

**Feature**

An article that goes into greater detail as opposed to spot reporting.

**Follow-on**

A product, service or article, for instance, that results directly from a previous product, service or article.

**Font**

Computer or Internet typeface [though it's technically interchangeable with "typeface," font actually means a specific instance of a typeface including point size, pitch (width) and spacing; "Helvetica, 10 pt. with pitch value of 9," for instance.]

**Frequency**

It is the average number of times that your TARGET AUDIENCE could be exposed to your message. People consume more than one type of media, and frequency calculations take this into account (for instance someone may read the Financial Times and Marie Claire and also watch television). Frequency is often linked with REACH. "This many people saw my message this many times". For example, 20 per cent of my target audience potentially saw my message 4.75 times on average", "10 per cent saw it 2.01 times", etc.

**FUD**

Short for "Fear, Uncertainty and Doubt," FUD is using positioning of one's own products or services to cast fear, uncertainty and doubt on the competitor's. For example, by calling Mike's Auto Shop the "home-grown" auto shop, we created the doubt that other auto shops weren't home grown, and the fear that if a customer didn't go with a home-grown shop, they might not receive good service.

**Goal**

The primary result a company is attempting to achieve through its public relations efforts.

**Headline**

The title of an article or press release.

**Hit**

A visit to a particular page on a website by a web visitor.

**House Organ**

A newsletter produced by a company for the employees of that company.

**Hype/Hyperbole**

Overdone exaggeration implied endorsement: the character the public often assigns to non-paid neutral or positive media coverage of a company, its products or services, industry authorities: respected individuals or publications within an industry.

**Impressions/Impacts**

Often thought to be readership, but is a multiplication of the number of times a marketing message is seen by the number people who see it. 10 people seeing a message 10 times = 100 impressions. 1 person seeing a message 100 times also equals 100 impressions (see CIRCULATION, OTS and READERSHIP).

**Index**

An index is a measure of suitability, and is not related to REACH. Especially useful when trying to match whether the profile of a type of media matches the profile of your TARGET AUDIENCE. The base is always 100. The measure (the index) can be any number above 100, or any number below 100, down to zero. For example, a figure of 220 means that the profile of, for instance a monthly woman's magazine, is 120 times more likely to match the profile of your target audience than a magazine with an index of 100. An index of 80 means that it is 20 times less likely to match. An index of 120+ is deemed to be significant.

**Ink**

Space devoted to a company, its products or services in the print media.

**Institute of Public Relations (IPR)**

The UK's leading public relations industry professional body representing the interests of people working in public relations in the UK and abroad.

**International Public Relations Association (IPRA)**

The IPRA provides professional development and personal

networking opportunities on a global level and promotes the practice of public relations in 95 countries.

### Inverted Pyramid

Journalistic style of writing where the most important information is written first, followed by information of decreasing importance (this allows the reader to stop reading having gained the most important information; it also allows editors to cut or edit the story from the bottom up without omitting vital information).

### Jargon

Language known only to members of a specific group, company or industry.

### Key Influencers

Individuals, groups or publications whose opinion or coverage of a product, service or company can significantly affect public perception within a specific market.

### Key Messages

Choose three to five main points that are most important to tell your audience about the company and its strategic direction. Judging by the Detroit Regional Chamber's marketing, one key message would be "small businesses mean big business to Michigan's economy."

For ease of use, develop bulleted statements that are easy to remember and to weave into any conversation with your target audiences.

### Keywords

Specific words or phrases, often lifted from a PRESS RELEASE, that then feature within the EDITORIAL coverage. Alternatively, words or phrases a media-monitoring agency will use to find your press cuttings.

### Link

A portal to another website or to another area within a website.

### Marcom

Marketing communications.

**Marketing**

Marketing is the wide range of activities involved in making sure that you're continuing to meet the needs of your customers and getting value in return. These activities include market research to find out, for example, what groups of potential customers exist, what their needs are, which of those needs you can meet, how you should meet them, etc. Marketing also includes analyzing the competition, positioning your new product or service (finding your market niche), pricing your products and services, and promoting them through continued advertising, promotions, public relations and sales.

**Mechanical Data**

The layout details of a particular publication in terms of page size, number of column and their widths, and other layout criteria on which pagination is organised and advertising rates are calculated.

**Media**

Members or tools for disseminating the news; unbiased third parties (press representatives).

**Media Coverage**

Mention in the media of a company, its products or services.

**Media Policy**

Organizational directive as to how company representatives will communicate with the media.

**Media Relations**

The function of gaining positive media attention and coverage.

**Media Type**

National press, consumer magazines, regional and trade press, broadcast and the Internet are all types of media.

**Mind Share**

Amount of thinking an individual or group does about a particular product, service or company.

**News Conference**

A scheduled presentation to a group of media representatives.

**News Feed**

Electronically transmitted broadcast information.

**Newspaper Licensing Agency (NLA)**

The NLA represent the copyright interests of several hundred publications, mainly newspapers, from the UK national press through to the major regional press and quite a few foreign ones as well. They issue licenses to companies like Paperclip so we can make copies send royalty fees to the NLA on your behalf.

**Noise**

Confusion caused by too many messages trying to be delivered at one time.

**Objective**

A specific, measurable goal.

**Opportunity to See (OTS)—Opportunity to Hear (OTH)**

A calculation determining the number of times an individual is likely to see a marketing message. Advertising relies on a large number of messages to be seen, whereas a specific PR campaign may only have one opportunity per publication. However, any number of PR messages within any number of publications can be calculated to produce an overall 'OTS'. (see CIRCULATION, IMPRESSIONS/ IMPACTS and READERSHIP).

**Overlap**

Households living on the edges of one or more ITV regions will be able to view one or more ITV stations.

**Pass-along Rate**

The number of times a received document (article, newsletter, brochure, report, etc.) is shared with other individuals.

**Pitch**

A prepared sales presentation, usually one-on-one (in public relations, it's generally an attempt to get positive coverage or analyst review).

**PMS**

PMS is the acronym given to colour codes associated with a specific ink colour library. Print shops often refer to a PMS colour such as "PMS 328," a nice teal colour. PMS stands for Pantone Matching System.

**Positioning**

(1) Placement of a company, its products or services in a market category or in relation to its competition.

(2) The location a company's web page appears on a search engine after a searcher enters key words to search.

**Press**

Members or vehicles of the media.

**Press Kit**

Several press deliverables combined in one package (usually a folder).

**Press Release**

A statement issued to the media to either describe a product or service, or to state a position on an issue. The intention being that the media will use the press release wholly, or in part, and reproduce it as their own editorial. Often accompanied with graphics.

**Pro-active PR/Re-active PR**

EDITORIAL that appears as a direct result of the PR input as opposed to re-active PR where the editorial has appeared as a result of the publication's initiative.

**Product Demo**

A physical run-through of a product or service by company representative (usually to analysts or members of the press).

**Promotion**

Promotion keeps the product in the minds of the customer and helps stimulate demand for the product. Promotion involves ongoing advertising and publicity (mention in the Press). The ongoing activities of advertising, sales and public relations are often considered aspects of promotions.

**Proofread**

Carefully reading a document to weed out errors.

**Pub**

Publication.

**Public Affairs**

The public policy aspect of public relations. *See* expanded definition.

**Public Relations**

Public relations includes ongoing activities to ensure the company has a strong public image. Public relations activities include helping the public to understand the company and its products. Often, public relations are conducted through the media, that is, newspapers, television, magazines, etc. As noted above, public relations is often considered as one of the primary activities included in promotions.

**Public Relations Advisor**

A person who provides public relations guidance (may work inside or outside a PR firm).

**Public Relations Consultant**

Independent professionals who provide public relations guidance.

**Public Relations Firm**

A company made up of public relations advisors and their support staff.

**Public Relations Plan**

A document that details specific actions to achieve a public relations result.

**Publicity**

Publicity is mention in the media. Organizations usually have little control over the message in the media, at least, not as they do in advertising. Regarding publicity, reporters and writers decide what will be said.

**Publics/Target Audiences**

An organization should develop effective relationships with the following publics/target audiences — employees, members, customers, local communities, shareholders, national, state and local government officials and with society at large. The better you define the target audience, the easier it is to choose the best medium to deliver your message. The definition should include demographics such as geographic area, age range, race, sex, job title and company size. Psychographic information including personality type and emotional and behavioural characteristics of the audience is useful as well.

**Q and A/Rude Q and A**

A document that lists predictions of difficult questions that may be posed to a company spokesperson, and the best answers the spokesperson can give to answer the questions and meet the company's objectives.

**Query Letter**

A letter sent to a publication asking whether the publication would be interested in receiving a bylined article.

**Radio Joint Audience Research (RAJAR)**

Operates a single audience measurement system for the radio industry. Encompasses the BBC, UK licensed and other commercial stations.

**Rate Card**

The published cost of advertising in any media.

**Reach**

The reach of a campaign is the total number of people within your TARGET AUDIENCE that may see your message. Sometimes referred to as 'COVERAGE'. Most often expressed as a percentage, and the actual number together. For example, "this campaign will reach 10.71 per cent of my target audience which equates to 258,000 people."

**Re-active PR/Pro-active PR**

EDITORIAL that appears as a result of the publication's initiative as opposed to re-active PR where the editorial has appeared as a direct result of the PR input.

**Readership**

The number of times a publication is shared with other individuals. The difference between readership and impressions can sometimes be confused (see CIRCULATION, IMPRESSIONS/IMPACTS and OTS).

**Repositioning**

Changing the placement of a company, its products or services in a market category or in relation to its competition.

**Research**

Marketing research can be done in a variety of ways — via communication audits, surveys of customers and industry competitors, private interviews with key customers and other audiences, focus groups with a cross-section of your key audiences or via the Web with online research tools. Research helps you define your key messages and to determine the best method for reaching your audiences.

**Retraction**

Media correction of information previously and erroneously reported.

**Return on Investment (ROI)**

A measure of budget spent to achieve an objective, versus the income generated through the activity.

**Run of Paper (ROP)**

An advertising package where there is no guarantee of position and thereby charged out at a lower rate.

**Running Columns**

Regularly appearing articles of a specific theme or topic in a publication.

**Sales**

Sales involves most or many of the following activities, including cultivating prospective buyers (or leads) in a market segment; conveying the features, advantages and benefits of a product or service to the lead; and closing the sale (or coming to agreement on pricing and services).

**Sans Serif/Serif**

These terms apply to typeface and whether a particular typeface has "tails" on it or not. Serif typefaces have "tails" on them—Times Roman is an example of a serif typeface. Sans serif typefaces have no tails; Arial and Helvetica are examples of sans serif typefaces.

Here is an example of sans serif.
Here is an example of serif.

**SCC Rate/Single Column Centimetre Advertising Rate**

The width times the height of a newspaper column on which advertising rates are based.

**Script**

Prepared speech written on paper.

**Sector Analysis**

An overall measure of an industry sector's media coverage. For instance retail. What is the retail sector achieving and how do we measure up against the sector's performance?

**Self-mailer**

A brochure or other document that contains postal information (return address, bulk mail insignia or room for postage) and room for an address label so that it can mailed by itself, without having to place it in an envelope.

**Series — Regional Newspapers**

A number of regional publications covering a geographical area represented by a single publisher.

Series advertising rates are available. Series circulations are often provided (See SYNDICATED ARTICLES below).

**Share of Shout**

For example, 6 companies feature in one article, who dominates the page, in ranked order?

**Shelf-Life**

How long a document is held onto by the receiver.

### Sig File

A signature block consistently used that includes a tag line about your company. Example:

> Janet Jacoby
> **THE PR ACADEMY**
> ***Our courses change lives***
> **http: / / www.learnpr.com**

### Simultaneous Submission

Sending a bylined article to more than one publication at the same time (often frowned upon).

### Snapshot Document

Combines an EXECUTIVE SUMMARY and best of press. Possibly will include PRESS RELEASES and a short overview. Creates an awareness of a larger project using key elements from it.

### Strategic Partner

A company or organization that another company or organization aligns itself with to benefit both parties.

### Strategy

The strategy is the recipe for developing a successful action plan to reach the objective of creating a better understanding and more awareness of your company. Like any good business plan, key components of this strategy include research, definition of target audiences, key messages, measurable objectives, tactics and evaluation. To get the best results, create strategies that are measurable so they can be properly evaluated.

### Syndicated Articles

The same article published across a series. The copy and layout can sometimes change within the series. ACE £'s calculations are based on the series ratecard.

### Tactics

To effectively develop understanding about your company, you can employ a variety of tactics.

- Submit a case study or feature article to editors of trade publications covering your industry or business in general.

- Exhibit at a tradeshow and/or speak at an industry conference where you can help create a better understanding of the company's expertise to a captive audience.
- Prepare a press kit with executive biographies and press releases that feature the latest company news and issue to editors of industry and business publications.
- Press releases are documents written in a format that journalists prefer. The most important information is detailed in first few sentences of the release. Editors take just a few minutes to decide if the story is interesting so write the release concisely, usually no more than two pages.
- Submit an opinion editorial (op-ed) piece to a business publication or local newspaper on a topic that affects your business.
- Network with your industry trade association or local businesses at a chamber event to make more people aware of your products and services.
- Engage your company in community relations activities that help promote your products or services. If you are a technology company, use your technology to help the community at large.

**Tag Line**

A sentence or phrase that provides a creative description of an organization's position (e.g., Red Cross: *We Save Lives*).

**Target Audience**

The key groups or individuals that a company most wants to receive its public relations messages.

This is the group of people you are trying to reach with your message. Can be defined by socio-economic groups, and/or any number of other criteria that defines the people you are trying to reach. Also referred to as 'target market'.

**Target Publications**

Newspapers and magazines whose readership profile best matches a company's target market.

**Tonal Bias**

Denotes whether an article has a positive, neutral or negative slant.

**Tone of the Media**

An analysis tool that accurately reflects the mood of the press, by any number of CORE MESSAGES and subjects, and other criteria, such as publication and journalist, and incorporates the associated degrees of editorial bias.

**Trade Publication**

A magazine, newspaper or newsletter published by members of a specific industry.

**TV Regions**

The transmission areas of each of the ITV companies cover specific UK areas. Viewers can only receive the terrestrial ITV station if they live within its transmission area. Households living on the edges of one or more ITV regions will be able to view one or more ITV stations. This is known as OVERLAP.

**TVR Television Rating**

A Television Rating (TVR) is a percentage of the total number of people viewing a TV programme or advertising break at a particular time. 1 per cent of the audience = 1 TVR. Ratings can be added together and can total more than 100 per cent. For example, an advertising campaign can achieve '400 ratings', because people may see the same ad more than once.

**Typeface**

Printing type (e.g., Helvetica, Times New Roman, Courier).

**Unique Selling Proposition (USP)**

A one-line description of your company's products or services that differentiates it among your market from the offerings of its competitors.

**White Paper**

A technical document that explains how a product or service functions and its purpose.

**Writer's Guidelines**

A list of do's and don'ts, including word length, topic choice, and format that publications provide for writers who wish to submit articles.

# 1

# Public Relations in Media and Journalism: An Introduction

## PUBLIC RELATIONS: AN INTRODUCTORY OVERVIEW

Public relations is, simply-stated, the art and science of building relationships between an organization and its key audiences. Examples include:

(i) Corporations use Marketing Public Relations (MPR) to convey information about the products they manufacture or services they provide to potential customers to support their direct sales efforts. Typically, they are supporting sales in the short run, i.e., to boost immediate revenue, and the long run, i.e., to establish and burnish their brand name for a strong, ongoing market.

(ii) Corporations also use public-relations vehicles to reach legislators and other politicians, seeking favourable tax, regulatory, and other treatment, and they may use public relations to portray themselves as enlightened employers, in support of human-resources recruiting programmes.

(iii) Non-profit organizations, including schools and universities, hospitals, and human and social service agencies, use public relations in support of fund-raising programmes and staff recruiting, and to increase patronage of their services.

(iv) Politicians use public relations to attract votes and raise money, and, when successful at the ballot box, to promote and defend their service in office, with an eye to the next election or, at career's end, to their legacy.

### The Case of Public Relations vs. Publicity

Although many people believe that "public relations" and "publicity" are synonyms, that view is outdated. Publicity is certainly an important tool in the public-relations professional's kit, but not the only tool. Publicity refers to activities designed to generate favourable editorial coverage of a product, service, candidate, etc., in the print, broadcast, and online media. The most widely known and used techniques are the news release (press release), news conference (press conference), spokesperson interview, and ghost-writing of articles and essays. The common factor in these and other publicity techniques is that the public relations professional provides information and expert sources to journalists. The journalists then combine what is provided to them by competing public relations professionals with their own independent research. In the best cases, the resulting report in the mass media is a balanced, authoritative and accurate. If the public relations person's product, service, or client receives a fair shake from the journalist, and is portrayed accurately, the PR person (or publicity agent) has done his or her job.

Major techniques that public relations encompass besides publicity are the following:

(*a*) Direct communication (carrying messages directly to constituents, rather than through the mass media) with, e.g., newsletters—in print and e-letters.
(*b*) Collateral literature, traditionally in print and now predominantly (in most cases) as Web sites.
(*c*) Speeches to constituent groups and professional organizations; receptions; seminars, and other events; personal appearances.

Public relations is often misused as a synonym for deceptive or unscrupulous efforts to mislead people. But, like other disciplines, such as accounting, sales, and research, public relations is not inherently good or evil. Sincere, honest people use public relations techniques to convey their beliefs, opinions, and recommendations. Dishonest people with talent and experience in public relations sometimes use it to deceive. The same is true of not only other disciplines mentioned above, but also the three learned professions—law, medicine and the clergy. We all known good lawyers, doctors and priests—and bad ones who abuse their abilities, status and professions. In this respect, public relations is no different from accounting or the law.

**Explaining the History of Public Relations**

Precursors to public relations can be found in publicists who specialized in promoting circuses, theatrical performances, and other public spectacles. Later, most PR practitioners were and are still recruited from the ranks of journalism. Journalists concerned with ethics question former colleagues for using their inside understanding of news media, helping clients receive favourable media coverage. Highly paid PR positions remain a popular career change choice for many journalists. PR historians say the first PR firm, the Publicity Bureau, was established in 1900 by former newspapermen, with Harvard University as its first client.

The First World War also helped stimulate the development of public relations as a profession. Many of the first PR professionals, including Ivy Lee, Edward Bernays, and Carl Byoir, got their start with the Committee for Public Information (also known as the Creel Committee), which organized publicity on behalf of U.S. objectives during World War I. Some historians regard Ivy Lee as the first real practitioner of public relations, but Edward Bernays is generally regarded today as the profession's founder. In describing the origin of the term Public Relations, Bernays commented, "When I came back to the United States, I decided that if you could use *propaganda* for war, you could certainly use it for peace. And propaganda got to be a bad word because of the Germans using it. So what I did was to try to find some other words, so we found the words Council on Public Relations."

Ivy Lee, who has been credited with developing the modern news release (also called a "press release"), espoused a philosophy consistent with what has sometimes been called the "two-way street" approach to public relations, in which PR consists of helping clients listen as well as communicate messages to their publics. In the words of the Public Relations Society of America (PRSA), "Public relations helps an organization and its publics adapt mutually to each other." In practice, however, Lee often engaged in one-way propagandizing on behalf of clients despised by the public, including Standard Oil founder John D. Rockefeller. Shortly before his death, the US Congress had been investigating his work on behalf of the controversial Nazi German company IG Farben.

Bernays was the profession's first theorist. A nephew of Sigmund Freud, Bernays drew many of his ideas from Freud's theories about the irrational, unconscious motives that shape human behaviour. Bernays authored several books, including *Crystallizing Public Opinion* (1923), *Propaganda* (1928), and *The Engineering of Consent* (1947). Bernays saw public relations as an "applied social science" that uses insights from psychology, sociology, and other disciplines to scientifically manage and manipulate the thinking and behaviour of an irrational and "herdlike" public. "The conscious and intelligent manipulation of the organized habits and opinions of the masses is an important element in democratic society," he wrote in *Propaganda*. "Those who manipulate this unseen mechanism of society constitute an invisible government which is the true ruling power of our country."

One of Bernays' early clients was the tobacco industry. In 1929, he orchestrated a legendary publicity stunt aimed at persuading women to take up cigarette smoking, which was then considered unfeminine and inappropriate for women with any social standing. To counter this image, Bernays arranged for New York City débutantes to march in that year's Easter Day Parade, defiantly smoking cigarettes as a statement of rebellion against the norms of a male-dominated society. Photographs of what Bernays dubbed the "Torches of Liberty Brigade" were sent to newspapers, convincing many women to equate smoking with women's rights. Some women went so far as to demand membership in all-male smoking clubs, a highly controversial act at the time.

### PR Industry in Contemporary Times

According to the U.S. Bureau of Labour Statistics, there were approximately 122,000 public relations specialists in the United States in 1998, while there were approximately 485,000 advertising, marketing, and public relations managers working in all industries. Public relations agents or "officials," most often called "executives," deliver info to the media or directly to the public to convey messages toward wider audiences, or to specific demographic segments within the public, called "target audiences." Because similar opinions tend to be shared by a group of people rather than an entire society, research may be conducted to determine a range of things such as target audiences, appeal, as well as strategies for coordinated message presentation. PR may target different audiences with different messages to achieve an overall goal. Public Relations sets out to effect widespread opinion and behaviour changes.

Modern public relations uses a variety of techniques including opinion polling and focus groups to evaluate public opinion, combined with a variety of high-tech techniques for distributing information on behalf of their clients, including satellite feeds, the Internet, broadcast faxes, and database-driven phone banks to recruit supporters for a client's cause. According to the PRSA,

> "Examples of the knowledge that may be required in the professional practice of public relations include communication arts, psychology, social psychology, sociology, political science, economics, and the principles of management and ethics. Technical knowledge and skills are required for opinion research, public issues analysis, media relations, direct mail, institutional advertising, publications, film/video productions, special events, speeches and presentations."

Although public relations professionals are stereotypically seen as corporate servants, the reality is that almost any organization that has a stake in how it is portrayed in the media employs at least one PR manager. Large organizations may even have dedicated communications departments. Government agencies, trade associations, and other non profit organizations commonly carry out PR activities.

Public relations should be seen as a management function in any organization. An effective communication, or public relations, plan for an organization is developed to communicate to an audience (whether internal or external publics) in such a way the message coincides with organizational goals and seeks to benefit mutual interests whenever possible.

## The Issue of Specialization in PR

As industry consolidation becomes more prevalent, many organizations and individuals are choosing to retain "boutique" firms as opposed to so-called "global" communications firms. These smaller firms typically specialize in only a couple of practice areas and thus, often have a greater understanding of their client's business. And because they deal with certain journalists with greater frequency, specialty firms often have stronger media contacts in the areas that matter most to their clients. Added benefits of smaller, specialty firms include more personal attention and accountability and as well, cost savings. This is not to say that smaller is always better, but there is a growing consensus that specialty firms offer more than once considered.

## Specializations

- food service PR
- health care PR
- technology PR
- public affairs PR
- on-line PR

A number of specialties exist within the field of public relations, including:

- crisis management
- reputation management
- issue management
- investor relations
- labour relations
- grassroots PR (sometimes referred to as Astroturf PR)

## Methods, Tools and Tactics of Public Relations

### *A. General*

#### *(i) Understanding Audience Targeting*

The most fundamental rule in public communications is to know who one's audience is, and to tailor every message to appeal to that audience. An "audience" can be a general, nationwide or worldwide audience, but it is more often a segment of a population. Marketers often refer to economy-driven "demographics," such as "white males 18-49," but in public relations an audience is more fluid, being whoever someone the client wants to reach. For example, recent political audiences include "soccer moms" and "NASCAR dads."

In addition to audiences, there are usually stakeholders, literally people who have a "stake" in a given issue. All audiences are stakeholders (or presumptive stakeholders), but not all stakeholders are audiences. For example, a charity commissions a PR agency to create an advertising campaign to raise money to find a cure for a disease. The charity and the people with the disease are stakeholders, but the audience is anyone who is likely to donate money.

Sometimes the interests of differing audiences and stakeholders common to a PR effort necessitate the creation of several distinct but still complementary messages. This is not always easy to do, and sometimes — especially in politics — a spokesperson or client says something to one audience that angers another audience or group of stakeholders.

*(ii) Conducting Press Conferences*

A press conference consists of someone speaking to the media at a predetermined time and place. Press conferences usually take place in a public or quasi-public place. Press conferences provide an opportunity for speakers to control information and who gets it; depending on the circumstances, speakers may hand-pick the journalists they invite to the conference instead of making themselves available to any journalist who wishes to attend.

It is also assumed that the speaker will answer journalists' questions at a press conference, although they are not obliged to. However, someone who holds several press conferences on a topic (especially a scandal) will be asked questions by the press, regardless of whether they indicate they will entertain them, and the more conferences the person holds, the more aggressive the questioning may become. Therefore, it is in a speaker's interest to answer journalists' questions at a press conference to avoid appearing as if they have something to hide.

But questions from reporters — especially hostile reporters — detracts from the control a speaker has over the information they give out. For even more control, but less interactivity, a person may choose to issue a press release.

*Making Press Releases*

A press release is a written statement distributed to the media. It is a fundamental tool of PR work. Press releases are usually sent via a newswire service (such as PR Newswire or Business Wire) to media outlets, where journalists may pick them up and use them as they see fit. Very often the information in a press release finds its way verbatim, or minimally altered, to print and broadcast reports. If a media outlet reports that "John Doe said in a statement today that...", the "statement" was almost always a press release.

The text of the press release is usually (but not always) written as a news story, with an eye-catching headline and an article written in standard journalistic inverted pyramid style. This style is effective for reaching hurried, and often skeptical journalists who rarely read entire releases. It also makes it easy for journalists to lift entire passages from a release and insert them into their own article. While this practice is frowned upon in newsrooms, journalism is a deadline-driven industry, and it is not uncommon for reporters to occasionally copy or modify a line or two from a press release. PR practitioners, on the other hand, design releases to encourage as much "lifting" as possible, so in essence, the less professional a journalist is, the more successful the release is judged to be.

The only time that journalists may copy from a press release in good conscience is if the release provides a direct quote, as in: *Senator Smith said, "This is the most fiscally irresponsible bill that the Congress has passed since the Buy Everyone A Mercedes Act."* In this case, a journalist may copy the quote verbatim into his or her story, although most reporters prefer to try soliciting an individual quote from the speaker before filing their story.

However, because press releases reflect their issuer's preferred interpretation or packaging of a story, journalists are often skeptical of their contents. Of course, the level of skepticism, if any, depends on what the story is and who's telling it. Newsrooms receive so many press releases that, unless it is a story that the media are already paying attention to, a press release alone isn't always enough to catch a journalist's attention.

With the advent of modern media and new technology, press releases now have equivalents in these media—video news releases and audio news releases. However, many television stations are hesitant to use VNR's as they appear slighted and not actually newsworthy.

*Press Release Format*

The typical press release announces that the statement is "For Immediate Release" across the top (some may instead be embargoed until a certain date), and lists the issuing organization's media contacts directly below. The media contacts are the people that the release's issuer wants to make available to the media; for example, a press release about new scientific study will typically list the study's lead scientist as its media contact. The bottom of each release is usually marked with ### or-30- to signify the end of the text.

*Understanding Other Tasks*

- Publicity events or publicity stunts.
- The talk show circuit. A PR spokesperson (or his/her client) "does the circuit" by being interviewed on television and radio talk shows with audiences that the client wishes to reach.
- Books and other writings.
- After a PR practitioner has been working in the field for a while, he or she accumulates a list of contacts in the media and elsewhere in the public affairs sphere. This "Rolodex" becomes a prized asset, and job announcements sometimes even ask for candidates with an existing Rolodex, especially those in the media relations area of PR.

### *B. PR Politics and Civil Society*

*(i) Identifying and Defining Your Opponent*

Political campaigns are peak times for defining one's opponents, though the process occurs continually. Organizations and other groups of people can be defined just as easily as candidates.

In the 2004, US presidential campaign, George W. Bush defined John Kerry as a "flip-flopper," among other characterizations, which were widely reported and repeated by the media, particularly the conservative media. Similarly, George H.W. Bush characterized Michael Dukakis as weak on crime (the Willie Horton ad) and as hopelessly liberal ("a card-carrying member of the ACLU"). In 1996, President Bill Clinton seized upon opponent Bob Dole's promise to take America back to a simpler time, promising in contrast to "build a bridge to the 21st century." This painted Dole as a person who was somehow opposed to progress.

In the debate over abortion, pro-abortion rights groups defined their opponents by defining themselves instead: "pro-choice." Anti-abortion rights groups responded in kind, branding themselves "pro-life." Extrapolating their respective rhetorics, pro-choice groups refer to their opponents as "anti-choice," and pro-life groups refer to *their* opponents as "pro-abortion."

More recently, opponents of same-sex marriage in the U.S. have declared that their opponents are not the gay couples suing for the right to marry in various state courts, but rather the judges who rule in their favour. They are now calling them "activist judges," implying that they impose their personal beliefs instead of objectively interpreting the law. This sidesteps the thorny issue of making millions of gay people an "enemy," and instead focusses attention on the much smaller judiciary, who all Americans can ostensibly agree should be prevented from being "activists" on the bench.

### *(ii) Understanding and Managing Language*

If a politician or organization can use an apt phrase in relation to an issue, such as in interviews or news releases, the news media will often repeat it verbatim, thus furthering the message. (This may be considered an example of a meme.)

"New Deal" became a description of President Franklin D. Roosevelt's anti-Depression economic plans, and "states' rights/ state sovereignty" became near-code words for anti-civil rights legislation.

Recent examples come almost solely from Republican politicians: "death tax" for estate tax, "racial preferences" for affirmative action, "faith-based" instead of religious, among others.

## *C. PR Entertainment and Celebrity*

### *(i) Identifying and Playing up One's Weaknesses*

A famous saying goes "Any publicity is good publicity," and celebrities tend to be fans of this dictum. If a celebrity says or does something embarrassing, he or she will often turn it into a strength and make it part of his or her "image." Of course, this tactic is used just as much with favourable situations as much as with unfavourable ones.

A current (2004) example involves the entertainer Jessica Simpson, who gained nationwide prominence when she wondered aloud on a reality show if "Chicken of the Sea"—brand tuna fish was actually chicken or tuna, garnering her a reputation for being slow-witted. But by the summer of 2004, she was being paid to endorse a brand of breath mints called "Liquid Ice." In the product's television commercial, Simpson replicates her earlier confusion by debating whether the mint is really liquid or ice. So although she was previously ridiculed, she (and her advisers) turned her nationwide embarrassment into a lucrative endorsement deal.

Top US entertainment publicists include Lizzie Grubman, Karen Ammond (KBC Media Relations) and PMK Public Relations.

*(ii) Time for Branching Out*

As Oscar Wilde is supposed to have said, the only thing worse than being talked about is not to be talked about at all. Many celebrities seem to take this truism to heart, because when their popularity (and income) wane, they take on new projects that attract media attention. Considering that a celebrity's celebrity is a brand unto itself, many celebrities are under constant pressure to "reinvent" themselves, as a prophylactic against obscurity.

A current trend among American celebrities is the transformation of musicians, comedians, and almost every other sort of performer into children's book authors. Madonna, Jay Leno, Billy Crystal, and several other celebrities have recently written children's books, accompanied by much media coverage.

A more traditional way of branching out is the celebrity restaurant. This is especially common among professional athletes, whose time in the spotlight is often limited by the physical demands of their jobs. Basketball player Michael Jordan opened a restaurant in Chicago, Illinois, and singer Britney Spears opened an ill-fated eatery in New York which closed a few months later.

Male celebrities like Tim Robbins, Sean Penn and Charlton Heston seem to gravitate toward politics, although some female celebrities, such as Susan Sarandon and Barbra Streisand, also become strong political voices.

Younger female celebrities on the other hand are often drawn into the fashion world. Hotel heiress Paris Hilton recently announced that she was starting her own line of jewellery, and Jennifer Lopez has started a line of clothing. And fading star Elizabeth Taylor launched a fragrance called "White Diamonds" several years ago, bringing renewed interest from the media.

## Public Relations: Ethical and Social Issues

Many of the techniques used by PR firms are drawn from the institutions and practices of democracy itself. Persuasion, advocacy, and education are instruments through which individuals and organizations are entitled to express themselves in a free society, and many public relations practitioners are engaged in practices that are widely considered as beneficial, such as publicizing scientific research, promoting charities, raising awareness of public health concerns and other issues in civil society.

One of the most controversial practices in public relations is the use of front groups—organizations that purport to serve a public cause while actually serving the interests of a client whose sponsorship may be obscured or concealed. The creation of front groups is an example of what PR practitioners sometimes term the third party technique—the art of "putting your words in someone else's mouth." PR Watch, a non profit organization that monitors deceptive PR activities it considers to be deceptive, has published numerous examples of this technique in practice. Critics of the public relations industry, such as PR Watch, have contended that Public Relations involves a "multi-billion dollar propaganda-for-hire industry" that "concoct(s) and spin(s) the news, organize(s) phony 'grassroots' front groups, spies on citizens, and conspire(s) with lobbyists and politicians to thwart democracy."

Instances of the use of front groups as a PR technique have been documented in many industries. For example, the coal mining corporations have created environmental groups that contend that increased $CO_2$ emissions and global warming will contribute to plant growth and will be beneficial, trade groups for bars and beer distributors have created and funded citizen's groups to attack Mothers Against Drunk Driving, and tobacco companies have created and funded citizen's groups to advocate for tort reform and to attack personal injury lawyers.

Current issues in ethical and social arenas have been brought to the attention of people from all stratas of the population when it was determined that more than one journalist with a platform had received money from a Public Relations firm for espousing a certain point of view.

## SYNTHESIZING PUBLIC RELATIONS IN MEDIA AND JOURNALISM

In a rapidly changing environment, both social and technological, the Public Relation man's job is a challenging one that calls for creative talents and professional techniques. Public relations functions differ from one organisation to another, depending on its purpose and its publics. However, that basic goal of the Public Relations is to attract public attention, win belief, achieve understanding and earn goodwill.

**Understanding and Explaining the Objectives**

This chapter introduces to Public Relations (PR), its nature, scope and process. The term "Public Relations" and other associated terms are defind besides the publics are, how important they are, how one can communicate with them. In short, we will take a wide look at what Public Relations does for the organisation, the publics and the management. While going through this chapter you will be able to state the factors that have contributed to the need for Public Relations; define Public Relations to bring out the various functions it serves; explain various terms used in Public Relations context; describe the nature and purpose of Public Relations; map out the scope of Public Relations and its limitations; relate the role of Public Relations to management function; define 'public' and analyse the nature of publics; identify the publics of various organisations; list the tools and media available to a Public Relations person; describe how Public Relations can being about mutual understanding through strategic communication and explain the increasingly greater challenge for the Public Relations professionals according to the changing environment.

As science gives us greater control over matter, machines, and methods, we must learn to deal with people with increasing effectiveness. Public Relations, as a means of inculcating attitudes, can greatly expedite the social adaptations required for our material advancement by influencing public opinion.

There was a time when experience in newspaper writing was practically a requirement for a job in public relations. Although this is no longer true, there is still emphasis on use of a journalistic writing style. This is because much of what the public relations writer produces is directed to the news media. A solid understanding of journalistic principles and concepts is needed, but public relations writing should never simply consider themselves "journalists in residence". Public relations writing differs from journalistic writing in its objectives, audiences and channels.

The purpose of a journalist is to inform an audience in the most impartial way possible. Personal bias may affect the choice of words, but in general the reporter tries to maintain an attitude of strict neutrality. The public relations writer, by definition, is an advocate. His or her purpose is not only to inform but also to persuade and motivate—to make something happen. All public relations writing should begin with the question: How does this help the organisation attain its objectives? For example, in choosing subjectives. If one of these is to increase productivity, the editor may decide to run several features about employees who are outstanding workers.

Although a public relations writer carefully chooses facts and story angles that help attain the objectives, this should not be done in a deceptive or misleading way. There is no excuse for writing that is not frank and honest.

The journalist writes for one audience—readers, listeners, or viewers of the medium for which he or she works. The composition of this audience is usually well defined. For example, a daily suburban newspaper circulates primarily among people who share a common residential area but have a broad range of backgrounds and interests. By contrast, the readers of a special-interest magazine share a very strong interest in only one particular group. The newspaper reporter writes about many things for a general audience. The special-interest reporter writes about just one subject for a limited and highly interested audience.

The public relations writer may write for numerous and radically different audiences, such as employees, professionals, customers, business class, home makers, travelers, bankers, politicians, stockholders, farmers, etc., many others. Effective public relations writing is based on defining the audience and its composition properly, so you can tailor your information to its interests and concerns. The media must be remembered as an audience and its concerns. Their positive response to your writing is what opens the channels. The journalists reaches his or her audience through one channel—the medium that publishes or broadcasts his or her writing, whether this comprises news or features, there is only one channel that conveys the writing to the audience.

The public relations writer, with many audiences to reach, will probably use many channels. Here is a listing of some of the channels of communication that you may use: metropolitan daily newspapers, weekly newspapers, general magazines, business magazines, trade magazines, special-interest magazines, radio stations, television stations, letters, pamphlets, brochures, profiles, newsletters, internal magazine, speeches, audiovisual presentations, posters, direct mail and telephone calls.

In writing for public relations, you need certain basic equipment, references and files.

You will need an electric typewriter or a personal computer to produce written materials of professional quality. A standard electric typewriter equipped with a high-yield self-correcting ribbon is an economical purchase; thousands of business offices use such machines. A new generation of electronic typewriters, controlled by microcomputers, brings a whole new set of skills to the typing table for much less than the cost of a personal computer.

An electronic typewriter cannot only correct mistakes but also tell the typist when a word has been misspelt or even overused. A built-in dictionary can provide correct spellings on a display screen, and a thesaurus can offer alternative words or phrases. The machines can remember and later print out what had typed earlier. Centering and tabulation can be done automatically, eliminating the need to count spaces.

A basic electronic typewriter costs about $200; its internal memory has a capacity of about 7,000 characters. For $1,500 IBM offers an electronic typewriter that has a 25-line display, a 25-page storage memory, and a host of other functions. The application of laser technology also allows faster printing and other functions. The application of laser technology also allows faster printing of documents on electronic typewriters.

Studies by Smith-Corona and Princeton University have found that personal computers are used 70 per cent of the time for typing rather than computing functions. Thus, manufacturers of electronic typewriters make the point that it is wasteful to purchase a personal computer if the primary purpose is writing.

The point is well taken, but more powerful word processing is available in personal computers. Consequently, more and more professional writers are using personal computers, can store large amounts of information, and software programmes like Word Perfect and WordStar permit maximum flexibility to write, edit format, and merge information into one complete document.

One of the most popular worked processing programmes is WordPerfect. It contains 115,000-word dictionary that enables you to examine documents for spelling and typographical errors as well as for unintentional double words. The programme's thesaurus (10,000 words) can be used to find synonyms and antonyms for specific words in a document or for individual words typed from graphic symbols into the text, compile and format statistical tables, vary the size of type and font, format the document into various column, widths, and even automatically insert names and specialized information into standard letters. The ability to do all these things almost instantly with a few instructions on the keyboard significantly increases a writer's productivity.

In addition to a personal computer and the appropriate word processing software, you must also have a printer. A better-quality dot-matrix printer is more economical than the more expensive laser printers, but advances in technology may bring laser printers down in price and make them the standard. Laser printers have the advantages of exceptionally high speed (an average of eight pages per minute) and extremely high resolutional. If you're preparing newsletters and brochures, laser printers allow you to write camera-ready copy complete with large-type headlines. The electronic scanners can input photographs and artwork directly into your computer disk for integration into your newsletter layout.

A basic library is a must for any writer. First, you should own a dictionary, preferably an unabridged one but at least a collegiate edition. This will answer questions of spelling and also help you select just the right word. A thesaurus (there are several good ones available) will supply synonyms, thus helping you to avoid repeating the same word too often. If you do speech writing, a copy of Bartlett's familiar quotations will be helpful.

Another necessity is a stylebook. Among the most widely used are the Associated Press Stylebook and Libel Manual, the United Press Stylebook, and the New York Times Stylebook. Of the three, the Associated Press Stylebook is used by the most weekly and daily newspapers. A stylebook helps you prepare copy that meets the standards of the media. It tells you how to handle things like titles, acronyms, punctuation, abbreviation numerals, and so on. If you do any writing for radio or television, you will need the Associated Press Broadcast Stylebook.

Other useful volumes on your bookshelf might include a current issue of the Reader's Digest Almanac, a Rand McNally word atlas, a Pocket Guide to the World (a Facts on File Publication) and a Statistical Abstract of the United States, published by the U.S. Government Printing Office. These sources are available in paperback, and they often save a hurried trip to a library for basic facts. A visit to the references that you may want to own.

Last but not least are media directories and listings of public relations services. If most of least work is geared to the local are, directories on the state or regional level. Western Media Contacts, for example, lists magazines, newspapers, radio stations, and television stations in California, Nevada, Arizona, Washington and Oregon.

For media listings on the national level, popular sources are Editor Publisher Yearbook, Bacon's Publicity Checker, and Working of the Nation. The latter is a five-volume set that contains listings of (1) newspapers, (2) magazines. (3) TV and radio personnel, (4) feature and photography syndicates, and (5) internal publications. Another popular references source is Standard rate and Data, a six-volume set that contains citations about a media outlet's market, audience demographics and advertising rates. National media directories can cost several hundred dollars. Therefore, an independent freelance writer might find it more economical to use the local library.

For listings of public relations services in photography, printing, distribution, and so on, a standard source is the Professional's Guide to Public Relations Services, published by Prentice-Hall. Another good source is O'Dwyer's PR Services, a monthly publication that contains articles and advertisements about vendors. Advertisements in the monthly publications of Public Relations Society of America (PRSA) and International Association of Business Communications (IABC)—Public Relations Journal and Communication World are also good sources. The national membership directory of each organization contains a section listing companies that specialize in public relations services. You won't be able to remember every pertinent fact, idea, or event, but a good, well-indexed file will help you find what you need. No two writers will need the same system, but the following list should provide some guidance: statics—about the organization or its industry; history—records, reports (annual or special) historical publications; publications house magazines, newsletters, leaflets, booklets, and so on; speeches—by organization people or by others in the same field; release—news items and features, plus clippings from those releases; clippings — based on other sources, giving information about the organization or affecting the organization; fact sheets—about the organization; position papers—on issues or situations affecting the organization; biographies—of key personnel; photos and art.

Three categories of books can help you become a more professional writer. First, there are those, that describe, current linguistic usages and give helpful hints about improving your general writing ability. Two of the most popular are: The Elements of Style by Strunk and White, a book that never seems to go out of style, and the newer On Writing Well by William Zinsser. Another outstanding work often used by professional writers in John B. Bremner's Words on Words: A Dictionary for Writers and Others Who Care About Words. Having these books on your reference shelf is not enough you should take the time to read them from cover once a year so as to avoid developing sloppy writing habits.

A superior backgrounder is— The Story of English by McCrum, Cran, and MacNeil, which offers excellent descriptions of regional variations in vocabulary and pronunciation. As public relations expands to international scope and English becomes more and more an international language, this book should become ever more useful.

Other helpful books on how English is currently used in America are by Ruolph Flesch, who has produced four Theodor Bernstein, who has also produced four; and Edwin Newman, the television commentator, who has written two.

Books about semantics, the connotative and denotative meaning of words, make up a second category. A knowledge of semantics will help you choose words that will be effective and persuasive and to avoid those that may have negative effects. S.I. Hayakawa has written two classics in semantics: Language in Thought and Action and Through the Communications Barrier. Mario Pei wrote another, calling it Weasel Woids: The Aret of Saying What You Don't Mean.

Third in the category of educational reading are the classics or semi classics. Our everyday writing and conversation is liberally sprinkled with phrases and expressions from these books. They are all interesting and many are highly entertaining; any writer who hopes use the language with skill should read them. Sir Winston Churchill was a master of both spoken and written English, he read voraciously in the classics and freely borrowed ideas and phrases from them.

In addition to books, you should read newspapers and news magazines to learn how they use the language. Also, it is imperative to read any publication in which you hope to place news items or features. The purpose is two fold: to learn what kind of material is used and how it is written.

Writing starts with facts and reading can supply you with many. Read the daily and weekly news media to know what is going on in the world. Read the trade of professional journal bearing on the organization for which you work, so you will know what is going on in your field. By reading books and booklets on pertinent subjects, you can gain a large amount of information that will help you produce more informative and complete materials.

Another source of current information is the "bestseller". Whenever, any books is widely read, it may have a strong influence on the public. Harriet Beecher Stowe's Uncle Tom's Cabin was a best seller in the mid-eighties. It aroused Civil War. In the 1960s, Rachel Carson's Silent Spring first ignited public concern for the environment. And Ralph Nader's Unsafe at Any Speed in the 1970s marked the beginning of today's consumer movement. In the 1980s; Allan Bloom's The Closing of the American Mind helped to spur public demands for improvements in American liberal arts education.

The revolution in communication, mentioned above, is more than an accelerator of change. It has created a whole new pattern of human dynamics. Changes are being felt in various areas of the society, particularly in the lifestyles and attitudes. For, the current changes in society are basically because of shifts in public attitudes, whether they be in government, in business, education, in science or technology. It is because of this that Public Relations is rapidly gaining attention worldwide.

In India, the new leadership in all organizations, government or private, has become aware of the importance of public attitudes. Some are either aware of Public Relations, or are receptive when it comes to their attention. As they gradually replace the old guard, the significance and dynamism of the concept of Public Relations is like to increase in scope and effect. The changes will create a human climate in which all organisations must exist. Understanding and coping with human climate is as vital for an organisation as dealing with the weather is for a farmer. In true democratic traditions, today's organisations and institutions, political parties and associations, the church or the temple, groups and unions, all work with the avowed aim of serving the interests of the people. Therefore, the people's attitude towards these social groups gain importance. Public Relations acts as a "link", placed as it is between an organisation and the people.

The process of development in society creates certain problems. The resolving of these problems require the mutual understanding of the goodwill between many groups, often having conflicting interests. As long as these societal processes operate, Public Relations hold great promise for the future. Therefore, the purpose of Public Relations practice is to establish a two-way communication to resolve conflicts of interest by seeking common ground or areas of mutual interest, and to establish understanding based on truth, knowledge and full information.

The scale of activity to promote good Public Relations may vary considerably according to the size and nature of the interested parties, but the philosophy, the strategy and the methods remain very similar, whether the Public Relations programme is designed to influence international understanding or to improve relations between a local company and its customers, agents and employees.

Attempts at defining the concept of Public Relations have resulted in people primarily referring to one or a few elements, or describing only a few of the many functions that "Public Relations" performs. Let us first clarify the meaning and definition of the term "Public Relations". We will take up a few of the major definitions given by eminent persons in the field.

Examine the dictionary meaning of PR: In its three fold definition of the term, the third edition of Webster's New International Dictionary describes Public Relations as:

— the promotion of rapport and goodwill between a firm or institution and other persons, special publics or the community at large, through the distribution of interpretative material/development of neighbourly interchange, and the assessment of publics.

— the degree of understanding and goodwill achieved between an individual, organisation or institution and the publics.

— the art or science of developing reciprocal understanding and goodwill.

One of the earliest definitions of the term is coined by Denny Griswold, published of "Public Relations News", a pioneer newsletter of Public Relations.

"Public Relations is the management function which evaluates public attitudes, identifies the policies and procedures of an organisation with the public interest, and executes a programme of action to earn public understanding and acceptance."

The above definition places responsibility for the Public Relations function upon the shoulders of management. The term "management" is used broadly, to cover all managements, and applies to non-profit as well as profit-making institutions and organisations. Further, the function and process are tied together in an orderly fashion to provide a step by step analysis or Public Relations in action.

Another important definition is carved out by two American Public Relations professionals, Scot M. Cutlip and Alien H. Center, authors of the famous book, "Effective Public Relations." According to them "Public Relations is the planned effort to influence opinion through good character and responsible performance, based upon mutually satisfactory two-way communication.

The Institute of Public Relations in the UK devoted prolonged attention to evolving a comprehensive definition of Public Relations. Their exercise yielded a definition, which now generally finds favour with Public Relations practitioners in many parts of the world, including the majority of practitioners in India. According to the Institute, Public Relations is defined as: the deliberate, planned and sustained effort to establish and maintain mutual understanding between an organisation and its public.

Sam Black in "Practical Public Relations" says that, "the fundamental purpose of Public Relations practice is to establish a two-way flow of mutual understanding based on truth, knowledge and full information.

Edward L. Bernays, the doyen of Public Relations in USA, defines it as "the attempt by information, persuasion and adjustment to engineer public support for an activity, cause, movement or institution."

An interesting and modern definition of Public Relations is the Mexican statement made at an International Conference of Public Relations institutions held in Mexico city in 1978.

> "Public Relations practice is the art of social science of analysing trends, predicting their consequences, counselling organisation leaders, and implementing planned programmes of action which will serve both the organisation and the public interest.

This is very helpful and practical definition. First of all, introduces the need for research, to audit or assess the situation, and to consider the implications what is discovered. Second, it stresses the advisory role of Public Relations, its service to management. Third, it shows that Public Relations programmes must be planned. Finally, it states that PR action must not only benefit its sponsors, but must also be in public interest, that is it should be socially responsible.

D.S. Mehta defines Public Relations, "As an attempt, through information, persuasion, adjustment, and contacts, to seek support for some activity, cause, movement, institution, product or service."

In the foregoing definitions, you will find though they may differ in their emphasis on certain elements, they have a great deal in common. Let us see what Public Relations is as seen in these definitions:

(*i*) A planned effort or management function;
(*ii*) The relationship between an organisation and its publics;
(*iii*) Evaluation of public attitudes and opinions;
(*iv*) An organisation's policies, procedures, and action they relate to its publics;
(*v*) Steps taken to ensure that these polices, procedures-and actions are in the public interest and socially responsible;
(*vi*) Execution of an action and/or communication programme and
(*vii*) Development of rapport, goodwill, understanding and acceptance through a two-way communication. This analysis should be helpful to you in identifying the purpose, functions and the scope of Public Relations itself.

To avoid confusion in terminology it would be better to differentiate Public Relations from other elements or functions that it performs. It would be worthwhile to keep in mind these working definitions of terms that are likely to be used in the course of discussion.

**Working Definitions**

- *Advertising:* Use of a hired or paid medium of communication, such as medium for conveying a message, information of a product or service. Although, it is basically a function of sales, advertising is regarded as an important tool of Public Relations.

- *Community relations:* Dealing and communicating with the citizens and groups in the vicinity of an organisations geographical.
- *Ethics:* The science of moral duty in conformity with principles of conduct accepted in a culture.
- *PR Professional:* The agent of management assigned to describe and interpret policies and procedures to public and seek their response and convey the same to the management.
- *Government relations:* Dealing and communicating with the employees of an organisation.
- *Industry Relations:* Dealing and communicating with firms within the industry of the organisation.
- *Professional public relations:* The art of convincing people that they should adopt a certain attitude or pursue a certain course of action; usually associated with management.
- *Profession:* Practice of a skilled art or service based on training, a body of knowledge, and adherence to agreed-on standards of ethics and procedures.
- *Public:* A group of people who have a common interest, goal, vocation and occupation.
- *Managing:* The art of conducting an enterprise or programme in the interest of the publics, owners and management and in accord with policy.
- *Policy:* The plan by which management sets out to accomplish its objectives.
- *Mass media:* Vehicles of communication designed to convey information, ideas and impressions to many people simultaneously; e.g., newspapers, magazines, television, radio, motion pictures.
- *Lobbying:* The attempt to influence the voting behaviour of legislators on behalf of specific interests or causes.
- *News:* Information about current events—accidental, incidental, or planned.
- *Publicity:* Dissemination of purposefully planned and executed message e.g., news releases, articles, features through selected media to further the particular interest of an organisation or person, without specific payment to media. Publicity is a significant tool of Public Relations.

- *Press-agentry:* Creating news events of a transient of nature, often of a sensational or attention-catching nature.
- *Promotion:* Special activities, such as sponsoring events, designed to create and stimulate interest in a person, product, organisation or cause.
- *Media relations:* Dealing with the communications media in seeking publicity or responding to their interest in the organisation.
- *Propaganda:* Efforts to influence the opinions of a public to propagate a doctrine, an ideology, a cause or an interest.

## Understanding and Explaining the Nature and Scope of Public Relations

Public Relations as a process serves a number of functions. While the definitions may vary, the nature of Public Relations indicate that it is essentially a task promoting rapport and goodwill between a person, firm or institution and the community at large through dissemination of information. It seeks to earn support, mobilise or solicit favour for an-idea, a cause, a problem, for an institution or an individual. It uses a two-way communication in dealing with public opinion. First, it assesses the attitudes of the public towards the organisation. Next, it executes communication programmes to gain public understanding and acceptance of the managements point of view. Public Relations aims to bring about harmonious and mutually advantageous adjustment between an organisation and the community through dissemination of ideas and also by providing feedback from the public to the management. It also evaluates public attitudes, identifies policies that interest public and executes the programme of communication.

Good Public Relations implies a sound moral base, i.e., communication must be sincere and based on facts. Harmless conduct is not enough. Action is required to gain favourable recognition. This may be expressed as striving for three objectives: (*i*) to attention; (*ii*) to win belief and (*iii*) to impart understanding.

These steps are taken to reach a goal: to convince people that they should adopt a certain attitude or pursue a certain course of action.

To perform this feat, Public Relations must begin at the heart of the organisation it serves the management. It must find the answer to these three questions: (*a*) What is the message that the management wants to impart? (*b*) To whom? (*c*) How?

And a fourth question is implied in these three: what is the purpose? These questions, although innocent-looking require great deal of thought. It is no good to engage in some Public Relations activity in spurt because someone else is doing it. Public Relations activity has to be a planned and sustained programme with the goals worked out clearly.

Without knowing what, whom, how, and why, a Public Relations programme can serve no purpose. A purposeful Public Relations programme should: (*i*) Understand the organisation's nature and purpose thoroughly; (*ii*) Communicate this understanding to others, that is, the publics; (*iii*) Observe and evaluate the effect of the communication.

Many people get all their news from television, and the entertainment programmes often reflect the attitudes of the viewers. You should know that what is being presented to the public. Communications scholars—like Dr. Max McCombs of the University of Texas pointed out that media coverage sets the agenda for people's thinking.

Watching the news will show what kinds of stories are used and how they are handled. The most popular programmes will give an indication of the social climate and possible public attitudes. For example, because they are now see as a threat to health, cigarettes have almost disappeared from the screen.

Listening to radio news will reveal the kinds of items that are used and the way they are presented. An awareness of this will enable you to prepare suitable material. Other programmes, especially talk shows, will show you what sorts of stories get on the air and indicate the kind of audience that listens to such programmes.

As a consequence of Public Relations activity on this sound base, management can gain the opportunity, to make such internal changes in the organisation, product, service, or method as will enable it to survive and prosper in a public climate of goodwill.

Briefly, Public Relations involves four major elements. They are interrelated and overlapping. In fact, one tends to lead to another. These are: (*a*) Two-way Communication; (*b*) Mutual Understanding; (*c*) Caring for Public Opinion and (*d*) Social Responsibility.

## Importance of Two-way Communication in PR

Public Relations philosophy puts great emphasis on the need for two-way communication. It is not fairly well accepted that feedback is important. How does one set it?

Many misunderstandings spring from a total lack of or an inadequate communication. The foremost objective in any Public Relations Programme, therefore, is to improve existing channels of communication and to establish two-way flow of information. However, this is not as easy as it sounds! Even if you have a strong desire to communicate, there may be great difficulties in achieving success because of the barriers in communication process.

Many of the human problems in organisation are ascribed lack of communication. Managements are constantly advised to give prompt and regular information to employees and the public. Public Relations methods can do much to resolve such conflicts to reconcile differences or even as a preventive measure but let nobody underestimate the difficulties involved.

## The Factor Like Mutual Understanding

Mutual understanding requires, by definition, a two-way communication. A Public Relations policy for any organisation, for example, should include both inward activity and intelligence to assess the policies and behaviour of the management, to see whether action is necessary to improve the organisation's image; and outward activity to inform the public about its achievement. You may be curious about one point—where does the question of 'mutual interest arise'? In any Public Relationship, there are at least two parties involved. First, there is the organisation which has something to promote. Often in competition with others. Second, there are the "publics" to which the organisation directs its efforts.

Thus, there are two interest to be met: The private interest and the public interest. Generally, these interests are often in conflict. Each party interprets the public interest in terms of its own self-interests. Let us take an example of a manufacturing industry. It is exposed to pressures from different sides. The consumer who wants to pay the lowest price for the goods he needs. The worker who wants the highest wage of salary for producing goods. The stockholder who wants the maximum dividend or profit for his investment in the machinery used to make the goods. The government which wants you to pay the sales and excise taxes on the good you are selling. Each group has its own interests in mind. Resolving these conflicts of interests is the essential part of Public Relations because satisfying those interests in essential to the enduring success of the organisation. This can only be done by achieving "mutual understanding" between the organisation and all these interests. For this two-way communication is necessary by providing information to the people and seek "public favour" through an informed "public opinion".

**The Factor for Like Caring for Public Opinion**

Public opinion has been described as the "source spring" of Public Relations. Public opinion, is the consensus of individual opinions of the majority among the masses, based on their attitudes and widely held beliefs, moulded by public interest. Abraham Lincoln once said: "Public-sentiment is everything. With public sentiment, nothing can fail; without it nothing can succeed." Public Relations practice requires ungrudging and unwavering faith in the wisdom of an informed public opinion. Public Relations provides the necessary information to various public interest groups, in the interest of the organisations. Satisfying the public interest, to the "mutual" advantage of all parties in conflict, is a basic requirement of sound Public Relations. Arriving at this definition of mutual interests requires satisfactory two-way communication as a pre-requisite to achieving goodwill.

As mentioned earlier, public opinion impinges on an organisation at many levels: with official bodies; contacts with stockholders; relations with distributors, wholesalers, reactions of buyers or consumers; and internal relations with employees. In all these fields there is a need for constant endeavour to establish and maintain mutual understanding and to keep a watch for possible cause of disharmony. Dissent and murmurs should not be ignored. The basic problem is to adjust the relationships of an organisation to serve both public and private interests and make it "socially responsible."

**The Factor Like Social Responsibility**

The social responsibility of any organisation stems from what has been discussed earlier that all organisations work in the name of the people with the main aim of serving their interests. For the organisation to profit or gain through its efforts, it has necessarily to first achieve the acceptance and approval of the people for its role. Many organisations, through getting profit from society, do not show their concern for the latter's welfare and thereby end up having problems. Public Relations seeks to attune itself to the needs and aspirations of the community it serves and identifies the interests of the organisation with that of the community's e.g. participating in festivals, sponsoring local sports events instituting scholarships, bus shelters, promoting local causes, etc. This is the social responsibility role of Public Relations.

What is the scope of Public Relations? Public Relations consists of a number of little things and a few big things. It is the daily application of common-sense, common courtesy and common decency. It is doing a lot of favours to others, so that they will be as important as providing counsel and advice that leads management to solve a crucial strike situation. It can be organising a health camp for the children of the employees of your at large, as in the case of Union Carbide's Bhopal gas tragedy. It could be just writing a letter to a parent whose child was reprimanded for neglecting studies, or providing information to potential investors in your company. It can be snuffing out a spark or putting out a big bonfire. Public relations is a multitude of things.

Many crises occur due to communication breakdown. This can happen due to lack of communication for inadequacy of such communication which has not satisfied the information needs of the receiver. To assess the information needs of the public it is important to be a good listener. A piece of gossip can generate a humour. A rumour unchecked can bring the production machinery to a standstill and cost the organisation dearly. If only, one had cared to listen, one could have possibly also detected the first murmurs of discontent and perhaps prevented the labour strike.

Much of what is usually labelled as Public Relations is actually "publicity"—the dissemination of facts, ideas about individuals and institutions for various purpose, such as to attract attention, gain prestige, publicize products, or to satisfy public interest an institution or for an individual. Often, people tend to confuse the publicity tool with the broader—aspect of Public Relations. Public Relations practice is still concerned with getting publicity, for somebody or something. Many Public Relations 'practitioners do little else. But publicity, a one way proposition, is not Public Relations. It is only a tool of Public Relations.

It is imperative to ascertain to get facts confirmed from reliable sources before making it public. Research may yield the real facts. In general, research for this purpose is divided into four categories:

(*a*) *Personal inquiry:* Asking questions of people who know something about the subject.
(*b*) *Interviews:* Detailed questioning of someone who has a thorough knowledge of the subject.
(*c*) *Reading:* Systematic reading of available printed material and use of computer data banks like Dialog and Nexis.
(*d*) *Survey:* Planning and conducting a thorough investigation.

### *Conducting Inquiries*

Your telephone is one of your best research tolls. Call experts in the field or people who are knowledgeable about the subject. Although you may think this is an intrusion, most people will be flattered and pleased to provide information. In addition, they can give you names, places, and examples that will add flavor to your publicity.

### *Doing Interviews*

Before the interview, you should look over your information about the subject of the interview. This should reveal what is not known and suggest questions to be asked. You should have a list of specific questions and ask them one by one. If the answers are not clear, you should continue to probe until they are.

If the interviewee goes off on a tangent, this may contribute information that you had not thought of. Pursuing these unexpected leads may yield valuable ideas, so digressions should not be squelched. Taking notes is a must, and a tape recorder can help you keep an accurate account of what was said. As the interview progress it is important to watch the interviewee and listen to his or her tone of voice. Tones, facial expressions, and gestures often reveal more than the words alone.

A good start would be to consult a comprehensive encyclopedia such as the Brittanica or Americana. The next step is to use a library. A reference librarian can direct you to get proper source of information about what you want to find out. A vague request for information generally produces unsatisfactory results. When you use books, try to select the latest publications/editions.

A number of major daily newspapers also have their own indexes, available in many libraries. These include the Journal of Indian Science, Times of India, and Hindustan Times, Christian Science Monitor, Los Angeles Times, New York Times, Wall Street Journal and Washington Post. A comprehensive newspaper index is Business News Bank, which indexes articles about companies, industries products and business people.

Another kind of reference will help you when you have to write about eminent personalities. These are the who reference books. They give detailed information about people, their careers, accomplishments, honours, and so on. In addition to Who's Who, there are several other books that list prominent people by profession or by general area of residence. These are normally grouped together in the library and, if you can't hit your target in one book you may do so in another.

Expect for a few classified documents, public records of local, state and national governments are open. For example, the National Library in India and of Congress in America are a large and helpful source. The Publication Division of the Government of India has a large number of publications on all subjects. State and local governments, too, publish bulletins, reports, and statistics that can be helpful.

Other sources of facts and figures include trade and professional associations, trade journals and publication of academic interests. The key to getting at this material is to ask the simple question: Who might know something about his subject?

### *Conducting Surveys*

Surveys can produce valuable information, but they are costly and time consuming. A very simple survey might be conducted without the use of a specialized research firm, but it will usually be necessary to get professional help. Among the things that will be involved in deciding to do a survey are questions like these: What is the objective? Who will do the survey and how much will it cost? How long will it take? Who will be surveyed and what sort of questions will be asked? How will the questions be asked?

### *Patient Listening*

Quotations add interest to news items or feature stories. On one day, a metropolitan newspaper use the word "said" 19 times on its first page. This shows that what people say can be a major factor in the news, and it suggests that you'll do well to use direct quotations whenever possible.

This suggestion is coupled with a warning to be sure that your quotations are accurate. It is also necessary to prevent misunderstandings. A misquotation may not lead to legal repercussions, but it can still cause confusion. The only way to make a quotation accurate is to listen carefully. Did the president say "possible" or "probable"? Did the contractor say that the job "would be finished by June 6" or that he "hoped, that it would be finished by June 6?"

If there is any doubt as to what was said, you must go back to the speaker and ask for clarification. Most people hate to be misquoted and are willing to correct a statement that might be misunderstood. Misquoting is not only inaccurate but also dangerous, because it can mislead the reader and the reaction of the person who has been misquoted can lead to repercussions.

Likewise, "corporate communication" and "Corporate Relations" are clearly limited to the "corporate sector"—the field of industry, trade and business. It relates to customer-investor relationships and is used in corporate-sponsored reports. While Public Relation's scope extends to policy and strategy and counselling managements, "corporate relations" is limited to the company's relationships with specific target groups, among clients, stockholders, commercial interest groups and sometimes liaisoning with government officials to secure mutually acceptable objectives, the last falling in the area of "public affairs", another term which impinges on the scope of Public Relations, all these terms are functional in nature. Choice of a term that deals with a function labels its practitioners as technicians and not as "professionals".

The broadness and non-specificity of the term "Public Relations" prevents it from becoming associated with any one type of function. As it is a general word, it remains suitable an "umbrella" term covering many types of functions that it performs. Public Relations, more accurately defined and described, would include the following, if we were to be referring to an industrial organisation, for example, Creating publicity for the organisation, its products and services; Employee publications like a house journal; General Body meeting reports; Preparation of booklets, Pamphlets, Advertising; Community work, Corporate donations;

Public-speaking; Radio and TV programmes; Direct mail; Arranging, Exhibitions, Tours, Open houses; Training employees in customer relations; Answering queries from media and public; issuing of press release; Making films, Documentaries, Video; Company policy formulation; Interesting with legislators and government; Company correspondence; Personal calls; Sales training; Promotion.

The broad variety and scope of Public Relations functions, ranging from doing small favours for people, being just visible in a social gathering, to devising a broader strategy to gain public favour, can encompass many things that come under the "umbrella" term of Public Relations. But one thing should be borne in mind. No two Public Relations practitioner's programmes or functions are exactly the same. They differ from organisation to organisation and person to person.

You may rightly feel like enquiring as to what, then, is the proper role of Public Relations in a democratic, agro-based, but industrialized society like India? For what tasks may the Public Relations professionals lay claim?

In a developing society like India with vast size and population, linguistic diversity, culture, religion and innumerable ethnic groups coupled with illiteracy, ignorance, superstition, diverse beliefs and faiths, Public Relations assumes a greater significance as the government is socially accountable for its various policies and programmes. This is also vital for shaping public opinion. Public Relations help our complex, pluralistic society to reach decisions and function more effectively by contributing to mutual understanding among various groups and institutions.

Public Relations serve a wide variety of institutions in society such as business, trade unions, Government agencies, voluntary agencies, foundations, hospitals, educational and religious institutions. To achieve their goals, these institutions must develop, effective relationships with many different audiences or "publics" such as employees, members, consumers, local communities, shareholders, other institutions and with society at large.

"Public Relations is the communication and interpretation of ideas and information to the public of an institutions; the communication and interpretation of information, ideas and opinions from those publics to the institution in the effort to bring the two into harmonious adjustment."

The Public Relations professional, is a specialist in communication and in public opinion. Thus defined, Public Relations meets a vital need in democratic society—the need to bridge the gulf which separate those having mutual interests and common causes. This concept of Public Relations must be the inevitable response to the changing nature of Indian Society which is now transforming itself from a "mixed economy" to a capital and technology-driven "market economy", increasingly becoming privatised."

**Public Relations as Management Function**

Among the multitude of roles and functions that Public Relations performs, one of the most important is identifying the "public interest" and keeping the organisation informed about it. But, in the final analysis, determining what is public interest, is decision for the management. This leads to the conclusion that Public Relations is management function.

While this is a reasonable claim, it is often misconstrued leading to confusion and mistaken assumptions. Ms. Denny Griswold in her definition begins as: "Public Relations is the management function...". G. Edward Pendray asserts ".... Public relations is not only a management function: it may well be the heart and core of modern management." Such assertions, common among Public Relations practitioner and the management he is employed to serve. The actions and policies of an organisation is determined by the policy-makers. The confusion lies in locating the boundary line where the responsibility of the Public Relations practitioner ends and the management takes over the task of fixing policy and implementing it. This cause a lot of friction.

Irrespective of where Public Relations fits into an organisation it is generally considered a STAFF rather than a LINE function. What do these terms mean? Line people are involved in carrying out the basis functions of the organisation while staff people are experts in policy planning and techniques which help supervise the line people do a better job of achieving and organisation's goals. In order to achieve this, management must make a continuous effort to understand the true role and status of Public Relations. It must accept Public Relations as a staff function and facilitate it to be more effective.

As a management function Public Relations encompasses the following:

(*a*) Anticipating, analysing and interpreting public opinion, attitudes and issues which might affect, for good or ill, the operations and plans of organisations.

(*b*) Counselling management at all levels in the organisation with regard to policy decisions, courses of action, and communication, taking into account their public ramifications and the organisation's social or citizenship responsibilities.

(*c*) Researching, conducting and evaluating, on a continuing basis, programmes of action and communication to achieve informed public understanding, necessary to the success of an organisation's aims. These may include marketing, financial fund raising, employee, community or a government relations and other programmes.

(*d*) Planning and implementing the organisation's efforts to influence or change public policy.

(*e*) Setting and implementing the organisation's efforts to influence or change public policy.

(*f*) Setting objectives, planning, budgeting, recruiting and training staff, developing facilities—in short, managing the human resources to meet all of the above objectives and goals.

If public attitudes and opinions are negative or hostile toward organisational policies, procedures and actions, the Public Relations practitioner:

(*i*) can utilise its skills and resources in an attempt to change or modify public attitudes and opinion through communication.

(*ii*) can inform line authorities and top management about the negative or hostile public attitudes and opinions and subsequently attempt to change them. This is based on the assumption that Public Relations is an intelligence-gathering and communicating agency. It recognises that evaluation of public attitudes and opinions and subsequent communication with public as its important duties.

Public Relations in this way is placed in the same category as personal management, finance department, etc. It is the Public Relations function to provide skilled assistance and advice to management and from its publics, internally and externally.

Public Relations and "Publics" are inseparable. Without publics there cannot be any Public Relations. What does the term "Publics" mean? To limp together 900 million of Indian under the umbrella term the "public" is to misconstrue and oversimplify the term. For the sake of convenience, practitioners prefer to segmentize public into broad, general groups. These are terms referred to as employees, stock-holder, customer and community publics. In precise terms, "a public may be defined as any group of people tied together, however loosely, by some common bond of interest or concern", for example, the shareholders of a company.

In additional Public Relations usage, Publics are divided into two categories—External and Internal. External Publics are those outside an organisation that have some relationship to the organisation and can have widespread impact on its functioning, like government officials the media, retailers, suppliers, customers, competitors, investors, bankers, local community organisations.

Internal Publics are those which an organisation most closely relates to—one shares the institutional identity, such as the management, stockholders, employees, dealers, sales representatives and other marketing personnel.

The nature of an organisation usually dictates its publics and one can draw some major distinctions applied to the nature of organisations and its publics.

Organisations with similar goals and purposes have similar publics. For instance, every daily newspaper in the country sustains itself by attracting readers and advertisers; hence, reading and advertising publics are basic publics for daily newspapers.

As organisations change in nature and purpose, so do their publics. For instance, if a textiles manufacturing firm switches over to readymade garments, the nature of its publics also changes.

It should also be noted that there are publics within publics and many of them are hidden from you. These are in a latent state. As issues arise which affect them, these latent publics begin to stir, surface and organise. They may cause innumerable problems if their presence is not detected and steps not taken to handle them. For instance, booksellers are the immediate public for a college. But the people who supply paper to these book-sellers form a latent public (hidden from view). Suddenly, due to government policy, there may be a crisis in the paper industry. These paper merchants may then create problems for the book-seller and therefore for the college indirectly.

Public is amorphous, every changing and virtually infinite in number. Also, the multiplicity of publics can cause internal conflicts, as different publics have interests and needs. These conflicts cannot be easily resolved. For instance, the employees as a public are interested in knowing more about an organisation, its personnel policies, wage policies, incentives for the workforce etc. The customers want to know the product range, quality of products, prices, after sales service, etc. What is true of the divergence of interests among these two publics, such as employees and customers, is also true of others publics.

The Public Relations practitioner must carefully identify each public pertinent to a particular project and determine other publics that might affect it. To achieve this, sometimes the Public Relations practitioner will have to undertake research to fined out who these publics really are, what they think, and what they want, in order to communicate appropriate messages effectively. Also, Public Relations should not assign importance to major public alone. While it must gauge the majority opinion it must also consider the view point of the smaller or minor publics. Sometimes, the Public Relations practitioner has to study the psychographics—the emotional and behavioural characteristics that define each group. Psychographics generally show how one public may be similar to another in interest or actions. Then identification and segmentation of publics is an important step to effective and meaningful communication in Public Relations.

The discussions so far reveals that Public Relations practice is the continuing effort to effect a harmonious adjustment between an organisation and the various interests it serves. This can be achieved through two-way communication resulting in mutual understanding of each other's interests. In this process, the Public Relations practitioner plays the role of communicators, catalyst and counsellor.

Communication is the art and science of sending or transmitting message, information, ideas, emotions from one person to another and obtaining a feedback (reaction) of the message sent. This means that the act of "communication" involves various elements, viz. source/Communicator (the sender of information); Context; Message (use of symbols, like words, gestures); Channel (a medium of transmission like voice, radio) etc.; Receiver (one who receives and comprehends the message; Feedback (Response of the receiver to the message, transmitted back to the sender, through medium).

Public Relations today involves complete analysis and understanding of all the factors that influence people's attitudes toward an organisation. This is achieved through what has been popularly called "Public Relation's four-state process." The stage are:

(*a*) Fact-finding—research analysis of opinion, environment,
(*b*) Planning-policy formulation, programming, goal setting,
(*c*) Communication—implementing planned communication activities, execution, and
(*d*) Evaluation—feedback and adjustment/course modification.

The gamut of Public Relations operations are targeted towards diverse publics with varied information needs so as to help the publics have a right perspective of the organisations and its goal. The Public Relations practitioner works through the printed word, the spoken word and the image to communicate and interpret messages to the publics.

In order to become the PR as an effective and vibrant communicator, catalyst and counsellor, one should develop the art of conveying the messages. One of the first steps in writing is to know exactly what idea is to be conveyed. It should be possible to express this in one brief sentence. Once you have this basic idea clearly in mind, all the words you choose should serve to expand and explain the basic message. For example, "The way in which a person drives can makes a big difference in the amount of gasoline consumed." This theme could be amplified into a feature article.

The message should be aimed at a specific audience. Is it the general public? A group of educators? Hospital administrators? Automobile drivers? Donors to charity? Regardless of who the target audience may be, the message should be coined in words that they will understand. Furthermore, the medium in which the idea is to be conveyed must be considered. Psychology Today is quite different from Popular Mechanics. The Wall Street Journal is not like the Toledo Blade. Radio uses material very differently than a newspaper would. You must not only aim at a specific audience but also tailor your message to the intended medium.

Sentences should be clear and concise. Longer sentences may often be necessary, but a good test is to go back over the material and see how many sentences can be cut down. Don't hesitate to use some sentences of eight or ten words. Mixing long and short sentences improves the rhythm. The typical paragraph should normally include only one idea. As a general practice, it ought to be no longer than six or eight lines. If necessary, a longer paragraph may be used, but brevity is preferable. Writing that goes on and on without a pause creates monotonous on the reader.

Word length is a good measurement of readability, and every writer hopes that his or her writing will be read. In readable writing, most words are short. A message containing and average of 1.5 syllables per word is considered to be very readable. Some states have required this 1.5 syllable average for consumer information about purchase contracts and monetary loans.

For the general public this guide should be kept in mind. For a more technical audience, it is permissible to use longer words, but even here, brevity is desirable. Whenever, there is a choice of two words, it's better to use the shorter one. Don't try to show off your knowledge by using long and complicated words. Remember that Lincoln's Gettysburg Address consisted of 267 words, of which 202 had only one syllable.

Greek Anglo Saxon word is more understandable than the longer one derived from French, Greek, or Latin. "Buy" is better than "purchase." "Home" is better than "residence." "Hire" is better than "employ." Most readers will react favourably to this kind of writing. In law, education and science there is a different standard. The language of lawyers is commonly loaded with repetitious and cumbersome words. Educators often seem to love concealing their thoughts behind words that are strange, such as "multi-ethnic individualized learning," and "continuum." Scientific writing, too, is loaded with esoteric words. To make them understandable to the general public is a difficult task, but it can be done.

Public relations writing should be natural. If it does not sound clear when read out loud, it should be rewritten. Every piece of copy should be reviewed to see if any words can be cut. Active rather than passive language is preferable. "Smith took every possible precaution" is better than "Every possible precaution was taken by Smith."

In many offices where people are engaged in writing, it is the practice to post a large sign bearing the letters KISS. Underneath, in smaller type, is the definition of this acronym: "Keep It Simple, Stupid."

This is good advice for any writer at any time. It becomes especially important when you must translate technical information into something that lay people will understand. Here the sign should change from KISS to MISS and the words beneath should read "Market It Simple, Stupid," because there is nothing to keep simple. Instead, there is something complicated that must be made simple.

Simplifying a complex idea is a hard work. First you must research the information until you really understand it. It is impossible to explain anything that you do not understand. To gain understanding, you must read the material and question the people who created it.

In explaining a complicated subject, it is important not to overload the reader. He or she should not be given any more than is needed. The language of explanation must be plain English. Jargon has no place here. If possible there should be no technical terms, but sometimes they must be used because nothing else will serve the purpose. It is necessary to use technical terms, they should be described in layman's language.

In describing something new and different, use familiar words and go step from a base of common understanding. A foolproof test of any writing that is meant to simplify a complex subject is to pretest it. If several people who know nothing about the subject do understand the explanation, it is probably adequate, provided that the experts approve. And if the experts disapprove, it is probably because the simplification is inaccurate. Here again, a rewrite is called for.

For news items or features to be published, they must conform to the writing style preferred by the mass media. The stylebooks mentioned in this chapter will help you get on the right track. Beyond this, however you should conform to the style of the specific media for which you write. Some may want hard facts, others may prefer a more breezy approach. Some will accept lengthy material, others insist on terseness. Some use pictures, some don't. If you read what they publish, you will soon learn what to send to them.

Before you start writing anything, you should make an outline of what you are going to include in your message. It may be brief or comprehensive. You will probably modify it as you gather information, but an outline will help to keep your thinking in order.

In the simplest terms an outline is a list of topics to be written about in the order in which they will be presented. Usually an outline has major topics, and within each major topic there are likely to be minor topics. This book is an example of an outline. Each chapter covers one general subject. Within each chapter there are several major topics. Each of these is identified by a major subhead in capital letters. Under each of these major subheads there are minor topics identifies by secondary subheads in capital and lowercase letters.

Errors in your writing will brand you as careless, illiterate, or inconsiderate of the readers. Be sure to think about the potential errors.

Credibility is sacrificed when spelling errors appears in public relations materials. Media gatekeepers, in particular, are critical of poor grammar and spelling.

Metaphors add sparkle and clarity to writing if they are appropriate and conceptually correct. But they can be unintentionally funny when they are made up of incompatible images.

The subject and the words that modify it often become separated in a sentence, causing some confusion as to what exactly is being discussed. An example is quoted below from news release:

> "The proposed budget provides salary increases for faculty and staff performing at a satisfactory level of two per cent".

Another gross error in writing is the use of redundant words. It is not necessary to use the word "totally" to modify words like "destroyed" or "completely" to modify "demolished." A lot of writers also say that "something is" some what or "very" unique. Unique by definition means one of a kind. Something is either unique or it isn't. The following redundancy appeared in a news release is given below for your understanding:

> In addition, the company lists $50 million in receivable that it hopes to collect. These are unpaid bills, largely from customers, that have yet to be paid.

Another common error is the misuse of percentages. The price or value of anything can be expressed in clear figures. The price can go up 10 per cent. 150 per cent, or 1,000 per cent. It cannot go down more than 100 per cent. Even if the price has gone up 1,000 per cent from a given base, the new price becomes a new base. If the price then goes down to nothing, it has gone down only 100 per cent of that new base. There can be no greater loss than 100 per cent. In spite of this, writers may say something like this: "The price is now 327 per cent less than it was ten years ago." What they mean is the price ten years ago was 327 per cent higher than it is today.

A couple of generations ago, it was a common practice in writing to use stereotypes. Today such stereotyping is certain to provoke violent resentment. Avoid suggesting that all members of any racial, ethnic, or sexual group have the same personal characteristics—ambition, laziness, shrewdness, guile, intelligence, or what have you. Don't suggest that some characteristic sets an individual apart from a stereotyped norm. For instance, it is inappropriate to write," Although he is black, he has excellent qualifications for the job." One should avoid racial identification unless it is absolutely necessary.

The other tools that can be used by the Public Relations person, are House Publications, Letters and Bulletins, Bulletin Boards, Posters. Photographs and billboards, Institutional advertising, Meeting, Speaker's bureau, Public address systems, Films, Video and slide films, Displays and exhibits, Visitors for open house, Plant tours, Staging special events, etc.

### Enumerating the Benefits of Public Relations

Every institution and function fares in relation to the values it provides to others, rather than in merely pursuing its own gain. The primary benefits derived from Public Relations are:

(*i*) Public Relations is a means for the public to have its desires and interests felt by the institutions in our society. It interprets and speaks for the public to otherwise unresponsive organisations. It also speaks on behalf of those organisations to the public to help create public acceptance and recognition.

(*ii*) It help promotion of a company's goods or services and builds up 'image'.

(*iii*) Public Relations is a means to achieve mutual adjustment between institutions and groups, establishing smoother relationships that benefit the public.

(*iv*) It can help to attract talented personnel for the organisation.

(*v*) Publication Relations is a safety valve for freedom. By providing means of working out accommodation it makes arbitrary action or coercion less likely.

(*vi*) Public Relations is an essential element in the communication systems that enables individuals to be informed on many aspects of subjects that affect their lives. It can stimulate attitudes and bring about changes.

(*vii*) Public Relations personnel can help activate the organization's social conscience and thus foster the goodwill of community.

(*viii*) It can help overcome public misconceptions about the organisation by disseminating correct information.

(*ix*) It can help earn the goodwill of employees by showing interest in their welfare. Thus, it may prevent labour problems and solve any disputes with greater ease.

Public Relations, consciously practised, is a universal activity. It functions in all aspects of life. Each of us, basically, practice principles of Public Relations in major areas for seeking the acceptance co-operation, or affection of others. Public Relations professionals only practice it in a more professional manner.

It is increasingly being recognised that Public Relations require professional attitudes in India within the context of a rapidly changing social environment. As the institutions of government, industry, and politics intensify their concern with increasingly articulate and preoccupied publics, the need for wise counsel and guidance is mandatory if the communications process is to be conducted with clarity. It is encouraging that a growing number of PR practitioners are becoming aware of the social and political implications of their profession. The work of the Public Relations Society of India is beginning to bear fruit. Another pointer to the growth of professionalism is that PR practitioners in India are developing "the problem-solving approach." This process requires that the PR professional be able to cope with not only the increasing degree of public awareness but also the advanced sophisticated communication technologies. To merit advanced status, to validate one's claims to deal with public opinion one cannot but function in a highly organised, professional manner and keep abreast of developing trends.

In the years ahead, Public Relations—and professionalism in Public Relations—are bound to increase. As the sophistication of the media grows, so must the ability of the PR persons increase to match the newer resources at their disposal. This is particularly true in this age of social transition. Since development in any sector, triggers off changes in many other sectors, the PR person is challenged as never before.

This growth of Public Relations and its obligations are a natural corollary to the great boom in electronic media which is staggering in its implications. New modes of communication are evolving rapidly. Cable television, satellite broadcasting, video and audio cassettes have become regular media of communication. Newspapers and magazines are bringing out specialised columns to combat the pressures of television competition, special-interest publications particularly in business, finance and trade are booming. It will demand the highest skills and creative imagination to choose the right medium and the right message and get it across to one's target audience in this highly competitive situation.

Besides coping with the new communication technologies, the PRO will need to be possessive to handle problems relating to environment, social conflict, international affairs, and the rising tensions that afflict our society at every turn.

A new age, of course, calls for talents and techniques appropriate to entirely new social situations, Public Relations professionalism must match the obligations with adequate resources. We are certainly on the road already but have a long way to go.

Public Relations undoubtedly is an effective way to achieve smooth relationships, safeguard reputations, promote sales and build a corporate image. However, it should not be seen as a panacea for all ills. It is to be borne in mind that Public Relations can help to achieve recognition only when there is a matching performance. Public Relations efforts are not composed of stunts or gimmicks. It is not a magical remedy like a coat of white-wash applied to the soiled walls. It is propaganda. It cannot afford to disregard ethics, truth or public good. It is not hollow publicity efforts directed at achieving, sales. It is not also a fire alarm service that can help reverse a crisis because goodwill cannot be established overnight. Hence, Public Relations is a sustained long-term and sincere effort, which along with genuine performance and concern can earn public goodwill.

# 2

# Origin and Growth of Public Relations in Media and Journalism

## INTRODUCTION

In this chapter one may examine the growth and development of Public Relations in the light of history of the PR movement, and mention factors that led to the evolution of Public Relations; history of Public Relations in ancient India; describe the early use of Public Relation in the USA; explain how Public Relations played a role in the World Wars I and II; analyse the evolution of the concept of social responsibility in Public Relations; state the different stages of growth of Public Relation in India; outline the first organizational Public Relations attempt in the Indian Railways; and to describe the role of Public Relation in the World War I through the Government of India's Information and Broadcasting Department and Audio-visual publicity.

You are familiar with the basis of Public Relations, its nature and the process involved in the practice of Public Relations. The Public Relations differs from advertising and the winning of public trust was realised in winning of the Press and all other functions of the public by giving them concrete and truthful information.

Public Relation is the newest area of the management discipline, and is considered a rather late arrival on the stage of our present day industrial society. In this unit, we shall examine what factors led to the origin of PR. Since PR, in the modern sense of the term, developed first in the United States, we shall therefore, begin with a study of its various phases of development in that country. Looking back at the past is not just an academic exercise. It should enable you to understand the strengths and weaknesses of PR. You would also be able to see clearly how the distinction between advertising and propaganda, on the one hand, and PR, on the other, gradually arose. By doing so, you would also be in a position to relate the subject of Public Relations to the existing social environment, and to appreciate that any modem management science needs to be studied in relation to the environment, and never in isolation.

Public Relations, is of recent origin, not only in India, but also in the West. PR relates itself to the social and economic environment. In America PR developed as an off-shoot of the growing industrialization and modernization process noticeable in their large business corporations the rationale behind that America is the world's leading exponent of the system of free and private enterprise, it was but logical that American business had a greater responsibility—a responsibility to conduct its affairs in the "public interest" and to win "public understanding and support." This has been one of the very important factors that helped avert the tide of "socialism" sweeping the world in the 50s. America rose to the occasion, as its business had no recourse but to use PR effectively, forthrightly, and skillfully.

While Writing the Introduction to the first edition of the "Handbook of Public Relations", in 1960, John Hill, opined that,

> "In such an unstable, human environment, the American Corporation must find ways not only to earn profit that keeps it alive but also the means to achieve the economic stability that is absolutely essential to the security of corporate life and health.
>
> "Around the globe, people are now rising in the underdeveloped nationals to assert their own rightful intent to industrialize and to consume on a much larger scale. The destiny of our corporate system of free enterprise is inescapably related to these newly emerging determinations... When we speak with pride of our own production records, we forget that we consume over three-fourths of the world's available supply of key raw materials.... produced in other lands. Suppose other peoples move forward to consume at a similar rate?... Even Nehru has ventured to enquire why America must consume so much... the one potent instrument left with us for coming to terms with conflicting opinion and concept, is Public Relations."

Virtually America made PR as their philosophy of life, and, more significantly, for their survival itself as we have been witnessing in the beginning of the 21st century.

Public relations is the twentieth century phenomenon, but traces of PR were present in human societies since the dawn of civilization.

The rulers of ancient Egypt, Babylon, Sumeria and other ancient kingdoms are known to have/made systematic efforts to tell the people how great they were. In many cases, they succeeded in making the people believe that they had a mandate from the gods, or were themselves god-like. The rulers of ancient kingdoms instinctively resorted to various forms of communication to maintain their hold over their kingdoms and their people.

Bards and wandering minstrels sang of the greatness and valour of kings and heroes, thus using the popular media of those days to communicate to the people, and create a favourable image of the rulers and the heroes. The Greeks are known to have realised the importance of public opinion like the Romans which is evident from the relics of the medieval period. It was the Romans who coined the expression, "Vox Populi, Vox, Dei, which means 'Voice of People is the Voice of God".

The Industrial Revolution began in the seventeenth century spreading across Europe, and reached North America by the eighteenth century. Mass production and selling of goods had already become a feature of the industrial societies of the world by the nineteenth century. Free enterprise and laissez-faire became the driving force for the manufacturing industries. A few people, enterprising enough, used their skills and expertise to harness the natural resources to produce marketable products. A new class of people emerged, ostensibly with the motive of serving the others in society. The reduced number of such entrepreneurs gave rise to monopolies in trade and commerce of different products. These captains of business and industry made huge profits by sheer dint of effort and aggressive marketing techniques, usually at the expense of the common man.

The nineteenth century had witnessed an apparent development in PR and averages it as on of the powerful weapons in the hands of the rulers and industrialists.

**Explaining the Factors which Contributed to the Rise of PR**

One has to appreciate the fact that any form of human activity develops only as the need for it arises and only when suitable environment has been created for it. It was only when public opinion became a potent force in society that it became necessary for organizations to win the support and goodwill of the public. The public could only become such a force in society when certain democratic institutions has developed. The mass circulated newspapers, adult franchise, organs of elected representatives of the people, such as the parliament, the legislatures, elected local government institutions, made it possible for the common man to make his voice heard. The public opinion emerged as a force to be reckoned with.

Why winning public support and goodwill was not considered important by the captains of business and industry in the past? It was only when it became impossible to ignore or disregard public opinion that they began to look around for ways to woo the public. And this stage was reached only in the twentieth century, when the democratic institutions and the media of mass communications developed and began to make people more aware of what was happening around them. The development in levels of literacy and education, which made people conscious of their rights was also an important contributory factor.

The growth of PR, having extended over several decades, is difficult to pinpoint exact factors responsible for its development. The factors are varied, interdependent and complex. Basically, it may be said that power struggles served as catalysts for the growth of PR as every group, desirous of dominance, wanted to have the public opinion titled in its favour. This is what led to the use of PR techniques even earlier in the USA: in the American War of Independence, and, subsequently, in the Civil War.

As was inevitable, the settlers from Britain and other parts of Europe in the American colonies came into conflict with the British authorities. To win public support for their movement for independence the settlers used many techniques which were later to be adopted as the tools of Public Relations. Pamphlets and newspapers were widely circulated tc further their cause. Letters were sent to important people within the country and abroad. The spoken word was also extensively used in the mass and committee meetings. Demonstrations were organized, plays were staged, and songs were composed and sung in support of their struggle.

The British authorities tried to curb the movement by enacting laws to censor the press by imposing taxes on the newspapers, and insisting on licences for publishing. The demand for a free press naturally became a rallying point for those demanding independence.

You might have hears of the famous "Boston Tea Party", a memorable event in the history of the American Revolution. In 1796, the British Parliament imposed duties on various imports into the American colonies. In the face of opposition, some of these were withdrawn, but not the duty on tea. To express their resentment and in support of the demand, "no taxation without representation," the people of the colonies boarded the British ships in the Boston harbour, and threw overboard their cargoes of tea. The staging of an "Event" to dramatise a popular slogan has since become a standard PR device to attract public attention, and to rally the people in support of a campaign.

Similar use of the PR techniques was seen in the American Civil War (1861-65). One of issues separating the north and the South of America was slavery. While the southern states, generally, supported the institution, the northern states pressed for its abolition. Both sides, made extensive use of the PR techniques to win public support. All available means of communication were pressed into service, and appeals were made, separately, to various segments of the public, calculated to win them over.

While all these events were helping to develop some of the tools of PR, and prove their efficacy in harnessing the public support, this could not yet be called the "Deliberate, planned and sustained effort" that emerged later, and developed into what we call PR. Surprising as it might seem, the dominant attitude of business and industry in the United States during the closing years of the nineteenth century and the beginning of the twentieth was exemplified in what has come to be known as "the public-be-damned" attitude.

The rapid expansion of trade and industry, the emergence of large corporations, controlling financial and physical assets unheard of before, gave the American businessmen a feeling that they were on top of the World. "Laissez faire" economic theories were favoured. Business wanted to be left upto itself, and was not prepared to brook any interference from the Government. The public did not enter into their calculations, exactions, except as a market for their goods. In any case, selling was no problem. It was at this time that William Vanderbilt, the head of the New York Central Railway, is reported to have used the expression "public-be-damned" in reply to a reporter, who asked him why he had withdrawn a railway service between New York and Chicago, despite its usefulness to the public.

The furore caused by this remark was unprecedented. This was because the United States was just entering a period when a free press was beginning to have its impact. A large number of writers came out with a series of exposures on the ways of big business and its unscrupulous methods of fleecing the public to enhance profits. This group of writers, amongst whom were Jack London, David Graham Phillips, Ida, Tarbell, Upton Sinclair and Lincoln Stephens, popularly known as the muck-rakers, exposed the excesses and corruption prevailing at that time. The muck-rakers received some support from President Theodore Roosevelt, and later from President Wilson.

A new era had started. Every action of business and industry was now under scrutiny, and the public could no longer be brushed aside. The new era was based on the maxim "the public-must-be-informed." The ground for the emergence of Public Relations had been laid.

The study of the development of Public Relations in the United States would not be complete without reference to Ivy Lee, generally referred to as the father of Public Relations. Operating in the firm of Parker and Lee, it was he who impressed on American businessmen that the public was not to be ignored, rather the public had to be informed. His statement to the press on behalf of the mineowners, in 1906, and his "declaration of principles," issued to the press the same year, are regarded as milestone in the development of Public Relations. The Declaration said:

> "This is not a secret bureau. All our work is done in the open. We aim to supply news. This is not an advertising agency. If you think any of our matter ought properly to go to your business office, do not use it. Our matter is accurate." Ivy Lee's open approach and forthrightness won him accolades from the media, which, in turn, help build a rapport between the organizations and the media.

**Elaborating upon Public Relations in World War I Phase**

The outbreak of World War I (1914-18) witnessed many significant developments in the field of Public Relations. For the first time in world history, a new kind of war started, a war in which the role of the people behind the battle lines, the people engaged in production, the people running the economy, was no less important than that of the combatants at the front. This was a war that needed that total mobilization of the human resources for the effect behind the war.

The problem of persuading people within the country, people in neutral countries and even those in enemy countries became central to the war effort. You would easily appreciate that this represented both a challenge and an opportunity to all those who had acquired some experience and expertise in the field of public communication.

Soon after the United States entered the War (April 1917), the U.S. Government set up a "Committee on Public Information" under the direction of George Greel, a form newspaper editor. Apart from the representatives of the government, there were many others with skills in this field, who were drawn into the activities of the Committee.

Amongst those who served on the Committee were people, like Edward L. Bernays, and these men subsequently, emerged as the first generation of the PR professionals in the United States. The rich experience gained by them in the war years in communicating with the public, in persuading them to support the US war effort through contributions to the war bonds, by participation in the civil defence activities, and by keeping the wheels of production in American moving, proved extremely valuable. It was on the basis of this experience that they were able to make a lasting contribution to the theory and practice of Public Relations.

The techniques developed during the World War set an example to people in other counties also, and helped to spread the PR activities to other parts of the world. The economic crisis of 1929-33, generally referred to as the Great Depression, lent further support to the Public Relations movement. Beginning in the United States, the crisis spread across the world, shaking the economies of every country. Stock markets crashed, banks closed their shutters, millionaires became paupers overnight, production came to a standstill in thousands of factories, and millions were thrown out of jobs. This event shattered the complacency of the businessmen and those in the government, who believed in laissez faire policies. It became clear to all that business could not be left along. The government was forced to intervene. Franklin Delano Roosevelt, U.S. President between 1933-45, came out with his New Deal which involved massive spending by the Government to revive the economy.

Public criticism, expressed through books and newspapers and from other platforms, forced the government and the industry to reviews their policies and attitudes war against this background that the concept of social responsibility was born, a concept that is central to the practice of Public Relations. The basic idea behind this concept is that a business organization should not concern itself with profits alone. It owes a responsibility to society, to the public at large, and must discharge its debts to the public by working the public interest.

Before Public Relations arrived at defining an ideal relationship between organizations and the press, there was a period characterised by the press agentry. The term denoted the use of the press to further a cause by trickery and by use of methods that sometimes amounted to cheating or fooling the public. It was a systematic effort to divert public attitudes or to exaggerate. Practices such as the press agentry gave a bad name to Public Relations because of the exploits of some press agents who became successful showmen. It was only the patient efforts of the genuine PR professionals like Ivy Lee, Edward Bernays and many others, that succeeded in giving the profession a good name.

## Elaborating upon the Public Relations during World War II and Post-World War Phases

By the time World War II started, Public Relations had already matured into an important profession. The invention of the radio and sound films, and further development in the techniques of printing, threw open vast opportunities of using Public Relations.

The efficacy of Public Relations techniques in communicating with different sections of the public relations. The efficacy of Public Relations techniques in communicating with different sections of the public, in changing the public attitudes and winning support for a cause, or an organization, came to be recognized and appreciated. The American business magazine, 'Fortune', which has first taken not of the emergence of Public Relations, in 1938, was sufficiently interested in the profession to conduct a survey on PR 1949, the results were published in its May issue.

The report stated that business in the United States was still in trouble, and that only good Public Relations, which denoted good performance, properly understood and appreciated, could assure its future.

By this time, PR had made its impact on university education, and had become an area of study. The American journals, Public Relations News and PR Journal, began publication in 1944. The Public Relations Society of America, formed after the merger of some earlier organizations, was established in 1948.

The bombing of Hiroshima and Nagasaki during World War II set important world leaders thinking about the need of a better understanding and humane approach to international issues. This led to the setting up of the United Nations, in 1945, and its character making the human being the axis, by reaffirming its faith in fundamental human rights, in the dignity and worth of the human person, was a landmark. Its declaration of faith in human rights has been adopted in its International Code of Ethics by the Public Relations practitioners of all the member countries, comprising the International Public Relations Association (IPRA).

## Public Relations in India

The various stages in the growth of PR in India and its links with changes in the political, social and economic environment will enable you to see clearly the relationship between developments in society and the stages of growth in PR.

A proper understanding of this mutual relationship will not only add to your knowledge about the origin and growth of PR, but will also provide valuable insights into the practice of Public Relations.

With the industrial development and introduction of modern management techniques, the need for Public Relations was felt as an essential aid in creating mutual understanding and faith between an organization and its various constituent 'publics'. You will be able to realise that Public Relations is equally useful to the government. In a developing country like India, which is beset with a multitude of problems, our government needs PR, perhaps more in comparison to the governments of highly developed counties.

Another interesting aspect of the situation is the mutual relationship between the media and Public Relations. As the existing media extend their reach and the new media come into existence, the Public Relations professionals are provided with new tools and new opportunities to reach out to the target audience.

As in other countries, the PR techniques of communication were instinctively used in ancient India. The best example is that of the Emperor Ashoka. His edicts inscribed on rocks, that have survived till this day, informed the people of the policies of the government, and exhorted them to carry out certain tasks.

Interestingly, an important principle of Public Relations was practised by Ashoka. The edicts for different regions were written in regional scripts that were in use in that region, making royal communication language and region-specific for better understanding and acceptability. We also have evidence of Mughal kings using spies to obtain direct feedback from the commoners.

True to the Indian tradition and ethos, one of the pioneers of Indian industrialisation, Jamshedji Tata, builder of the Tata Iron and Steel Company, adopted a number of measures with great foresight that reflected his spirit of service to the community.

When he conceived his project, it was not limited to the construction of a factory. He had a vision of township that would be full of shady avenues where the workmen employed in the factory could live in a serene and healthy atmosphere. Although he died before his vision could be translated into reality, his successors saw to it that this dream was realised. Not only was a beautiful township built for the employees, with the necessary civic amenities, but also numerous welfare schemes for the employees and their families were established. Community relations and good employees relations, important aspects of public relations were, thus, spontaneously practised by the House of Tatas, long before professional PR arrived on the scene.

In the Indian Railways, the Public Relations efforts in the pre-World War II period, were perhaps dictated by commercial needs. Having built the railways at a considerable cost, mainly for the purpose of carrying raw-materials from the hinterland to the ports, the British companies which were then running the railways, realised that without promoting passenger traffic the railways would not be commercially viable. Records show that in the early 1920s the GIP Railway in India carried on a Public

Relations campaign in England to attract tourists to India. For this purpose they published pamphlets and carried out an advertising campaign. Within the country the Publicity Bureau of this railway company introduced a travelling cinema, which gave open air shows of films at fairs and festivals. Subsequently, publicity officers, with similar functions were deputed to other railways. The Railways Board established publicity bureaus in London and New York also. Both the bureaus used to advertise extensively in newspapers and journals. These offices also participated in exhibitions held abroad to popularise the Indian Railways, and attract the tourist traffic.

Another form of Public Relations was practised directly by the Government during World War I. As in other parts of the world, the War made it necessary to mobilise public support, and the Government of India felt it necessary to disseminate information. It was also considered necessary to set up an organization to feed the press, and supply news about the war to the people. A Central Publicity Board was established, again, as in other countries, a newspaper editor was appointed its Chairman. In this case, it was Sir Stanley Reed, editor of The Times of India, Bombay. The Board had on its representatives from the army and the foreign and political departments of the Government of India. After the War this Board was dissolved and its functions were taken over by the Central Bureau of Information established in 1921. Professor Rushbrook Williams, from Allahabad, was appointed its first Director. In 1923, the Central Bureau was redesignated as the Directorate of Public Instruction. Later, as this nomenclature did not correctly reflect the activities of the department, the organization was renamed "The Directorate of Information and Broadcasting."

### Explaining the Relationship between PR and the National Movement

As we have described the beginnings of P R techniques in India, and brought the story up to the World War. Before we take up the subject of PR in the post-independence phase, which is the main concern of this unit, we shall discuss briefly, the developments during World War II, and the use of PR techniques in the National Movement. This is necessary in order to complete the record of various stages in the development of Public Relations in India, as they have a bearing on the events that took place in the post-independence period.

Not much progress was made in the development of professional PR during the period between the two World Wars. The public did not have any forum for expressing themselves except for a few nationalist newspapers, which were often subject to harassment by the Government. Many of these also forced to close down.

During the Second World War, however, the government again felt the need to reach out to the public. To mobilize support in favour of the war effort was difficult in situation, where the Indian National Congress and the National Sentiments were, generally, against the war effort. The government, therefore, took a number of measures.

A Ministry of Information and Broadcasting was created, and the Directorate of Information, which had been formed already was amalgamate with the new ministry. The ministry tried consciously through the use of PR techniques to create opinion in favour of the war effort. A National War Front was also set up, and a number of units were created under the Ministry, such as the war purposes Exhibition Unit, the Films Division and the Central Bureau of Public Opinion.

Just as in Europe and the United States, the need for mobilizing the public opinion in favour of the war efforts gave a fillip to organised and conscious public relations activities in Indian also.

We would do well to take note of certain other features of the pre-independence phase, which influenced events in the period after independence, and are significant from the point of view of the growth of PR in India.

In the American Independence and, later, in the American Civil War, extensive use of the PR techniques was made even before professional PR arrived on the scene. In India too, we must not fail to note, the PR techniques played a significant role in the national movement. In particular, it would be extremely rewarding to consider briefly how our great national leader, Mahatma Gandhi, was able to communicate with the masses and win public support despite the problems of cultural and linguistic diversity overcoming the serious obstacles laid by the alien government. Many of the methods, adopted by him to communicate with the masses, are now part of the standard practice of PR all over the world.

First, the importance of getting the public to identify themselves with a cause, and with the leader espousing that cause. The London-educated Barrister had no hesitation in discarding his European dress and dressing himself in the briefest of garments such as the poorest of the poor use in our country. He realised that it was only by doing so that the masses would be able to identify themselves with him and the cause he represented.

Second, the use of symbols. Apart from the fact the 'half-naked fakir' himself became a symbol around which the nation could rally. Mahatma Gandhi, a born communication understood the value of symbols. The 'charkha' (spinning wheel) symbol, which he adopted, became, as it were, the logo of national movement, symbolising self-reliance and people's participation in the cause of the freedom struggle.

Third, the staging of 'events'. The 'Dandi March' to make salt, and thus, throw a challenge to the British rulers was one such event, which captured the imagination of the whole national. The 'bonfires' of foreign cloth was another such device. Like the Boston Tea Party, which we referred to in the previous unit, 'events' such as these, proved far more effective in taking the message to the masses than the routine harangues, printed posters or leaflets.

Mahatma Gandhi did not, however, neglect the conventional means of communication either. Besides, holding meetings, giving speeches, he regularly published a journal Harijan, and continued throughout to write articles focussing attention on problems of interest to the people. Indeed, he made use of all possible media, and devised imaginative forms of communication to circumvent restrictions placed by the government on the official.

This brief interlude, which might perhaps be considered a digression from the main story of the development of professional PR, has important lessons for the PR practitioners, and you would agree that we have much to learn from this unique example of Gandhiji's art of effective communications.

### Position of PR in the Post-Independence Period

The scenario changed completely with the attaining of independence. On the one hand, there was the tragedy of partition and widespread disturbances, on the other hand, the leaders of the national movement who had realised only too well the importance of communication in winning the support of the people, they set about the task of laying the foundations of the Indian state. The first task before the country was to frame a democratic Constitution, a task that was performed by the Constituent Assembly. This body, which has been set up in 1947; completed its task in November, 1949. The Constitution framed by it came into force on 26 January, 1950. It was under this Constitution that the new Indian Republic came into being. The Constitution proclaimed the Indian polity as a Parliamentary Democracy, federal in structure but with unitary features.

Significant, from the point of view of PR, were two features of the new Constitution. One was the guarantee of certain fundamental rights, including the right to freedom of speech and expression; freedom of assembly, association or union, of movement, residence and the right to practise any profession or occupation. The second was the adult suffrage, whereby all citizens who are not less than 18 years of age (originally it was 21 years, but, in 1989, the franchise was extended), have the right to be registered as voters in any election to the Lok Sabha and legislative assemblies of the States.

With the establishment of an elected Parliament and elected legislative assemblies, along with the establishment of a free press, the two essential prerequisites for the growth of PR had been fulfilled. The stage was now ripe for the development of the professional Public Relations in India.

Some other developments, which also contributed to a conducive environment for the spread of PR in the country, also need to be noted. One was the planned industrialization of the country, which started soon after independence, and the other was expansion of the diversification of the media. We shall discuss these two developments in the sections that follow.

Prior to independence, there were very few industries in the country. We relied on imports to meet most of our requirements. In 1948, the total production of finished steel was only 845,000 tons, of cement only 1.6 million tons, and of coal only 29.8 million tons.

To correct this situation, the Government set up the Planning Commission in 1950. Its task was to prepare a blue print for development. By the end of Second Plan (1957-62), a sea change had taken place in the industrial scenario as giant steel plants, heavy electrical and heavy engineering complex began to emerge. The infrastructure was also developed with the expansion of roads, means of transport and communication, and increased power generation capacity.

The guidelines for the pattern of industrial development were provided by the Industrial Policy Resolution of 1948. These were, later, more clearly defined in the Industrial Policy Resolution of 1956. These resolutions demarcated the respective areas for different sectors of industry. Certain important areas, termed the core sectors, were reserved for the public sector, i.e., for undertakings set up and owned by the Government, while others were open for the private sector. Within the private sector, there were industries reserved for the small scale sector.

The Government of India exercised a strict control over industry with the help of an Act passed in 1951, the Industrial Development and Regulation Act. It was made compulsory for an industry with a capital base above a certain limit to seek a licence from the government for its operations.

Subsequently, other legislations were introduced to control and regulate industry. Of the many pieces of legislation introduced, one could mention the Monopolies and Restrictive Trade Practices Act (MRTP) and the Foreign Exchange Act (FERA). Imports and exports, were strictly regulated by the Controller of Imports and Exports, and there was also a Controller of Capital Issues. The Companies' Act laid down an elaborate code for the functioning of companies including conditions under which the Directors to the Boards of Companies could be appointed, and the emoluments that could be paid to them.

The adoption by the Parliament of this elaborate framework of legislation and the setting of so many bodies to regulate the various aspects of the functioning of industry created a situation wherein it became necessary for industry to develop relations with the Government, its many regulatory institutions and with the Parliament.

In the background of these developments, both the government and business organizations had to adopt conscious and deliberate policies and programmes of public relations. It is from this period of the fifties that the PR practice in the modern sense of the term began in India.

Large international companies, which already had their own expertise in P R, began to make use of these techniques in India so that they would be able to survive and grow in the post-independence environment. In the fifties and early sixties, companies like Burmah Shell, ESSO, Dunlop, Philips, etc., set up departments to execute programmes of Public Relations to meet the new situation. Indian companies like the House of Tatas also began to set up their own public relations departments to carry on organised PR activity.

The Industrial Policy Resolutions that were passed had demarcated certain areas in which the private sector play a part. Certain other industries were reserved for the public or the government sector, e.g., public utilities like Post and Telegraphs, Power and Irrigation, the Railways, Defence Production establishments, etc., as also many departmental undertakings like the Integral Coach Factory. The objective set for public sector was "to gain control of the commanding heights of the economy". This resulted in the public sector emerging as a major factor in the country's economic growth with increasing number of personnel employed and mounting investments.

The fact that these enterprises had been entirely financed by the Government, made them constantly liable to public scrutiny. Besides many important policy decisions, being taken at the ministerial level, it involved an element of dual control. The Parliament and its various committees were constantly monitoring the performance of these undertakings. The media too was watchful and quick to point out any failings and deficiency in the public sector.

On the other hand, public sector undertakings were in an advantageous position, as far as publicity was concerned. The entire government infrastructure of information and communication was available to them, and the government media such as the radio and television were accessible for publicity. Public sector undertakings, therefore, as they came up, started setting up PR departments. However, this was done initially, in a haphazard manner with no uniform practice either in respect of the organizational structure of the departments or of the nature of the functions to be performed.

The Government of India had, meanwhile, set up a Bureau of Public Enterprises (BPE) to monitor the functioning of the public enterprises, to set targets of performance, and to frame guidelines for running them. In addition to this, the public sector undertakings felt the need for a platform to share their experiences, to coordinate their activities and to discuss common problems. For this purpose, a Standing Committee on Public Enterprises (SCOPE), was set up with representatives of the important public enterprises. Under the auspices of these bodies, a number of meetings of PR professionals of various public undertakings were held to discuss the various problems faced by them, and to evolve a uniform set of guideline.

The Public Relations Society of India (PRSI), the central association of PR professionals and practitioners, in the private as well as the public sector, discussed, at its conferences and committee meetings, the problems of PR in the public sector.

The Parliamentary Committee on Public Undertakings (CPU) took note of all these deliberations, and discussed the problems and issues confronting public undertakings in respect of their relations with the public. In their 47th report to the Parliament, they recommended that an expert's committee should be appointed to make a detailed study of the organizational structure of the public relations and publicity units in public undertakings and suggest guidelines for the set up of such organizations, keeping in view the need to inform the public not only of the products marketed but also of the functioning of the undertakings.

The other issues suggested for examination by the expert's committee were: (*a*) the question of having a joint cadre of PR and publicity officers for the public undertakings; (*b*) the minimum qualifications and experience required for the posts in the public relations and publicity departments in the public sector; and (*c*) laying down certain broad guidelines for determining expenditure on PR and publicity in such undertakings.

The expert's committee, in its recommendations, pointed put clearly that "the continued existence and growth of any public sector undertaking depends on the sanction of the people, who are its owners. Therefore, every public undertaking has already a clear-cut duty marked out for it, to tender to the public a full and frank account, at all times of the estate of its business, its progress and problems." It also suggested guidelines on the functions and responsibilities of PR officers. It, however, felt that "a joint cadre was not really feasible future," and that any practical guideline for expenditure could not be laid down as "the needs of different undertakings could vary."

An important result of these recommendations, which were accepted by BPE and SCOPE and which were circulated to all PSUs, was that the PR departments were set up in almost every undertaking, and a more less uniform pattern of functioning was established. This was an important step in the development of the PR profession in the country, as the number because while some private sector organizations had fairly elaborate and high level PR departments, many others ignored PR altogether, and felt they could get along with advertising and publicity alone.

**Explaining Major Objectives of Public Relations**

Like all activities, successful advertising and publicity in Public Relations are goal-oriented or activities based on objectives. The objectives of advertising are two fold, (*i*) as a marketing tool and (*ii*) as a means of persuasion.

As a tool of marketing, advertising is used to sell ideas, products and services of identified sponsor. This is achieved through communication of the product (or service) features, pricing, benefits to the customers, and the image (brand image) among other things. Apart from dissemination of information about products, advertising is also used as a mass persuader whether for creating popularity, whether used in election or in education, advertising seeks to bring about a change in attitude and behaviour. This is why advertising is also defined as controlled, identifiable information and persuasion by means of mass media. Advertising is thus tailored and executed towards achieving one or more of the objectives, depending on the product or service, the market for it, its customers, and the marketing organisation behind it. The execution, and its implementation in media to achieve the objectives is a science and an art in itself, requiring special skill.

The objectives of publicity are concerned with imparting information, through specific media to the specific target group. The information has to be intrinsically newsworthy, honest and credible, but made to be more authentic by the nature of the media in which coverage is obtained. The information is put across in such a way that it seems as if it is the media which are giving it out to the readers or viewers, rather than the Advertiser or Public Relations man in an organisation. To be able to do this successfully requires good knowledge of mass media, its editorial need and policies, the audience and the operation process. It requires planning, effective writing, and extremely good media relations to ensure that news releases receive favourable consideration.

The objectives of public relations comprise a subtle combination of advertising and publicity. Public Relations is concerned with achieving a shift in knowledge, perception, image and behaviour. Each Public Relations programme, therefore, can have different objectives depending on the situation, the target group (the "publics" it is meant for) and the timing. For instance, the objectives of a programme directed to motivate the employees of a company will be different for each internal situation, its timing, the structure and the organisation. Similarly, the objectives of Public Relations with the media (i.e., of the media relations) will vary from situation to situation, and company to company. Handling a crisis will demand one type of objective, whereas the launching of a new production unit will demand another type of objective when dealing with the media as a specific "public."

Another difference with regard to Public Relations objectives, when compared with advertising of publicity, is that in Public Relations the target group or the "publics" many often be more than one in a given situation, for instance, the employees, the press, the shareholders, and the government can be the target group in the case of a new project launch, or even a crisis. In advertising and publicity, the target group is generally one specific and large group, for instance, the housewives in the case of a consumer product, or the shareholders in the case of a financial crisis, or the government in the case of an industry issues.

## Explaining the Practices in Communication

Communication is easy; everyone does it all the time. Effective communication is difficult. It involves attracting attention, compelling interest, and conveying information with impact, accuracy, and lack of ambiguity. It also requires that the audience should be clearly defined and that means of reaching that audience should be identified and skilfully used, which involves understanding and operating a variety of techniques.

As if this was not problem enough, there are also the physiological and psychological barriers of the selective and subjective mechanisms of every individual member of the audience to be appreciated and overcome.

For example, it is usually accepted that colour is a subject of infinite difficulty to talk and write about without misunderstanding. Apart from those who are wholly or partially colour-blind, colours are seen differently by different people. Some shades of blue to one are green to another, and so on.

In other words, the physical apparatus of the eye and the nervous mechanism for transmitting its messages to the brain are unique to every individual and what one person sees is never seen as precisely the same by any other person.

What is seen is also selected by a variety of factors: alertness, experience, frame of mind, prejudices, physical surroundings and many more. The choice of facing fractionally one way instead of another immediately makes what is seen unique to the individual. No other person can be looking with the same eyes and attitudes at the same subject from exactly the same place at the same time.

A street scene containing all kinds of activity will be seen by different people in different ways. A nervous old lady will see a frightening rush of vehicles and people. A man who is late for an appointment will see the big clock outside an office. A house wife will see a supermarket sign. A youth will see only a pretty girl walking by.

The validity of these subjective factors has been amply demonstrated. Examine any two eye-witness accounts of a street accident; ask any two people to carry a verbal message and check on its delivery. The 1914-18 War joke about the message, "Send reinforcements; we're going to advance" being passed from man to man along the trench until it arrived as, "Send three-and-four-pence; we're going to a dance" has a sound basis in observable reality.

The spoken word has its own hazards and its peculiar differences from the written word are often overlooked. Any shorthand-writing reporter will confirm that he transcribes what the speaker meant to say, for if he wrote what he actually said the speaker meant to say, for if he wrote what he actually said it would often be gibberish. This is true of almost any unscripted speech, apart from that of the gifted few who are able to compose sentences to speak as others compose them to write.

Read any transcript of a radio or television unscripted discussion just as it comes from the monitoring organization and it becomes apparent that what sounds plain enough at the time is often confused, broken, and jumbled when seen in written form.

Facial expression, inflection and tone, the interplay between speaker and audience, the visual context of the occasion—all contributed to enhancing the meaning of the spoken word and none can be conveyed adequately in a written report. Only in rare case, such as Sir Winston Churchill's speeches, is the mastery of language such that the words are equally acceptable and effective whether read or spoken. Yet, however precise the words, there remains the obstacle of subjective reaction and interpretation to overcome.

At its most macabre, it is possible to postulate that each separate member of an audience thinks he hears what the communicator thinks he is saying, and the fear begins to develop that clear communication is not possible. It is possible, but it is not certain. As long as everyone whose work it is to convey messages remembers that uncertainty and guards against it, there is hope for effective communication.

Most communication is by word, spoken or written, or by some form of pictorial or visual presentation. That words are liable to be ambiguous, however carefully used, is obvious, but visuals can be equally ambiguous if their effect on the chosen audience is not the intended one.

A non-representational work of art may convey a variety of emotional 'meanings' to those who view it; it may also convey to some a representational meaning far removed from what the artist had in mind. The question 'what does it mean?' can produce many answers, according to the subjective interpretations put upon it by those who look at it. The question 'what did you mean?' addressed to the artist, may produce only one answer.

The differing interpretations put upon the words of a politician by professional commentators, who may or may not have been present to hear them, instantly illustrate both the potential ambiguity of even cunningly conceived speech and the selective acceptance of a message by those who filter it into their minds through fixed attitudes.

Subjective thinking is often a matter of believing that some things are 'right' and others are 'wrong' without necessarily defining at any time what those moral terms may mean. Even if it is not possible to establish what someone else means by his subjective reaction, it is vital in public relations to recognise that it exists, that it is, in fact, a part of the make-up of every human being.

To take a simple example, the steel-engraved company letter-heading with a vignette of the bearded founder looks just as right to the elderly manufacturer as it looks wrong to the graphically alert young manager. Either might in theory be collect in believing that his personal choice of what is right is also right for the company's audience. The only way to try to find out is to seek the advice of those who are trained in the visual disciplines involved and of those who are trained to the techniques of measuring attitudes.

In other words, subjective public relations judgement is dangerous—for all the value of flair and hunch—and the scientific approach of using available, proven techniques is more likely to produce useful answers to problems. Allied to this, there is a permanent need for the public relations man to retain a cold objectivity about his work.

This does not mean any lack of loyalty to client or employer, nor any lack of enthusiasm for a cause or a company. It does mean the ability to see and hear through the eyes and ears of the audience as well as those of the concern he serves. Loss of objectivity, lack of the scepticism which motivates the best in journalism, of criticism and social analysis, can be morally damaging to a public relations man's effectiveness. To believe cooly and calmly in what, after study, he propounds is one thing; to believe unthinkingly in what his masters wish the world to believe is quite another.

With as objective an attitude as he can retain, mastery of number of skills and an understanding of several more, the public relations man is still faced with the lack of objectivity of every member of his audience and almost certainly of his client or employer as well. Apart from the occasions when that lack of objectivity is on his side he has to overcome a barrier which he cannot, touch, for it is within the minds of his public.

In these circumstances he has to persuade, he has to engineer consent, to convey information that may not be wanted or welcome. His task is made easier by the developed techniques of analysis and communication which now exist, and by the specialized advice and help which is available to him. Many of the skills he must acquire for himself, although no man can be master of all the many methods of communicating which come within public relations.

He must learn to understand the attitude and reactions of his public as well as identify its location and habits. He must discover which techniques to use and when, in order to reach the minds of his audience. He must plan and he must work to a policy.

Technical skill alone will not carry his message all the way unless he has retained his objectivity, unless he is able to put himself in the other man's shoes and to listen to the other man's point of view. If he cannot identify himself with other people and with what they believe is right for them and for society, he will have little hope of overcoming the barrier of subjectivity which is in every man's mind.

In respect of communicating management policies, and in projecting the image of the organization, PR is generally active, and is called upon to plan and execute various programmes and projects. In the area of crisis management, too, the PR persons are now being sought for active participation though, at times, their role is limited to 'handling' the media. In the task of preparing organizations to face a crisis, and in deciding on policies and programmes to be followed for dealing with a crisis situation, PR generally has a very limited role to play. In problem-solving, too, PR is seldom asked to make a contribution as the effectiveness of the PR techniques in tackling major problems such as increasing productivity, preventing waste, reducing costs, improving safety consciousness, are not often appreciated.

Issue management is an area where PR can play a crucial role. With greater privatisation, the field of investor relations is rapidly expanding, and PR is being called upon to play a key role in the mobilization of finances. With the phenomenon of collaborations, having become a regular feature of the corporate scene, financial public service is in great demand. The highly complex scenario of the capital market is leading to a high degree of specialization in the field of financial public relations. Many advertising agencies are offering consultancy services in handling and managing all communication for equity/debenture/bond issues.

It is, however, in the area of monitoring the social, political and economic environment, and counselling the top management that PR could do much more than it is being called upon to do today. As a result of the rapid changes in the socio-economic environment, both within the country and abroad, new issues of public interest are coming to the fore, and a wide variety of pressure groups are emerging. This is affecting PR in two ways. Corporations are having to deal with new publics, to understand the emerging issues and to devise strategies to handle these publics. On the other hand, these publics are themselves in need of public relations to put across their points of view, and to communicate with the government and other sections of the people. Ecology is one such factor, which was hardly of any significance a decade ago, but is now of crucial importance.

Consumerism and the consumer movement is another trend that is acquiring importance. Pressure groups like the trade unions have been active for a long time, but are increasing their clout as a result of having representatives in the Parliament and Legislatures, and also because of their capacity to act unitedly on certain issues. The agriculturists lobby is also growing in strength, and has been able to get a considerable amount of legislation in its favour or to stall decisions that adversely affect its interests.

In addition, other minority groups, women's groups, the new class of the knowledge workers, the new media are emerging as publics, and the governments as well as the corporations have to reckon with them. While it is the corporations, as a whole, that would be required to face these issue, it is the public relations specialists who have to deliver the blue prints for strategies that need to be adopted.

The growing complexities of the social environment in India, and the variegated pattern of issues coming up, require the development of the Public Relations Consultancies in the country. So far, only a few have come up in Bombay, Delhi and Calcutta. Many more would be needed, once organizations realise the importance of tackling the emerging issues, and of taking timely action before crisis situations develop. The policies of economic liberalization announced by the Government would undoubtedly give a boost to the PR profession in India. The reliance on the market forces rather than on the bureaucratic regulation to run the economy, and the creation of a competitive environment would offer a much wider scope for the use of the PR techniques than has been possible so far.

## Explaining the Roles of Press and PR Advertising

With the dawn of independence, a democratically elected government started functioning in India. Realising the importance of keeping people informed, the government began to develop infrastructure for a vast information and mass communication network to suit its objectives and priorities. The Ministry of Information and Broadcasting serves as the nodal ministry in this field for setting up and monitoring the information network through its various media units like the PIB, DAVP, Akshavani, Doordarshan, Films Division, Publication Division, etc.

We have seen that the newspapers and journals existed even prior to independence. There were, however, only a few papers, and of these some were either directly run by foreign interests or were influenced by them. Independent newspapers, which supported the national interest, were under constant threat, and has to face restrictions and harassments of many kinds.

It was only after independence that there was a burgeoning of newspapers and magazines all over the country. The most rapid growth took place amongst the papers and journals in the regional languages. Although the press was now free, thanks to the fundamental rights guaranteed under the Constitution, the government still had a role to play, especially in the matter of import and allotment of newsprint and printing machinery as foreign exchange was scarce, and the newsprint demand far exceeded the indigenous capacity.

In July 1956, the Government of India, established the office of the Registrar of Newspapers. All newspapers and journals are to be registered at this Office. The number of newspapers and journals have steadily grown since independence, and today there are nearly 25,000 paper including dailies, weeklies, fortnightlies and other periodicals with a circulation of over 60 million. Most of these are privately owned.

You will appreciate that without the existence of a network for the dissemination of information and without a variety of the media reaching out to the people, it would not have been possible for the PR practitioners to play their role of creating understanding between their organizations and the public through sustained, planned and deliberate efforts.

Advertising for Public Relations is more commonly referred to as 'institutional advertising', and this is an important instrument for achieving Public Relations objectives. Public Relations advertising has been distinguished from the more commonly used product advertising. The latter is part of the marketing-mix of the organisation. It is intended to further sales of the company's products, either of a single product or a range of products.

Industrial advertising seeks to build an image of the organisation as a whole, the corporate image. Product advertising may also be sometime concerned with image building, but that will be to build up a brand image. Institutional advertising does not directly promote sales, or even help to popularise a brand, but by building the corporate image it creates goodwill for the organisation, makes for better relations with the publics such as government, the parliament and the press, and thus ultimately helps to improve the company's profitability by creating the climate in which its business operations can proceed in a congenial atmosphere.

Some of the objectives of Public Relations advertising include: improving the image of the company among specific publics; to bring about a change in attitude of audience towards the company or its products; to enhance the company's image by making known its achievements, e.g. increased production targets, export awards etc., educating the audience on company's various aspects etc. Its future plan, prices etc., establishing the organization's reputation as a responsible corporate citizen and its concern for the community; establishing itself as a good company to work for in order to attract more talent, and providing a unified marketing approach for all its products.

In deciding what to highlight in an institutional advertising campaign, one has to consider the public towards which the campaign is mainly directed. Is it the government or the parliament is it the press is it the shareholders, the capital market, or the employees of the organisation? The answers to these questions should be adopted for the campaign.

As in the case of all advertising, Public Relations advertising should be simple, and the message should be clear. Ideally, only one concept should be put across in one advertisement for the best effect. If more than one idea is to be conveyed, one could plan a series of advertisements tying up together into a total corporate message to the public or the publics concerned. In situational advertising, one must avoid complex messages and detailed explanation. Instead a brochure or pamphlet or even a book may serve the purpose of Public Relations better depending on the amount of material that has to be incorporated. However, where it is felt that a series of advertisements will be able to project the message, there should be some kind of inter-connecting link between them, so that the impact of the first is reinforced by each succeeding advertisement in the series of institutional advertising, is however, very expensive and the one should use it judiciously.

### *Understanding the Public Relations on the TV and Radio*

The introduction of sponsored programmes and the TV serials over the various channels of Doordarshan and Cable Network has provided an opportunity to the PR practitioners as never before.

It place at their disposal a very powerful medium, which has now a wide/reach throughout the country. Institutional advertising is used for purposes of image building, bringing about changes in attitudes, helping to mould the public opinion and popularising new concepts. As far as the marketers are concerned, the television medium also given them a powerful tool to develop the brand image and to sell their products and service through 'sports' as well as through sponsored programmes.

For most purpose, it is the commercial channel of Vividh Bharati which will have to be the main outlet for Public Relations purposes. Sponsored programme put across this channel, and, if intelligently produced, can evoke a high interest among listeners. Such programmes can be used for popularising brand products as well as for image building. Entertainment programmes, popular film based programmes and sports programmes command a high listenership and can be effectively used, for Public Relations advertising.

Most of the activity in Public Relations consists of publicity, with some promotion. Publicity material include news releases, pictures, articles and background material. It is important to prepare publicity messages keeping in mind the channels of mass media to be used—whether newspaper, trade magazines, specialised magazines, radio or television broadcast etc. Indiscriminate mailing of publicity material is a sheer waste of resources. Hence, it is important to have a good knowledge of mass media, their audience and editorial policies, besides keeping good media relations with the media personnel.

Publicity and promotion are highly creative fields. There should be no limitations set on the practitioners, innovativeness other than the ethical ones. The media is flooded with publicity messages. Hence, the publicity messages compete for attention. Editors have no choice but to reject mediocre material and use only such news releases which are worthwhile. It is here that the work of creative, skilled people will stand out. The best attention-getter is the targeted quality work.

It is important to remember that even the most creative work is only effective if it is in line with the organisation's strategy. Bright ideas that do not communicate the organisation's message to the proper audience are not worth publicising. Good publicity ideas come with experience and a Public Relations person must make good use of both publicity and advertising to achieve the Public Relations goals.

All communications—big or small in terms of size and effort in Advertising, Publicity and Public Relations—involve significant financial and manpower resources. Both are, today, not only scarce, but expensive. Hence, advertising, publicity, and Public Relations must be effective to the core. This requires professional planning in the following areas:

(*i*) *Objective orientation:* All advertising, publicity and Public Relations programmes must have pre-defined short-term and long-term objectives as a pre-requisite. These must be agreed to and accepted by the management.

(*ii*) *Target group orientation:* For any campaign (or even single but important activity), the target group to be reached must be clearly identified. There should be no ambiguity or vagueness in this. The definition of the target group should be in demographic and psychologographic terms.

(*iii*) *Message selection:* The message to be communicated must be directly linked with and focussed upon the objectives to be achieved (awareness, image, announcement, shift in attitude, behaviour, etc.) in respect of the target group and the media in which it is going to be transmitted. There must be a perfect match between the two to achieve the desired results.

(*iv*) *Media selection:* The media to be used must be those which reach the right target group, at the right time and at the minimum cost. Waste in reach must be minimal—and this is today easily possible with the detailed data and planning at the disposal of a professional. The right media have a significant role to play in publicity and Public Relations, where the communication is largely situation-led and the messages are broad-based and different, unlike advertising.

(*v*) *Creativity and innovations:* This step needs no elaboration as such. The more creative and innovative you can be (within the professional guidelines), the better your message will be noticed and the better will be the chance of your being able to achieve your goals. Creativity and innovation should be an objective on its own, in all forms of business communication, today and in the future.

(*vi*) *Adequate resources:* One of the biggest shortcomings in advertising and Public Relations is that companies tend to economise on the financial outlay? This often results in unsustained or sporadic communications. To be effective, and to make the desired impact, advertising, publicity and Public Relations programmes must be sustained and backed with adequate financial resources in creating the message as well as sending it out through the media.

It is often recommended that if you do not have adequate resources, it may be better that you do not undertake the programme, rather than do a half-hearted and low-impact job. Obviously, in this you have to weigh the consequences viz-a-viz your own particular situation and organisation.

(*vii*) *Manpower back-up:* Whatever your objectives and financial resources, the professional manpower support in advertising, publicity and Public Relations is most essential for the planning and execution of programmes and campaigns.

There is a need for professionally trained and effective people in all the three communication fields. Training and development, therefore, is an essential requirement at most organisations. Something is being done today about this, but much needs to be done still. The communication situation that prevails today in the market.

## Forming the Public Opinion

A 'public', from the standpoint of public opinion, is a group of people with similar interests, who have a common opinion on a controversial subject. Kuppuswamy defines public as "a spontaneous collection of people in response to a certain kind of situation." To clarify the concept to you further, it is issue/ controversy that holds the public together. You must however note that the members of the 'public' are heterogeneous and are not one composite group. 'Public' is not limited by size or enclosed within some geographical boundaries.

Opinion, according to Webster's Seventh New Collegiate Dictionary, is "a view, judgement, or appraisal formed in the mind about a particular matter." An opinion is stronger than an impression and weaker than positive knowledge. It implies a conclusion throughout, yet open to dispute. A more or less settled opinion is a 'sentiment' and, if held firmly, a 'conviction'. A 'view' is an opinion more or less coloured by bias.

*Public opinion* is an expression of a belief held in common by members of a group of public on a controversial issue of general importance. The public opinion—formed process emanates from the expressed individual opinions of members of a group. Whose views are subject to the influences exerted by the group.

*The Dictionary of Mass Communications* defines public opinion as the expression of all members of a group, who are giving attention to a given issue. The process starts with an interaction of individual attitudes, mind-sets, and beliefs concerning an issue.

Public opinion is usually expressed after controversy, dispute and debate over some controversial question, which concern the welfare, doctrines, and values system of a group. Public opinion is aroused, whenever a contemporary issue or question of some concern arises about which the member of the group are likely to have disagreement. An issue is a situation or occurrence which threatens to disturb the prevailing values, beliefs and attitudes of a group creating more or less of a crisis, and arousing discussion and the expression of public opinion. Reservations for the backward classes and the question of merit is one such issue. Which has begun to confront the Indian public. The testing of nuclear materials causing environmental pollution is an international issue, which causes people throughout the world to take affirmative or negative positions on the question. Similarly the issue of nuclear non-proliferation and India's stand on it and the GATT accord have also generated much heat.

Public opinion is not simply the opinion of the majority of a group. On each issue, the interested public will divide itself into two or more differing points of view, which will not necessarily be contradictory or mutually exclusive. The attitudes and previous experiences of the individuals making up the public as well as the complexity of the issue determine the cause of public opinion. The opinion must be representative of the group as a whole. Thus, public opinion is the complex of beliefs expressed by a significant number of persons on an issue of general importance. Public opinion is a potent force to reckon with particularly for a public relations functionary.

The basic objective of public relations is to measure, analyse, and influence public opinion which develops from the attitudes of individuals comprising the public. Therefore, it is important to understand the meaning of attitudes, why people hold the attitudes they do, and their role in the opinion-forming process.

*Attitudes* are the feelings or moods of a person or against some person, organisation, issue, or object. They represent the predisposition of an individual to evaluate controversial questions in a favourable or unfavourable manner. Simply stated, an attitude is a way of looking at situations. *An expressed attitude is an opinion.*

Change in attitude may occur under various conditions e.g. the existing attitude no longer provides us the satisfaction or if our aspirations get raised. Changes in attitude can be brought about through communications by creating new beliefs, or by appealing to the emotions to arouse favourable or unfavourable attitudes. Appeals to the physical, social and economic needs of people are considered to be effective in changing their attitude e.g. the ads for insuring life, property etc., have considerable acceptance and response by general public.

Attitudes and their expression in the form of opinions are the psychological phenomena of an individual. A group is not capable of forming an opinion. Since a group cannot form an opinion, how is public opinion formulated?

Public opinion is formed by individuals composing a group, who express their own opinion on a controversial issue. Public opinion is a composite opinion resulting from the interaction of the individual opinion, by group stimuli, is a distinctive characteristic of the public opinion process. This metamorphosis is sometimes referred to as the 'group mind', which is the combined opinions of individuals in the group. This is what we call public opinion.

Public opinion involves a transformation of individual opinion into group opinion, brought about by the influence exerted by the members of a group on an individual's opinion. The opinions of people in a group are influenced by what they here from opinion leaders, other members of the group, or persons outside, the group; what they read in newspapers, magazines, and books; what they see in life about them or on television. Apart from group pressures, individual opinions are influenced by their needs, emotions, experience, heredity, culture, economic status and education. Out of the interaction of individual attitudes, opinions, and the opinions of the group emerges public opinion.

Now you are aware of how public opinion is formed and how Public Relations efforts can help mould it. There is however, another spects to moulding of public opinion based on propaganda. It is important for Public Relations students to learn to distinguish Public Relations from propaganda and not confuse the two, as they operate at different levels and have different motives. Public Relations is not propaganda. So let us briefly look into this art also to make ourselves clearer.

Propaganda is defined as an expression of opinion by individuals, and groups which is deliberately designed to influence opinion or action by other individuals or groups with reference to pre-determined end. Although in its broadest sense, propaganda intends to advance a cause e.g, a religious faith, and hence can be considered as legitimate persuasion, it has come to acquire a negative image because it has been used to unleash hatred and fear during wars. It is still being used by suppressing facts. Propaganda has therefore gained notoriety as brainwashing and barbarity. It is characterised by the use of words with double meaning; appeals to prejudices of people and arousal of negative emotions like fear, hatred etc., evasion of truth, suppression of facts, distortion; provocation, playing up trivia; presentation of only one sided arguments and repetition.

Critics of Public Relations sometimes refer to it as propaganda to imply that this also manipulates public opinion. However, even though Public Relations attempts to influence public opinion, it is vastly different from propaganda. Public Relations is an honest, straight forward, long-term effort to create favourable image based on facts and performance. It has no malicious, short-term selfish gains to make by suppressing fact to mislead people. Unlike propaganda, it is based on an open two-way communication.

The importance of sound and significant Public Relations research to the management of all organisations is greater today than it has been in the past. Top executives are spending many hours studying how public attitudes towards their industries may affect their future operations, or turn into opportunities in terms of the market place and their growth.

The focus of opinion research and Public Relations research has been changing from the study of traditional public to a greater attention to the study of "issues", and how best to make an impact on public attitudes for their benefit. The tools of public relations research may not have undergone much change in the past decade. But there is an all-round effort to bring timely and actionable processed data into the hands of decision-makers quickly and effectively.

Public Relations research services these three functions: (*1*) Most frequently, it may simply confirm assumptions and hunches about the state of public opinion on an issue, or a company. This is a highly useful kind of back-up function, in many ways analogous to the use of quality control systems in the manufacturing end of a business. (2) A second role of research is to clarify questions on which limited information is available, or on which apparently contradictory data are to be found. Research can help sort out what people really mean and when they say they like or dislike an organisation—the reasons they cite for these feelings, and even the origin of the feelings. (*3*) Research re-orients our thinking and conceptualisation of Public Relations problems. It helps us to define and focus on our objectives and target group, and in assigning priorities to Public Relations, problems and Public Relations actions.

There are many research techniques available for conducting Public Relations and public opinion research. A very old and still useful method is to vary a content analysis of how an issue or a problem is treated in the press, published data and the like. Such desk research given a pretty fair measure of the saliency of the problem and often useful hints as to which aspect of it seem to be arousing the greatest public interest.

For many people, Public Relations research is synonymous with public opinion surveys, and their various market research and survey techniques, each of which has its merits and its limitations. Properly used, these different techniques can complement one another and produce a mosaic of data giving new insights into long-standing problems.

Another form of opinion research, which is a useful tool for Public Relations professionals is depth survey. This is nothing more than an effort to let the public tell the researcher how it views the Public Relations programmes. In these surveys the researcher carefully avoids imposing his point of view on the respondent. Depth studies are useful in the earlier stages of programme in giving clues to the perimeters of a problem. They can also provide some really valuable themes for the Public Relations campaign.

Good research takes time. And if undertaken must not be unnecessarily hurried, even if the findings are required in a hurry. It must take its own course with all the procedures completed fully and the analysis of data done properly to throw up the required leads to evolve the Public Relations strategy and programme.

The secret of managing effectiveness lies in "how to do it", or the methodology of doing things. Success in communication results out of managing four important steps:

(*i*) Right selection, (*ii*) Right motivation, (*iii*) Right evaluation and (*iv*) Training and development.

Selecting the right message, the right target group, and the right media is the first step. Motivating your target group to perceive and then act as you want them to, is the next. Having done that, evaluating what has been achieved, what has not been achieved, and what needs to be done further is vital. This may be part of the programme undertaken, but must be planned before hand. Feedback in communication is crucial—there should be one-way communication if one needs success.

With 'all this, admen, publicity men. and public relations men (and in three cases women too) must be constantly trained to be professionals in the techniques, think—inputs and the final execution of programmes and campaigns. Training should be an ongoing process, and not something which is done only when the going is tough, or when there is an acute need for qualified people. Because of the link of advertising with marketing, a number of training programmes-in-company and external are available to advertising people. But in the field of publicity and public relations there exists a big vacuum, which must be filled up in the coming years, especially when public relations is becoming more and more important in business and industry.

## Explaining the Roles of Social Marketing and Counselling

Public Relations professionals in increasing numbers have begun to realise that social causes can benefit tremendously from the Public Relations way of marketing, thinking the planning.

The term 'social marketing' has been defined as the "design, implementation and control of programmes, calculated to influence the acceptability of social ideas and involving considerations of product planning, pricing, packaging, communication, distribution and marketing research". In short, it means "the application of marketing techniques in moulding public opinion for or against a social issue, or 'selling' and idea to serve a social cause, or wherever specific public or social programmes and campaigns require significant changes in the attitudes and behaviour on the part of the relevant 'publics'."

The most successful example of employing marketing techniques for popularising a public programme in India has been the Nirodh commercial distribution, drawing on the marketing skills of a number of large consumer goods companies. Similarly, there have been several social advertisement campaigns, like the Bombay Municipal Corporation campaign on water conservation, or Indian Oil's "Save Oil" campaign, or Hyderabad Municipal Corporation's "Keep Your City Beautiful" campaign.

Let us take a practical example. Business houses design products and services in terms of the needs and wants of target groups of consumers. Similarly, in social marketing, target audiences must be studied and appropriate "products or services" designed by the organisation, so that the target audiences find it desirable to accept the product or service. Thus, if the National Savings Organisation wants income-earners to save by buying Saving Certificates, which in the long run will help to curb inflation in the country, many types of "Schemes" can be designed to contribute to this social objective. For instance, instead of cash incentives for buying consumer products, wholesalers, dealers and even retailers may be given Savings Certificates, or coupons for buying a certain volume of a product or products, a Savings Certificate worth a fixed sum is given to the buyer. Many such "products" can be designed to achieve the social objective of developing the saving habit.

Thus in social marketing, the Public Relations men can view it as a marketing problem requiring the designing of the "right product or service", offered at the "right place", at the "right price or effort" to the "right consumer or target audience" with the support of the "right promotion." However, it must be added that such an approach may not guarantee total success, but it does offer a systematic framework for planning the social efforts.

PR Counselling is a part of the PR profession. It is basically the functions of an external agency. The PR counsellor is retained to counsel and advice management on policy, financial and government relations, opinion research, educational services publication, press relations, TV, graphics and community relations, J. Walter., Thomson, Hill and Knowlton, Young and Rubican, Satchi and Satchi and Carl Boyer are a few but internationally well-known PR counselling firms. They employ 100 to 300 PR specialists to serve clients through their specialised PR services in most parts of the globe.

Prominent advertising agencies also provide PR communication counselling services in India. More than 50 major ad agencies are undertaking PR counselling along with their routine ad services. Famous Indian ad agencies Mudra O & M, HTA, Lintas, Blaze, Trikaya, PR Associates, Clariton have their own PR wings. Roger Pereira's firm and 'Good Relations India' are the two major PR counselling firms mentioned in professional circles.

These PR counselling firms and ad agencies with PR cells should be good enter-points for beginners as they welcome freshers to the junior positions. It is relatively easier to get an entry. Some ad agencies have at least 10 to 15 vacancies for PR jobs whenever they are hired for a PR event. Opportunities are wide open in this field. A good PR student should have no problem of making an entry in these firms. The salaries may be initially unattractive but with experience and service a PR graduate will have no regrets.

PR concept has gained more respectability, of late, mainly due to its empirical approach to the PR problems and public opinion measurement. Initially, few could foresee public opinion research as one of the thrust areas of social science theory "stemming from a study of public opinion process, that should guide a proper and beneficial public relations programme." That Research and evaluation is an integral unit of the total PR profession does not merit mention. About 70 per cent of professionals look for PR counselling precisely for its fact-finding, opinion research services. Research enable PR professionals to formulate sound policies and win public confidence, PR professionals use variety of research techniques such as Image survey.

"Motivation Research", "Effectiveness Surveys", "Content Analysis", "Individual Public Surveys", as part of the interest in PR and public opinion research. Social aspects of basic human relation research are other key research areas that employ sound methods used by social behavioural scientists. As a specialised area, PR research is new development and very few people are competent and experienced. Usually, outside PR counselling and Public Opinion Research Organizations help the PR department on a contract basis. Now, the trend is towards encouraging the PR practitioners to have good knowledge of PR research methods and techniques. This is an area which can provide a wide job opportunity not only with public opinion research firms and PR counselling firms, but also in the corporate PR units. Post-graduate communication researchers can easily find a good vocation as PR research specialists. In India, though relatively novel, our PR professionals are slowly becoming sensitive to this development. Agencies like MARG, IMRB, ORG, are some of the well-known Public Opinion Research Organizations.

## The Onset of Professionalism in Public Relations and its Evolution

The industrial development got underway in the post-independence period, and large professionally managed enterprises began to emerge, they began to feel the need for PR. In many private sector undertakings, in multi-national companies, and in the public sector undertakings the PR departments were set up, and a cadre of PR professionals emerged.

Since, in the initial state, there were no clear-cut codes of professional practice, and no standards had been laid down, the first requirement was to set up such standards and codes. For this purpose, it was also necessary to form an organization which would bring under its umbrella the Public Relations professionals from all fields. This led to the formation of central PR organization of the PR professionals from all fields. The Public Relations Society of India was formed in Bombay in 1958. The First All India Public Relations Conference was held in New Delhi in April, 1968. This conference took note of the fact that while Public Relations had been gaining currency, the reputation of the profession was sullied by the operations of some lobbyists and fixers, who were using rather dubious methods to gain their ends.

Understandably, the concern of the First All India Public Relations Conference was the adoption of a code of ethics, and defining the parameters of the PR profession. By and large, this conference succeed in achieving its goal, and Public Relations has, since, come to be recognised as a profession that is playing a useful and, in many ways, a crucial role in modern society.

The PR profession in India has benefited greatly from interaction with the PR professionals abroad. These contacts started in the sixties, and resulted in meeting of the Council of the International Public Relations Association (IPRA), held in Bombay in 1974. This IPRA central theme, "Towards a more responsible citizenship." Besides, it might be of interests to note that Prof. Scott Cutlip, a leading authority on PR in the USA, conducted a course on PR at the Indian Institute of Mass Communication, New Delhi in 1969, which was attended by many of the leading professionals in the country.

The first generation of PR practitioners in India in the fifties and sixties came from the field of journalism or advertising. Until then, there were no facilities for PR education in India. The PR professionals learnt from foreign books on the subject, from their own experience and through contacts with the PR professionals abroad. Some were fortunate enough to have undergone PR courses in the USA or the UK.

You would, however, appreciate that profession cannot develop without facilities for education and training. One of the first tasks, taken up by the Public Relations Society of India, after its formation, was to organise such training programmes. The India Foundation for Public Relations Education and Research (IFPR) was organized by the PRSI to provide an academic and educational base for education and training. In planning their educational and research activities, PRSI and IFPR have taken note of the recommendations of IPRA on the subject of PR education. To harmonies educational standards on a worldwide scale, the IPRA decided in 1980, to set up a working group for a systematic study of the state of PR education in different countries, and to make recommendations for education and standard in this field. The recommendations of this group were published in the IPRA Gold Paper No. 4 in 1982.

In the introduction to the Paper, the Chairman of the IPRA Education and Research Committee started:

> "In considering the elements of public relations education, it is essential always to respect the individual nature of a country's culture and historical background. The theory of public relations is valid everywhere, but its practical application must take into account national character, economy and

environment.... The curriculum for the education of a student wishing to enter the profession can be pictured as a series of three concentric circles. The smallest circle encloses the subjects specifically concerned with the practice of pubiic relations. The second large circle has the subjects in the general field communication. The third and the largest circle represents the general liberal arts and humanities background, which is essential preparation for a successful education."

Public Relations has come a long way from the days of 'Public-be-dammed' to The Public-be-Pleased'. The changing perspective of Public Relations as "management ideal" and "communication concept" has already been discussed in the previous units. We have noted that Public Relations is slowly responding to the environmental changes in society. The modern age is described as the age of inter-dependence. People's power is the ultimate power. It is this power in the form of public opinion which determines the role and scope of various organizations in our society. Institutional subordination to public opinion may be termed as a radical development in this industrialised age. As mentioned earlier this dependence is mutual. People depend on institutions for various services. The institutions, in turn, depend on their public's goodwill for survival. This mutual inter-dependence among the public and the social, economic, scientific, political, education, religious and other types of organizations, has created a need for constant communication. This is where Public Relations steps in to establish mutual trust and understanding.

Thus, Public Relations is a relatively new and emerging concept. While, there is no rigid and precise description as to its nature, its scope and need is to be understood from the various definitions used to explain it, it is rightly described as a management function in an organizational setting.

According to Webster's New Collegiate Dictionary, Public Relations is "The business of inducing the public to have an understanding for and general goodwill towards a person, firm or institution." The philosophy of modern Public Relations is that it is "applied communication concerned with human relationships." Essentially Public Relations is a communication approach to establish a better understanding between people and organizations in a dynamic society. Modern Public Relations is a scientific, rational and professional concept and philosophy developed to solve the problems of organizations and their human relational conflicts. As a profession, it is systematically practiced and conducted on sound communication principles and organizational methods. Consequently, education in Public Relations and its career avenues, have received greater impetus in India.

The contemporary world has witnessed the impact of Public Relations on our society. It is increasingly realised that individual freedom and public opinion are the key factors to social control. A greater status is assigned to those organizations which reflect the public spirit. "It is an era in which the management principles of participation by individuals is on the ascendant over the authoritarian approach." Therefore, a Public Relations professional has to understand the publics, mediate and respond to the situations, and achieve mutual adjustments.

This calls for a professional approach to its functions. Whether it is used systematically or casually, people have always recognised the need of Public Relations activity in every sphere throughout the world. "Each member of the public practices the principles of Public Relations in seeking the acceptance, co-operation, or affection of others." Public Relations professionals only practice it in a more professional manner.

Professionally, Public Relations had earned a new dignity and status for its members by promoting higher standards in business., banking and other institutional sectors. A substantial body of literature has been built around the discipline of Public Relations. A large number of associations of professional (PRSI, PRSA, IPRA, etc.), rigid admission rules, and administration of a code of conduct, promotion of education, training and research (IFPR), professional books, journals, papers, research reports, public service are the professional characteristics of modern Public Relations. Thus, Public Relations has emerged as one of the promising, enterprising and challenging field of communication, attracting multitudes of talented andyoung professionals.

A career, in public relations is a full-time employment available to a professionally qualified, experienced, talented and competent person. PR field is attracting younger and educated persons by its status and financial rewards. For a notice the job of a PRO either in Government agency or in a private organization entail perks and privileges apart from his salary. In India, a communication graduate may aspire for a career in PR more than in any other vocation in the line. Government of India and its auxiliary units, public sector enterprises and the State Governments provide a good job opening for a professionally competent beginner.

Big, medium and small business organizations in India have PR departments ranging from a full-fledged department to a one-man directed PR department. Two decades ago, a graduate would have came across only a few ads for PROs in newspapers. But, now ads for PROs have become a familiar sight in the Indian newspapers. In the USA, over 100,000 people are employed in the PR professional, with an accredited membership of 8000 to PRSA. We do not have reliable census data of PR professionals in our country. We may venture to guess that more than a lakh of people are employed in various PR slot, both in private and public sector organizations. A large chunk of PR activities have been undertaken by Government of India particularly through its field network of Departments of Field Publicity, Directorate of Advertising and Visual Publicity (DAVP), Song and Drama Division, Press Information Bureau (PIB), Research and Reference Division (RRD), Photo Division, Publications Division, Films Divisions, where job potential is enormous. Most of these jobs are highly proved and valued. PRSI, a professional association claims a membership of over 2000 through various chapters spread over the country.

Public Relations, which is a special philosophy of management in the western countries, has assumed new roles in the Indian context. Public Relations professionals are being sought after for the nation-building derive and development. They are expected to interpret the policies of the Government and harmonies the Government's actions with the popular sentiments. Every action of Government and its programmes are to be interpreted to the public from mundane "Family Welfare" messages to the inspiring science literacy campaigns. This calls for a vast reservoir or PR talents. PR is not to be mistaken as an effort for achieving greater profits. It should also be seen as service to the public. The outlook of our professionals should be different from their counterparts in the West. Therefore, a PR professional should be more empathetic and socially motivated than merely being a competent professional in the Indian context.

A formal degree in PR is merely a stepping stone to his career which involves "Engineering public opinion." Considering that the job involves interaction and effective communication, it is only natural that there are some prerequisites apart from education and training.

There are the personal traits of the candidate which give the capacity to deal with other people. These include a genuine interest in people around, a flair for communication, a positive mental make-up, charisma, motivation and drive, ability to fact challenges, leadership qualities, alertness and vitality. A candidate possessing these qualities can hope, with proper education and training, to up the professional ladder.

Education in PR, as a formal requirement for PR job is gaining importance throughout the world. A university degree in PR is a recent development and also an indication of the advancement of PR as a profession in India. There is no standard guidance or statutory prescription. Through any graduate from the liberal Arts. Science or Commerce/Management is eligible to enter Public Relations in India, it is better to have through background in social sciences. Of course, a Bachelor or a Post-graduate Degree on Communication/Journalism, with a strong doer of PR courses, is a must to the practitioners of Public Relations.

Yet, any graduate with Diploma in Public Relations (without a formal degree in journalism and communication) is also acceptable. The Public Relations Society of Indian also offers a Diploma in Public Relations through its Indian Foundation for Public Relations Education and Research, in many Indian cities through its local chapters, which is the best way to start your professional career. Bharatiya Vidya Bhavan's Rajendra Prasad Institute of Communication and Management also offers Postgraduate Diploma Course in Public Relations through its numerous centres all over the country. The Dr. B.R. Ambedkar Open University, Hyderabed, is running a Bachelor's Degree course in PR which has been accepted by many as standard course for a beginner.

It is appropriate to know that the education committee of PRSA has listed eight important job classification as a part of Public Relations professional activities. These may also be useful to Indian students as a vocational guidance. These are Writing; Editing; Placement (Media Relations); Promotion (of all PR activities); Speaking (As a spokesman); Production (of PR Communication messages); Programming (Counselling) and Institutional Advertising.

Finally, the field of PR requires various important elements from many disciplines, therefore, it is advantageous to have an understanding of behavioural science.

As pointed out earlier, it is not the formal education which perfects a student for a career in PR. That is only a means. Head work and dedication are important. So also the ability to think positively, speak clearly and coherently with an objective approach to the public, can take you far ahead. Besides, the basic PR skills, he/she should be able to develop innovative techniques of dealing with the relevant publics in the changing and competitive environment. Particularly, corporate relations, media relations, employee relations, community relations, communicating with shareholders, consumers, customers, government, industry, dealers, suppliers and other public each of these require a different and specialised approach altogether. Each public is different and hence their needs and characteristics are to be thorough understood by PR students. As the job of PRO, even a junior level are likely to be part of management executive cadre, the demands can be challenging. A PR person is expected to assume a variety of roles such as a writer, photographers, media specialist, marketing expert, financial analyst, protocol officer, exhibitor, interviews, speech maker, published, image maker, editor, psychologists, etc., besides being an expert communicator, PRO must establish a communication network together intelligence i.e., relevant information on public opinion so as to counsel the management. He/she is the spokes person of the organization and, therefore, must function as a representative of the organization, helping to interpret the policy of the management to the various publics.

Besides, mastery in public affairs, public opinion, social and public relation research are an asset to professional advancement. With commitment and diligence, these traits can be cultivated.

Extensive and excellent career opportunities are often for interested graduates in the Corporate PR sector in India. PR Departments have become an inseparable part of the management, and organizational manpower in thousands of industrial units, service agencies, educational institutions, private and public sector banks, business enterprises. Central, State and Local Governments set-up, hospitals, hostels, welfare agencies, trade associations, cooperatives, international diplomatic corps, armed forces and in every conceivable human organizations.

It is important to know that the designation may vary in various firms/organizations. A PR person may be called 'welfare officer' communication executive, industrial relations officer, information officer, publicity officer, customer relations officer, guest relations officer and so on, as considered suitable by the organization. The specific tasks may vary but the overall responsibility is one of coordination, motivation and persuasion, through dissemination of information.

On smaller scale, PR job openings could be explored in the PR cells of University, Labour Unions, Political Parties, Social Service Agencies, Farm Organizations, Medical Associations, Bar Associations, Chambers of Commerce and Industry, pressure groups, lobby, and countless other firms of all sorts. It is difficult to enumerate these agencies as no census data is available.

Moderately big industrial firms have bigger PR departments with PR personnel strength between 25 to 100. Juniors are usually assigned with the task of writing, production, and execution of various types of corporate PR activities whereas senior PR executives function as policy-makers and advisers. Salaries are highly rewarding in corporate PR, as compared to many equivalent mass media placements. A beginner will find the first job in corporate PR as a good start. But the experts sound a word of caution. It is better to enter corporate PR after a stint in the mediate. Otherwise, there is fear of stagnation.

**Public Relations in Industrial Services and Educational Institutes**

Indian industrial sector, comprising both the private and public sector enterprises, is one of the most competitive job markets for graduates. Indian industries, considered biggest in Asia, accounted for 1,98,533 companies in 1990 including 1,77,761 private and 20,972 public sector undertakings. India ranks 23rd in terms of its stock market with a billing of 23 million dollars per annum. The Indian Stock Market is the third largest in the world with 40 million shareholders. The top 20 industrial giants in the private sector are: Tatas, BK and A.V. Birla, Thapar, Bajaj, Ambani, R.P. Goneka, Mallya, G.P. and C.K. Birla, Chhabria, Mohindra, G.M. Modi, Arvind Mafatlal, Nanda, L.N. and S.K. Birla, Godrej, K.K. Birla, Hinduja, Walchand T.V.S. and M. P. Birla.

Indian Oil, Oil and Natural Gas Commission, Hindustan Petroleum, Coal India, Bharat Petroleum, BHEL are some of the public sectors industries ranked biggest in Asia and the World. Public Sector Undertakings include all organizational activities funded by the Government budget, like government companies both in Central and State Sectors, Irrigation and Power Projects, Railways, Post and Telegraphs, Communications, Ordinance factories, Departmental undertakings. Banking Insurance, Financial and other services. Indian industries provide employment to 11,175,000 people. Corporate Public Relations is a must in these bigger industrial companies. It is a highly specialised and promising career for a prospective graduate. A variety of professional PR services are expected from them like improving their relations, and image in the eyes of public, establishing goodwill with their employees, community, governments, ancillaries, shareholders dealers, customers, etc. Usually, opening are available at the junior cadre level for PR graduates. Promotional opportunities are also very high in the private sector undertakings.

With growing consumer awareness movements, many business houses have realised the importance of keeping customers satisfied and have set-up special cells to deal with consumer complaints and fill the consumer information gap through the use of various media.

Industries like tourism, hoteliering, airlines are getting increasingly professional in their approach and offering lucrative career opportunities to PR persons. In their effort to attract tourists and encourage travel by planning and offering special packages and other incentives, they need skilled motivators and persuaders as PR persons. With increasing privatisation of airliners, and consequent competition, the scope of PR career opportunities have only increased.

The defence system in India is one of the largest establishments of the world. The various wings of defence come under the Defence Ministry such as Air Force, Army and Navy. These defence establishments have maintained PR units for effective information management with various publics such as officials, soldiers, ex-servicemen, civilian staff, general public contractors, suppliers, etc. It is basically, a guarded PR activity for exclusive defence needs through its own network. A PR graduate can make an entry through the defence recruitment cadre for the services.

Education is an important aspect of our life. It is being conducted in an organized environment. Educational institutions are formal organizations which act as custodians of public knowledge. Education institutions reflect our social values. They provide not only education to individual but also supply a steady steam of man-power to socio-economic organizations in our society. Government, social leaders, private organizations have recognised the need for supporting a good educational system for the survival of knowledgeable citizenry.

The Indian Constitution has listed education as a state subject. Both the State and the Central Governments have a vested interest in Education as it is their national obligation to prepare the country for all-round progress.

Our Government has assumed, naturally, a great responsibility, authority and control over the educational policies, institutions and other aspects of higher education. Even though, there are several private educational institutions in the country, it is the Government which is directly involved in educational management in the Indian setting. India has the largest institution based educational network in the world. However, education is highly subsidised and is largely state-sponsored in India. We have about 5,43,677 primary schools, 1,41,104 middle schools, 71,305 higher secondary school, 4329 colleges (general), 876 professionals educational institutions, 198 universities. Most of these educational institutions have to interact with various publics such as governments, parents, children, teachers, staff, residents, civic groups, legislators, etc., without their active support, these institutions cannot survive. Besides there are non-formal adult education schemes. Literacy drives are being conducted to make the masses 'functionally literature. All this needs the services of people who can persuade and motivate the beneficiaries. PR is most important for educational institutions. Though our country hopes to achieve 87 per cent literacy by 1995, PR has not become part of the institutions of the secondary level and below. PR is being conducted at the higher levels by institutions of higher education. At present PR is being practised merely as press relation in most of our educational centres. There is tremendous job potential. If only our educational institutions realised the need of public relations and used the professional PR approach, a lot of problems at the campus could be resolved through communication resulting in a better image, for the universities.

The Government of India is one of the biggest public organizations legally elected and run by the people for themselves within the constitutional framework. Public administration through various levels of administrative hierarchy is nothing but an act of PR by the Government. Perhaps no other organization in the world has ever built and set-up such a large PR network and communication apparatus as that of Government of India. Both at the Centre and States, there is a vast multitude of "public servants" manning the bureaucracy, who should necessarily be PR-oriented. More than 50 per cent of this officials comes into contact with the public. This testifies to the government's involvement with the functional aspects of PR. A prospective PR graduate can explore opportunities in various governmental wings under different nomenclatures. Thousands of posts of PR specialists are advertised in various Government units performing essentially PR functions.

Central, State and Local Governments employ around 18.33 million people for a variety of governmental services in India. In 1947, Government of India had only 18 ministries, but today it has over 60 large ministries—the biggest establishment anywhere in the world.

With the Ministry of Information and Broadcasting taking the lead, the Ministry of Agriculture, Civil Aviation, Commerce, Communication, Defence, Energy, Environment and Forests, External Affairs, Finance, Food and Civil Supplies, Food Processing Industries, Health and Family Welfare, Home Affairs, Human Resources Development, Industry, Labour, Law and Justice, Parliamentary Affairs, Personnel, Public Grievances, Pensions, Petroleum and Chemicals, Planning, Programme Implementation, Railways, Tourism and Urban Development, Water Resources, Welfare, Women and Child Development, Atomic Energy, Electronics, Ocean Development, Space Technology and the Cabinet secretariat, Prime Minister's Office, Planning Commission—provide the biggest job scope for PR graduates. Besides, at State level, there are PR departments and at District levels, there are information officers who establish contact with the people?

Public opinion is the Foundation of Government of India's PR programmes. Since it is a statutory organization, people have a right to know the goings on the Government. Secondly, it must mobilise the public opinion in its favour to take the country forward in the community of nations. All these together constitute a gigantic task of applied PR for the Government.

Take the Union Ministry of Information and Broadcasting, it has an elaborately structured PR apparatus to provide specialised PR services to various units of government. The Information and Broadcasting Ministry has control over a vast empire—All India Radio, Doordarshan (Broadcast Media), Press Information Bureau. Research and Reference Division, Photo Division, Publications Division, Films Division, Central Board of Film Certification, National Film Development Corporation, Directorate of Film Festivals, National Film Archives of India, Children's Film Society, Directorate of Field Publicity, Song and Drama Division, Staff Training Institute (Technical) for Engineer of AIR and Doordarshan, Film and Television Institute of Indian and India Institute of Mass Communication.

These PR agencies offer centralised services and they are potential career centres of PR job seekers in different specialised branches. All the ministries and their constituent units, public sector undertakings also have attached PR units, employing thousands of PR specialists to cater to their own departmental needs.

The State Governments of India closely resemble the Central Government system and have their own Ministers of Information, Publicity and PR, operating closely with the central system, which offers thousands of jobs in Government Public Relations to prospective candidates.

Most of the States in India have Municipal Corporations for major cities under specific legislative acts. There is provision for a separate PR cell in the system except in the small town municipalities.

PR in Panchayat Raj, Local Self-Government is crucial for a meaningful dialogue between government and the public. Various government functionaries and extension workers carry the message of development to the people. A prospective PR graduate can explore the openings in these government department for a career.

There is wide scope for PR in the Banking in India. The banking industry broadly functions as "an instrument for promoting economic and development in a more purposive manner". We have about 274 scheduled banks and a 4 non-scheduled banks, out of which 224 (about 90%) are public sector banks. There are 58,417 branches of commercial banks. About 33,640 of them are located in the rural areas forming a vital link with Indian commerce.

Alongside, we also have non-banking financial institutions serving Banking Industry such as the Reserve Bank of India, Life Insurance Corporations, Financial Corporations, NABARD, Regional Rural Banks, Housing Banks, Industrial Development Bank of India (IDBI), Industrial Reconstruction Bank of India, Export and Import Bank of India (EXIM BANK), Industrial Credit and Investment Corporation (ICCI), Industrial Corporation of India (ICI), Small Industries Development Bank of India (SIDBI), Tourism Finance Corporation of India (TFCI), Credit and Investment Company Ltd. (CICI), State Financial Corporation (SFC), General Insurance Corporation of India (GIC), Unit Trust of India (UTI), and the Stock Exchanges in many bigger cities and towns.

Banks are actively involved in a competitive market environment to win their customers, dealers, industrial community. Almost all the Banking units have provision for corporate PR departments with a staff ranging between 20 to 100 PR professionals. These banks offer excellent career opportunities for a beginner with status, perks and rosy promotional chances.

Public Relations for hospitals and health organizations is a recent development in India. Organizational PR has been at work in the medical profession. The Doctor-Patient relationship is a classic case of PR. There is a greater need for effective PR management to accomplish the avowed objects for Government of India. With the newer and revolutionary trend of patients demanding to be treated as consumers, the need for information and better relationships is even more urgent, making it imperative for hospitals to adopt a professional PR approach.

"Health for all by 2000" requires crucial public understanding and citizen participation. The importance of PR for Hospital and Health agencies being recognised in view of the emerging problems resulting from factors like ignorance, over-population, illiteracy, lack of sanitation and remoteness of Indian rural life. We have one of the biggest state sponsored healthcare systems comprising 20,531 primary health centres, 1,30,390 sub-centres, 5.86 lakhs of trained Dais, 4,10 lakh health guides, 128 medical colleges. It is rather unfortunate that the PR concept is restricted only to big cities. Health and family welfare, however, has a well-structured extension communication wing performing PR functions in almost all the states. PR graduates with love for health communications and having dedication to social service can explore avenues for a career in these hospitals and organizations involved in healthcare.

The State-sponsored welfare programmes, through its thousands of welfare agencies and private voluntary organisations include women and child development (ICDCs), nutrition programmes, early childhood education programme, women's development programmes, welfare of the disabled, social defence, relief and rehabilitation schemes, government-controlled welfare departments, hundreds of voluntary agencies, and many international voluntary and aided organizations, in specific fields provide good job opportunities for PR personnel to provide a two-way channel of communication, to persuade and motivate the public, to bring about attitudinal change and thus aid the development tasks.

## MANAGING MEDIA AND PUBLIC RELATIONS: A CASE STUDY

### Explaining Public Relations

You have news to share—information that would benefit the Linux community. You have some idea of the people you want to reach with your news and views. Now the problem becomes: How to reach them in the most effective way? The better the communications between you and your audience, the higher the profile of your organization.

Generating publicity is not as complex as you might think. Most of the success of public relations centers on knowing what to do and when. Implementing these initiatives can dramatically increase awareness of your business.

Public Relations (PR) is often confused with advertising, merchandising, promotion, or any of a dozen other buzz words in the marketing communications vocabulary. (By the way, *marketing communications* is a broad term that encompasses all of these disciplines.)

Public relations is about doing something newsworthy that you want to communicate, and then telling your audience (or very likely, several audiences) what you have done.

One of the most common public relations vehicles is the brief "New Product" announcement you see in magazines and trade publications. Often only a few lines or a paragraph in length, these announcements herald the launch of future products or services. These short announcements are typically triggered by a new product release, which may be accompanied by various forms of communications such as internal announcements to the organization's employees and external news releases to the media, stockholders, user community and other groups. News releases trigger a chain of events that result in visibility.

There are some important terms that may help you understand public relations. *News media* refers to all the places where people read or hear about news, including newspapers, magazines, television, radio and the Internet.

A *news release*, sometimes referred to as a press release, is a printed or electronic document issued by organizations who want to communicate news to editors, journalists, industry writers, or other media groups. Journalists write about the story for publication (if it is considered newsworthy), while editors control whether the story actually appears in a newspaper, magazine, website, or broadcast.

A news release contains important facts, quotes from key people, dates that the news happened (or will happen), and contacts for additional information. The news release is concise and usually runs no longer than two pages.

Public relations, then, can be thought of as the process that delivers your news to the people you want to reach through a broad, influential, and far-reaching news media community.

### Difference between Public Relations and Advertising

International humorist Stephen Leacock defined advertising as: "the science of arresting the human intelligence long enough to get money from it." But the textbook definition of advertising is: "a form of persuasion that informs people about the goods and services they can purchase."

Advertising is very different from public relations. One key difference is that you always pay for the space and time of an advertisement (or commercial, which is an insert appearing on radio, television, or the Internet). By contrast, editorial coverage generated through public relations is not paid for by the organization issuing the news release. The media will pick up and publish the story because they consider it newsworthy, not as a paid advertisement.

Another crucial difference is that, in advertising, you have virtually full control over the message. Because you are paying for advertising, the ad or commercial runs your exact text (called copy), provided the copy complies with generally acceptable standards for advertising. In the case of public relations, the media outlet you are targeting is under no obligation to run the story in any form. If a media outlet does decide to run the story, an editor will generally rewrite the news release, or use pertinent information from the news release to create the news. (For instance, your news release might be used as part of a larger story on players in your industry or profession.) In addition, you have no control over when the release or news will run. All decisions are made by the editor.

As you can see, public relations is a cost-effective way of getting your story out. Taking the trouble to write effective news releases and to build a relationship with the relevant media will, in time, pay dividends in the form of exposure and prestige. Best of all, public relations probably costs less than a single advertisement.

**Role of Public Relations**

Since public relations communicates your messages through the news media, all the power of the media is brought to bear when the public—those viewers, listeners, or readers you want to reach—learns about your news.

Think of what this means: high interest level, credibility, implied objectivity, and possibly implied endorsement by the journalist or publication reporting the information. There is also an urgency conveyed when news is reported in the media—and that news has the potential to reach a tremendously large audience.

With exposure comes awareness. An important goal of public relations—in any medium—is to make people aware of what your organization is, what it offers, and what it does. Never underestimate the value of such awareness. In flashier terms, it's called *buzz*.

Creating awareness for your organization is important for the development and utilization of its programmes and initiatives. You must inform the public and educational and training institutions about what you offer and how you can meet their needs. Public relations is probably the most valuable tool in accomplishing this. A well-implemented public relations initiative will help present your organization's offerings to their best advantage.

Public and news media relations also positions you to enter new marketplaces and exposes new Linux programmes to new audiences—all without the expense associated with an advertising programme. A sustained public relations programme allows you to ensure your programmes are in front of appropriate decision-makers. This continuous flow of information creates a constant awareness and a constant influx of inquiries—especially when integrated with other powerful marketing communications tools such as brochures, trade shows, and so on.

## Taking into Account the Benefits of a Public and Media Relations Programme

Public relations is vitally necessary, perhaps even critical, in today's competitive marketplace. There are many ways a sustained public relations programme can benefit your organization:

- Public relations should not be a "we will do it if we have the time and resources" kind of effort. A sustained initiative can build your organization's profile in the news media and the local community.
- Editorial coverage gives your organization better stakeholder attention compared to paid advertisements.
- Editorial copy generated through effective public relations is far more believable and credible than paid advertising, due to media objectivity. Recent studies in North America suggest that positive editorial coverage generates up to nine times more visibility than paid advertising.
- Public relations is an economical means of promoting your organization.
- Regular and effective news releases can make your organization a "news media source" on the state of Linux. It is critical to develop relationships with the news media in the same way it is a good idea to develop other kinds of friendships in the community. Writers and reporters are always looking for reliable and respected sources to quote.
- Regular media exposure legitimizes your organization's work and enhances its reputation. There is a subtle but nonetheless real perception that mention in a newspaper

or on television must be important. Media coverage communicates to the business community that your organization's qualifications and programmes are worthy of "a serious look."

You must also be cautious when dealing with media outlets. Being overconfident or overly aggressive in trying to place stories with the news media can have damaging results. It is a lot easier to lose goodwill than to gain it back. The safest position is to understand what you are doing, work hard to accomplish predetermined and realistic goals, be courteous and respectful when dealing with your media contacts, and expect some disappointments along the way. After all, hard as you may try, the results of your public and news media relations initiatives are never predictable. But if planned and implemented correctly, the benefits are enormous. As below explains how to determine what you really want to accomplish.

### Issues in Public and Media Relations Planning

When you want to promote your organization, you are provided with a variety of options. The first step is to develop a plan. You must determine the following:

- What do you want to accomplish?
- Who do you want to reachneeds to know about your organization?
- What do you want to say?
- What kind of information is newsworthy?

#### *Tasks to be Accomplished*

The first and most important step in public relations planning is to understand and define what you want to accomplish through public relations. What are your objectives? Just as importantly, how will you determine (measure) your success in accomplishing these objectives? Creating a list of concrete goals can help you maintain direction in your efforts.

#### *Writing News Releases*

Who, what, where, when, why and how—these are the six critical ingredients of all news releases. But don't forget, a little spice can make your news release stand out from the crowd. In this part, you will learn how to write a professional-looking news release, the most important tool in any public relations programme.

### *Writing Headline*

The headline is the first thing—and sometimes the only thing—an editor will read. Releases are often rejected as a result of a weak headline.

Create headlines with impact. The most effective words in a news release headline are eye-catching words like "announces" and "new." Comparative words like "better" or "more" can also draw attention to your article. The headline is the "hook" that lures editors and reporters into reading more. Headlines must be compelling.

Many public relations novices make the mistake of embellishing their headlines. Your organization has to earn the respect of editors. Nobody owes you a reading. Too much information, or confusing information, is a turnoff. Most importantly, you should never sacrifice accuracy for the sake of a flashy headline.

Here are some guidelines for writing headlines:

(*i*) Determine the most significant benefit your most important reader will derive from the news.
(*ii*) Try and state those benefits in seven words or less.
(*iii*) Ask yourself if your statement is meaningful to someone not closely involved with your business.

When actually writing the headline, try to achieve the greatest impact using the fewest words. Your headline doesn't need to be quite as dramatic as a newspaper headline. Editors are looking for information in the headline, so try to at least include who, what, and why. Whatever, the headline, you must accurately reflect the content that follows.

### *Writing First Paragraph*

Many news releases are accepted or rejected on the basis of the headline and first paragraph or two. These introductory paragraphs are often all an editor will have time to read. Many releases are rejected due to simple downfall: failure to include any *news* in the first paragraph.

An important news-writing concept is *collapsible copy.* Collapsible copy reads well from the beginning to the end of any given paragraph. The information is "chunked" to stand on its own, if need be. Each sentence could be pulled from the news release and used as a quotation. This type of copy should be used as extensively as possible in all paragraphs.

Editors expect to see the five Ws covered in the first few sentences. Here's an example:

> *NEW YORK—January 22, 2003*—The Linux Professional Institute (LPI) (http://www.lpi.org/), the premier professional certification programme for the Linux community, and UnitedLinux LLC (http://www.unitedlinux.com/), an industry initiative to streamline Linux development and certification around a global, uniform distribution, have signed a cooperative agreement to market a UnitedLinux professional certification programme.
> Under the memorandum of understanding, LPI and UnitedLinux will work jointly to create new UnitedLinux specific exams which, when passed together with the current LPI Levels 1 and 2 exams, will lead to two new UnitedLinux certifications. The new exams are expected to be available during the first quarter of 2003.

Let's look more closely at this example. The *where* and *when* of this and most releases are specified in the *slug* ("New York—January 22, 2003"). The *who* is LPI and UnitedLinux. The *what* is signing a cooperative agreement. The *why* is marketing a UnitedLinux professional certification programme. And the *how* is LPI and UnitedLinux working jointly to create new UnitedLinux-specific exams.

These two paragraphs alone communicate the essential points of this announcement. In print, there may not be enough space for more than this. Some special-interest journals devote a column or a page to announcements, which are printed verbatim from the news release. Unless the announcement is deemed more newsworthy, this may be all the coverage you get.

*Writing Middle Paragraphs*

Limited space in publications and time in broadcasting means the first paragraph *may* get covered. Paragraphs should always be ordered by importance for two important reasons.

First, editors read through releases quickly and often will not finish entire releases. You must consider what things are most important, and place them next in the release. Often, a statement from your spokesperson explaining the expected impacts on the marketplace or something related can be catchy enough to be quoted. Follow this with the next most important thing, and so on to the end of the release.

Second, sequence frequently indicates importance (unless the story is an in-depth feature that can establish pacing and shape). Stacking your news, in what some editors call the "inverted pyramid," can show editors the relative importance of your details. By following the inverted pyramid, you will make the editor's job easier and also accomplish your goal of getting the most critical information covered.

*Writing Final Details*

You need to mark the end of your news release, so that editors know there is no further news. In journalism, this is traditionally done by putting "-30-" or "-end-" on a new, centered line, after the last line of copy, as follows:

After ending the release, it is important to include the *boilerplate*—standard, reusable background information about the organization issuing the news and contact information for editorial follow-up. The boilerplate includes the organization's web address where the editor can go for further details. Boilerplates can be reviewed and revised periodically, but they should maintain consistency. Wildly different boilerplates are unprofessional from one release to the next.

***Quality Analysis of News Release***

Print editors and journalists are notoriously overworked and underpaid. A well-written news release will often be used word for word, with may be a few changes for "objectivity" or to accommodate the publication's format.

The editorial staff at the *Los Angeles Times* says this about news releases:

> A good news release is a concise, complete description of an upcoming event; a timely report of an event has just occurred; notification of important personnel or procedural changes in an organization; or other news or feature tips.

Bad releases—the ones that don't get used—often have these common mistakes:

(*i*) Lack of a local angle.
(*ii*) Insufficient or inaccurate information (who, what, when, where, why, how).
(*iii*) Failure to include contact information for the organization.
(*iv*) Verbosity. (Try to keep the release to one or two pages, but balance brevity against failure to include necessary information.)
(*v*) Lack of timeliness—the editor's deadline has passed or the news is released too long after the event.

Writing a news release does not have to be painful. What you need is a little time to gather all the facts: the who, what, when, where, why and how (and any additional information necessary to support).

Sometimes your news won't be used right away or in the form you provided. A writer may need time to rewrite your outline into a news story. Or, if a feature is being developed on Linux, the writer may use many sources for depth and objectivity. They may use quotable quotes, first-person anecdotes, statistics, and causes and effects from your releases as well as those of your competitors.

Deadlines are hugely important because the news media cannot delay publication or broadcasting. Don't bother editors with untimely information. If you can't pitch your story in time, wait for another opportune moment to come around.

### *Listing Important Tips for Writing Releases*

To summarize what we have said so far, here are ten tips for writing an excellent news release:

#### *(a) Use an Active Headline to Grab the Editor's Attention*

The headline makes your release stand out. Keep the headline short, active, and descriptive, with the most positive spin. Write "Jane Doe Named Person of the Year" instead of "Jane Doe Gets Award."

#### *(b) Put the Most Important Information at the Beginning*

This is a tried and true rule of journalism. Remember that the first two paragraphs should contain the salient facts of who, what, when, where, why and how. Don't bury good information at the end.

#### *(c) Avoid Exaggeration and Unsubstantiated Claims*

A news editor can smell a sales pitch a mile away. Instead of making over-inflated statements, provide real, usable information. Find legitimate ways to set your organization apart, and stress those points.

*(d) Write in an Active, Engaging and Concise Style*

Use language that conveys your excitement about the news. If your release is boring or passively written, the editor may conclude the news itself is not very meaningful or you are not a good candidate for an interview. Interesting equals newsworthy.

*(e) Keep Your Release to Two Pages or Less*

Generally, if you can't state your message in two pages, you are not getting to the point fast enough. Editors are always looking for concise, easy-to-read releases that can be thrown onto a website or squeezed into a leftover space in a page layout. For highly important news with many details, you can include a third page, but this should be done sparingly.

*(f) Include a Contact*

Every news release should include a contact person who the media can reach for more information. This contact is your spokesperson and must be familiar with all the news in the release. They should be prepared to answer questions.

*(g) Keep Jargon to the Minimum*

Avoid using highly technical terms and buzzwords familiar only to Linux insiders. Jargon can date quickly, and complicated language irritates people who don't know what you mean. Your goal is to tell your story to as wide an audience as possible, not to unduly limit the audience. Even special-interest publications mostly write in plain language and only use jargon and acronyms generally familiar to their readers.

*(h) Stress "Benefits, Benefits, Benefits"*

This falls under the category of "show, don't tell." Avoid claiming something is "unique" or "the best" when you can't substantiate this. Instead, provide specific examples of benefits, supported by evidence and anecdotes.

*(i) Be Specific and Detailed*

Marcia Yudkin, author of *Six Steps to Free Publicity*, talks about the "Yes, but what *is* it?" syndrome. Nothing is more irritating than seeing constant references to a product name or service name, but no information on what that product or service is. The reader needs to be able to visualize a new product or understand what a service offers. This is particularly critical for launches (announcements of new offerings). You should ask someone unfamiliar with your product or service to read your release and then describe the product or service in their own words.

*(j) Proofread!*

This is easily forgotten, but extremely important. Always proofread your work before issuing the final release. Better yet, give the document to someone else (perhaps a copy editor) who can readily spot spelling and grammatical errors. Nothing signals unprofessionalism more than a typo-filled communication.

### *Process of Distribution of News Release*

Your media contact database is your best source for editors, journalists, and freelancers who should receive your news, but if you want to include a broader range of news media targets, you may consider using one of the many news release distribution services available. Asking one or two of your news media contacts will likely reveal a creditable service. These services can be expensive, so base your decision on how broad an appeal your news has.

In North America, the more popular distribution services include:

- PR Newswire
- Canada Newswire
- Business Wire

These firms will customize your distribution based on the subject- matter, and can target specific media such as technology editors, medical editors, daily news editors and so on. A customer service representative will explain your options and the cost involved.

News releases are very important in a public relations campaign. News releases give editors and the public a glimpse into your company. When these documents are done professionally, your organization will receive the recognition you deserve. Remember, though, that news releases are not the only tool of public relations professionals. In next section, we will examine the variety of other tools that can be used.

### Other Public Relations Tools

The news release is the most important form of written communications used by a public relations professional, but not the only one. There are many other public relations tools that should be used when appropriate.

News releases may suffice for most news stories, but other, lengthier forms of communication can give in-depth coverage of an interesting news item. Feature articles, bylined articles, and emails may be written to provide human interest appeal, to explore topics and issues in more depth, to raise your organization's profile in the local community, or for other reasons.

### Elaborating upon Bylined Articles

A byline is the line showing the author's name at the beginning of an article. Basically, a bylined article is attributed to a source rather than being anonymous.

Bylined articles can be any length, and they tend to be based on opinion. They articulate views and opinions that are clearly the writer's own, without requiring objectivity.

Issues, trends, and predictions regarding Linux and open source are ideal subjects for bylined articles. Moreover, forward-looking pieces are of high interest. Editors are always looking for "the next thing" to tell their readers about.

Opinion articles are important to position your organization as the leader and trendsetter in your field. To be a guru is to be watched, quoted, respected and followed. Editors like highlighting celebrated members of the community because they sell more issues.

Gauging the interest of the news media is very important. What's hot? What are they writing about? Check the topics listed in their editorial calendars. Try to match their interests to the activities of your organization in the community. Then start writing your opinion piece.

Typically, the author of a bylined article should be your organization's designated spokesperson and acknowledged authority for the media. That might be you or a senior official. Sometimes a public relations professional will ghost-write the piece for the spokesperson, whose name will appear on the article. When this occurs, the article must closely reflect the spokesperson's views and ideas. In other words, he or she "owns" the ideas expressed in the article, not the writer.

An added bonus of by lined articles is that they can be adapted into speeches for possible speaking opportunities. Conversely, any speech can be written as a by lined article.

**Elaborating upon Feature Articles**

Feature articles, which explore a subject at length, are not constrained by the tight deadlines of regular news articles. Features may be submitted at any time, depending on the editor's needs. Features often stem from a regular news item.

Imagine that the Linux operating system has been successfully implemented at a large organization in your community. This story is newsworthy, but begin to look for "the rest of the story." What difficulties did they experience in the transition, or what part did your organization play in their implementation? This could be the start of a feature article.

More research and creativity will go into a feature story, but this must still be accurate. You will provide more facts, more statistics, more examples and anecdotes, and more analysis than in a news release. You can humanize and dramatize what may appear unexciting at first glance (a Linux implementation). You can openly focus on a particular angle or viewpoint, so long as you avoid outright advertising. Readers dislike advertorials masquerading as "articles," and no editor will accept an article that blatantly sells.

Another bonus is that editors are quite open to features, because they provide much needed content for filling an issue. When the feature is written by a reliable source and does not require payment (unlike a commissioned article), the article becomes a real asset.

All writing needs to engage the reader. The first sentence or two must be compelling enough for the editor to read on. Features require a strong lead—something to hook your target audience. A headline or a photograph may help.

For a feature, you have a wide repertoire of leads to choose from. Some leads are designed to startle and shock, some will excite readers' curiosity, some will vividly describe a real or imagined scenario, and some will succinctly state the nature of the story.

The body of the feature then unfolds in a logical sequence, and ends with a strong and memorable close. Every feature will be different, depending on the subject, the anticipated audience, and the skill of the writer. Reading features written by others in the Linux community is a good way to learn and pick up possible story ideas.

You can direct a feature to the "feature editor" at a daily newspaper or your targeted trade magazines. Before going to the trouble of writing the article, you should pitch the idea to see if the publication has any interest at all. The pitch should include an outline, an estimated length (number of words), and a description of illustrations or photos you can supply. You could also include a selected portfolio of previously published articles about your organization.

The upfront consultation is invaluable. Since the editor knows their readership better than you do, they might suggest an angle of specific interest to their readers and indicate where this piece might fit in their publishing schedule. The more complete your package, the more seriously your work will be considered.

Another possibility is to plant the story idea with the editor, and let the publication take care of writing the feature. In this case, you can supply expertise and interview subjects.

Whatever your approach, keep in mind that the ultimate goal is to generate favourable coverage and visibility for your organization.

***Illustrating Email Writing***

Another effective way to communicate to a targeted audience is through an email campaign. The effectiveness of a good email should not be underestimated. Some fundraising experts, for example, can raise thousand of dollars with an effective email campaign. Exceptional letters have obtained contracts, sold properties and landed jobs.

Emails can be targeted to a specific audience for much less than you would spend on a regular mail campaign. Every email is an opportunity to effectively communicate to your target audience. For example, your organization might want to target recent graduates of local computer training courses with opportunities in their area. You will need to obtain the names and email addresses of recent graduates from the institutions offering those programmes. Cooperation with their institution can often be established if you provide something in return, such as a reciprocal link on your website, a mention in your newsletter, or even free advertising.

Hopefully, your email campaign will generate interest in your organization and your programmes. Be mindful of potentially spanning your intended audience—this could have a negative impact.

### *Other Communications Tools used in Public Relations*

There are numerous other communication tools you can use in a public relations effort. Here are just a few suggestions:

- A speech at a Linux trade show.
- A presentation at a local training institution or career development conference.
- A brochure or flyer describing the work your company does.
- A white paper describing the benefits of your company's work, posted on your website.
- A newsletter or email newsletter describing your organization's activities and achievements, aimed at current and prospective users.
- An advertisement placed in targeted magazines.
- Special events such as open houses and "media information" days.
- Regular tours of your facility.

The possibilities are limited only by your time, resources and budget.

### *Emphasizing Core Messages*

In all your public relations initiatives, don't lose sight of your core messages . These messages are the "essence" of your organization, defining your identity for users, the media, and the general public. Remember that the core messages should be woven into everything you do as a public relations representative. Consistency creates a bigger impact for your audience.

## PUBLIC RELATIONS SPECIALISTS: A CASE STUDY

- Nature of the Work.
- Working Conditions.
- Training, Other Qualifications and Advancement.

- Employment.
- Job Outlook.
- Earnings.
- Related Occupations.
- Sources of Additional Information.

*Significant Points*

- Although employment is projected to grow faster than average, keen competition is expected for entry-level jobs.
- Opportunities should be best for college graduates who combine a degree in public relations, journalism, or another communications-related field with a public relations internship or other related work experience.
- Creativity, initiative, and the ability to communicate effectively are essential.

### Nature of the Work

An organization's reputation, profitability, and even its continued existence can depend on the degree to which its targeted "publics" support its goals and policies. Public relations specialists—also referred to as *communications specialists* and *media specialists*, among other titles—serve as advocates for businesses, non-profit associations, universities, hospitals, and other organizations, and build and maintain positive relationships with the public. As managers recognize the growing importance of good public relations to the success of their organizations, they increasingly rely on public relations specialists for advice on the strategy and policy of such programmes.

Public relations specialists handle organizational functions such as media, community, consumer, industry, and governmental relations; political campaigns; interest-group representation; conflict mediation; or employee and investor relations. They help an organization and its public adapt mutually to each other. However, public relations are not only about "telling the organization's story." Understanding the attitudes and concerns of consumers, employees, and various other groups also is a vital part of the job. To improve communication, public relations specialists establish and maintain cooperative relationships with representatives of community, consumer, employee, and public interest groups, and with representatives from print and broadcast journalism.

Informing the general public, interest groups, and stockholders of an organization's policies, activities, and accomplishments is an important part of a public relations specialist's job. The work also involves keeping management aware of public attitudes and the concerns of the many groups and organizations with which they must deal.

Media specialists draft press releases and contact people in the media who might print or broadcast their material. Many radio or television special reports, newspaper stories, and magazine articles start at the desks of public relations specialists. Sometimes, the subject is an organization and its policies towards its employees or its role in the community. Often, the subject is a public issue, such as health, energy, or the environment.

Public affairs specialists also arrange and conduct programmes to keep up contact between organization representatives and the public. For example, they setup speaking engagements and often prepare speeches for company officials. These media specialists represent employers at community projects; make film, slide, or other visual presentations at meetings and school assemblies; and plan conventions. In addition, they are responsible for preparing annual reports and writing proposals for various projects.

In government, public relations specialists—who may be called press secretaries, information officers, public affairs specialists, or communication specialists—keep the public informed about the activities of government agencies and officials. For example, public affairs specialists in the U.S. Department of State keep the public informed of travel advisories and of U.S. positions on foreign issues. A press secretary for a member of Congress keeps constituents aware of the representative's accomplishments.

In large organizations, the key public relations executive, who often is a vice-president, may develop overall plans and policies with other executives. In addition, public relations departments employ public relations specialists to write, research, prepare materials, maintain contacts and respond to inquiries.

People who handle publicity for an individual or who direct public relations for a small organization may deal with all aspects of the job. They contact people, plan and research, and prepare materials for distribution. They also may handle advertising or sales promotion work to support marketing.

### Working Conditions

Some public relations specialists work a standard 35-to 40-hour week, but unpaid overtime is common. Occasionally, they must be at the job or on call around the clock, especially if there is an emergency or crisis. Public relations offices are busy places; work schedules can be irregular and frequently interrupted. Schedules often have to be rearranged so that workers can meet deadlines, deliver speeches, attend meetings and community activities, or travel.

### Employment

Public relations specialists held about 188,000 jobs in 2004. Public relations specialists are concentrated in service-providing industries such as advertising and related services; healthcare and social assistance; educational services and government. Others worked for communications firms, financial institutions, and government agencies.

Public relations specialists are concentrated in large cities, where press services and other communications facilities are readily available and many businesses and trade associations have their headquarters. Many public relations consulting firms, for example, are in New York, Los Angeles, San Francisco, Chicago, and Washington, DC. There is a trend, however, for public relations jobs to be dispersed throughout the Nation, closer to clients.

### Training, Other Qualifications and Advancement

There are no defined standards for entry into a public relations career. A college degree combined with public relations experience, usually gained through an internship, is considered excellent preparation for public relations work; in fact, internships are becoming vital to obtaining employment. The ability to communicate effectively is essential. Many entry-level public relations specialists have a college major in public relations, journalism, advertising, or communication. Some firms seek college graduates who have worked in electronic or print journalism. Other employers seek applicants with demonstrated communication skills and training or experience in a field related to the firm's business—information technology, health, science, engineering, sales, or finance, for example.

Many colleges and universities offer bachelor's and post-secondary degrees in public relations, usually in a journalism or communications department. In addition, many other colleges offer at least one course in this field. A common public relations sequence includes courses in public relations principles and techniques; public relations management and administration, including organizational development; writing, emphasizing news releases, proposals, annual reports, scripts, speeches, and related items; visual communications, including desktop publishing and computer graphics; and research, emphasizing social science research and survey design and implementation. Courses in advertising, journalism, business administration, finance, political science, psychology, sociology, and creative writing also are helpful. Specialties are offered in public relations for business, government, and non-profit organizations.

Many colleges help students gain part-time internships in public relations that provide valuable experience and training. The U.S. Armed Forces also can be an excellent place to gain training and experience. Membership in local chapters of the Public Relations Student Society of America (affiliated with the Public Relations Society of America) or the International Association of Business Communicators provides an opportunity for students to exchange views with public relations specialists and to make professionals contacts that may help them find a job in the field. A portfolio of published articles, television or radio programme, slide presentations, and other work is an asset in finding a job. Writing for a school publication or television or radio station provides valuable experience and material for one's portfolio.

Creativity, initiative, good judgement, and the ability to communicate thoughts clearly and simply are essential in this occupation. Decision-making, problem-solving, and research skills also are important. People who choose public relations as a career need an outgoing personality, self-confidence, an understanding of human psychology, and an enthusiasm for motivating people. They should be competitive, yet able to function as part of a team and open to new ideas.

Some organizations, particularly those with large public relations staffs, have formal training programmes for new employees. In smaller organizations, new employees work under the guidance of experienced staff members. Beginners often maintain files of material about company activities, scan newspapers and magazines for appropriate articles to clip, and assemble information for speeches and pamphlets. They also may answer calls from the press and the public, work on invitation lists and details for press conferences, or escort visitors and clients. After gaining experience, they write news releases, speeches, and articles for publication or plan and carry out public relations programmes. Public relations specialists in smaller firms usually get all-around experience, whereas those in larger firms tend to be more specialized.

The Public Relations Society of America accredits public relations specialists who have at least 5 years of experience in the field and have passed a comprehensive 6-hour examination (5 hours written, 1 hour oral). The International Association of Business Communicators also has an accreditation programme for professionals in the communication field, including public relations specialists. Those who meet all the requirements of the programme earn the Accredited Business Communicator (ABC) designation. Candidates must have at least 5 years of experience in a communication field and pass a written and oral examination. They also must submit a portfolio of work samples demonstrating involvement in a range of communication projects and a thorough understanding of communication planning. Employers may consider professional recognition through accreditation assign of competence in this field, which could be especially helpful in a competitive job market.

Promotion to supervisory jobs may come to public relations specialists who show that they can handle more demanding assignments. In public relations firms, a beginner might be hired as a research assistant or account coordinator and be promoted to account executive, senior account executive, account manager, and eventually vice-president. A similar career path is followed in corporate public relations, although the titles may differ. Some experienced public relations specialists start their own consulting firms.

### Job Outlook

Keen competition will likely continue for entry-level public relations jobs, as the number of qualified applicants is expected to exceed the number of job openings. Many people are attracted to this profession because of the high profile nature of the work. Opportunities should be best for college graduates who combine a degree in journalism, public relations, advertising, or another communications-related field with a public relations internship or other related work experience. Applicants without the appropriate educational background or work experience will face the toughest obstacles.

Employment of public relations specialists is expected to grow faster than average for all occupations through 2014. The need for good public relations in an increasingly competitive business environment should spur demand for public relations specialists in organizations of all types and sizes. The value of a company is measured not just by its balance sheet, but also by the strength of its relationships with those on whom it depends for its success. With the increasing demand for corporate accountability, more emphasis will be placed on improving the image of the client, as well as on building public confidence.

Employment in public relations firms should grow as firms hire contractors to provide public relations services rather than support full-time staff. In addition to those arising from employment growth, job opportunities should result from the need to replace public relations specialists who take other jobs or who leave the occupation altogether.

**Earnings**

Median annual earnings for salaried public relations specialists were $41,710, in 2002. The middle 50 per cent earned between $31,300 and $56,180; the lowest 10 per cent earned less than $24,240, and the top 10 per cent earned more than $75,100. Median annual earnings in the industries employing the largest numbers of public relations specialists in 2002 were:

| | |
|---|---|
| Advertising and related services | $48,070 |
| Local government | 42,000 |
| Business, professional, labour, political, and similar organizations | 39,330 |
| Colleges, universities and professional schools | 36,820 |

According to a joint survey conducted by the International Association of Business Communicators and the Public Relations

Society of America, the median annual income for a public relations specialist was $66,800 in 2002.

## Related Occupations

Public relations specialists create favourable attitudes among various organizations, interest groups, and the public through effective communication. Other workers with similar jobs include advertising, marketing, promotions, public relations, and sales managers; demonstrators, product promoters, and models; news analysts, reporters, and correspondents; lawyers; market and survey researchers; sales representatives, wholesale and manufacturing; and police and detectives involved in community relations.

# 3

# Public and Media Relations Management: An Overview of Practice

## PUBLIC RELATIONS AS MANAGEMENT FUNCTION: AN INTRODUCTION

Public Relations is a management function which attempts to create goodwill for an organisation and its products, services or ideals with groups of people which can effect is present and future welfare by highlighting the rewards of mutual understanding and the risks involved in misunderstanding between individuals, groups, Governments and Nations in this restless world of "Man the unknown".

PR is an important tool concept in the field of Business Management. It introduces the human factor into management. New thinking on management techniques have slimmed down the management team and have killed the theory of delegation of authority which led to top-heavy management with every executive having a deputy. However, small the controlling group in a company there should be room for an executive with Public Relations know-how and do-how.

Public Relations activity in a company varies according to whether it is carried out by its own Public Relations Department or by hiring PR consultants. It is necessary to differentiate between the advisory and executive features of professional Public Relations practice: the writing and issuing of press releases, the calling of a press conference or the editing of a house journal are one of the important aspects of Public Relations practice.

The managements want their Public Relations to project how good they are in running their organisations. It is true that it is one of the functions of PR to publicise the achievements of its organisations but it is not the only function.

Public Relations is meant not for projecting one's own image but for working to project the reputation (IMAGE) of the company he works, conjointly with it his own image automatically projected. Good Public Relations needs thought, planning and organisation. The best Public Relations will not compensate for weakness in these and in many important business areas.

Public Relations has been in existence for hundred of years: "Manu Samhita" and "Koutilya's Arthashastra" bear testimony to the existence of Public Relations. The study of the origin of Public Relations provides a helpful insight into its functions, its strengths and weaknesses. The effort to deal with the force of opinion and to communicate with other goes back to antiquity; only the tools, degree of specialisation, breadth of knowledge and intensity of effort required today are relatively new. The history of Public Relations cannot be told by simply averring that it grew out of press agentry.

## Major Objectives

Public Relations must be flexible, organic, responsive and creative. It may be most effectively handled by some of the most talented people. Care must be taken to eliminate any biasing factors. Public awareness was substantially higher than would have been the case in a city or the other side of the country.

The aims of the Public Relations campaign for any organisation must include:

(*a*) to project an aura of creditability and professionalism;
(*b*) to develop a higher profile and improved product awareness;
(*c*) to attract and recruit high calibre personnel;
(*d*) to create and instill a common purpose team spirit and enthusiasm;
(*e*) to encourage the sales force to increase the level of sales;
(*f*) to generate the maximum number of reader equiries to be followed;
(*g*) to project the company as a responsible ethical organisation and a fair and honest trader.

The more recently developed concept of issues analysis has some interesting implications for Public Relations planning.

To find agreed schedule of Public Relations objectives for any organisation which should try to cover.

(*i*) Quantified objectives for year one and, possibly, two.
(*ii*) Detailed aims for years two and three.
(*iii*) Outline aims to cover those issues predicted to arise during years two to five.
(*iv*) Broad aiming to cover alternative issues that might arise beyond year five.

## Need for PR in Government: A Valid Case

It is necessary for any government to keep up a constant link with the public in order to make them aware of its activities, decision taken on some important matters relating to the public, action plans, etc. Especially in India, where the percentage of literacy is less, the need for an organised communication programme is of utmost important. In order to get the public support for implementation of government plans and in order to motivate them, the PR section of the government at its Central, State and District levels must be strengthened.

Basically Public Relations works in government has to start with the preparation of annual PR plans, outlining the fundamental communication objectives of the year and outlining, in brief, the actual plans to communicate these objectives which at the end should be submitted to the Chief Executive for his approval. In sum, the need for PR in government can cover the following points:

(*a*) to inform about new government schemes to the public;
(*b*) communicate to all government departments the methods of handling the scheme;
(*c*) communicate to the general public to enlist its cooperation;
(*d*) to bring government department and mass media closer for better understanding between each other of the points of view;
(*e*) to win the support of mass media through editorials and articles; and
(*f*) to motivate employees at all levels for executing the government scheme.

## Explaining Basic Principles of PR

PR is a phenomenon that has emerged in modern society because of the nature of the social, political and economic institutions that have been developed in the world today and the behaviour of different groups of people within society.

PR is based on a social philosophy of management. It places the interests of people first in all matters pertaining to the conduct of an organisation. Public service is the foundation for the modern concept of public relations. The objective of a non-profit association is comparable to its publics. Mr. Paul W. Garrett, a pioneer in modern PR aptly expressed PR as the fundamental attitude of mind, a philosophy of management, which deliberately and with enlightened selfishness places the broad interest of the public first in every decision affecting the operation of a business.

Business corporations serve many public interests. In fulfilling the expectations of the publics in relation to their needs, wants and their interests differ and may, sometimes conflict. Employees are interested in steady employment, fair wages, good working conditions, recognition, opportunity of advancement, refinement and disability benefits. To serve these interests, the management should lay down the foundation for good employee relations. Customers are primarily interested in quality products and services, fair price and continuous supply. Stockholders are concerned with management and fair return on their investments. Suppliers are interested in profit, continuous relation and fair dealing. The community in which the company is placed is interested in generating employment, paying taxes, maintaining fair employment practices, protecting the environment, contributing to local charities and participating in community affairs.

In serving the interests of these various groups, corporate management must maintain a fair balance of benefits to all group so that one does not receive the advantages at the expense of another. A business that succeeds in satisfying the interests of its publics enjoys the understanding and goodwill of the general public, which is the primary objective of PR.

### Reiterating the Need for PR

There are still many who regard PR as an unnecessary frill that can be dispensed with a fed that should be ignored or a luxury which only the large and affluent organisations can indulge in. But the need for PR is inherent in the very nature of modern society and people can ignore it only at their peril. Society is made up of many groups of people, each with its own interests which are different from and in some cases even in conflict with the interests of other groups. In order that a society functions harmoniously, it needs the help of organised PR.

The need for PR arises from the responsibility that an organisation owes to the society which nurtures it and establishes it to function and operate. No organisation functions in a vacuum. It flourishes only because a particular kind of social environment exists. The world over business organisations which are forward looking and foresighted are trying to make a contribution to social causes apart from achieving their immediate and ultimate ends of producing goods for sale and marketing them at a profit.

**Explaining PR for Public**

PR is not something that is necessary only for business organisations. It is an approach to the problems—a management tool—that is equally valid for all organisations that function in a society even if they be non-profit making organisations, academic institutions, government bodies and the like. Even political parties, religious groups, social service or philanthropic organisations and trade unions need to have, and in many countries to have, PR set-ups to ensure that their communications lines with the public remain open and they are able to earn the goodwill of the people that they need so much.

A feature of modern society which makes the task of creating understanding between an organisation and the public a matter that requires professional expertise is the segmentation that has taken place in our society. The public today are no longer a homogenous society. It comprises numerous groups, each with its own interests and sometimes with conflicting interests. PR involves evaluation of attitudes of each one of these segments of the public that are relevant to an organisation and requires that a regular flow of communication be directed towards them so that they are kept informed to the organisations' policies. It is only by this means that a favourable attitude on their part can be ensured or in other words it is only by this means that their goodwill can be won.

Some of the relevant publics for a modern business organisation are:

- Shareholders.
- Government.
- Central Parliament and the State Legislatures.

- Municipalities and other Local Bodies.
- Customers.
- Dealers.
- Suppliers.
- Press.
- Community around.
- Organisation's own employees..

Even though PR is formally accepted, there is very little appreciation of the potentially of this discipline in achieving management objectives. There is hardly any areas of top management functioning where considerations of PR do not enter, hardly any aspect of management policy that does not have a PR angle. Any business organisation which tries to function today without understanding fully the environment in which it is functioning and the changes that are taking place in it is bound to end up in disaster.

The maintenance of proper PR set-up will help a management to understand and also to anticipate environmental changes which are likely to have a bearing on the functioning of the organisation. It will enable the organisation to prepare itself for the required changes and will also enable it to influence the environment in a direction favourable to it. PR can play a role in developing favourable equations with each of the various publics or segments of the public with which it is concerned.

Therefore, it follows from the above, that if PR is to be effective, it is essential that the closest rapport should exist between the top management and the PR set-up of the organisation. The PR department should be fully aware of top level management thinking and planning. It is only where this is so that PR will be able to advise management effectively on whether its thinking and planning is in tune with public moods and aspirations. PR can be most effective where it is not only has access to top management and is able to get information from it, but has an actual role to play in the making and implementation of policies.

## MAJOR MEDIA TRENDS

From the rise of transparency to the decline of newsprint, every PR pro needs to remain on top of the ever-changing media landscape.

**Portability of Video Content**

"It's an understatement to say that the news media have changed almost cosmically over the past several years," says Laurence Moskowitz, CEO of Medialink. And that change, he adds, is not a result of content or society's appetite, but is instead due to technology.

Indeed, technology is at the root of many current trends in the media landscape. But perhaps one for which it has the power to have the most influence is the portability of video content. It was not long ago that news programmes or entertainment TV programmes could only be viewed from the comfort of one's living room. Now, with the increasing popularity of video on demand, there is a lot of talk about video content on cell phones, says Lela Cocoros, cofounder and partner of October Strategies, a marketing and communications firm that counts a number of cable content providers as clients.

While such technology is already the norm in Japan and parts of Europe, Cocoros says it will be a reality in the US within the next year.

"Probably the next step is a video version of an iPod," says Steve Lanzano, EVP and GM of Havas-owned media planning and buying firm MPG. He adds that this ties in with the overall trend of consumer control of communication. "They get what they want, how they want it, and where they want it," he says. "Distribution can be anywhere."

Giving video the portability feature that print has always enjoyed makes it the dominant content, adds Moskowitz.

Cocoros says that providers likely will have different programming on cell phones or broadband sites, as well as programming specifically designed for those outlets. For marketers, the key to taking advantage of this rising trend is determining the consumer's preferred mode of communication, Lanzano says.

Moskowitz adds that PR pros must attain fluency with technologies and with the kinds of content that can be communication vehicles for clients. "The PR industry remains far less technically adept than its marketing and advertising brethren," he says. "We need to be minding the traditional processes, but we certainly can't be looking in awe—and only awe—at the new ones."

### Blogs

In the past couple of years, blogs have grown from an outlet for tech-savvy geeks to something that has reached an almost mainstream level. Indeed, corporations and even media outlets are making blogs part of their marketing strategies. They reached news-breaking entity status when a group of bloggers debunked Dan Rather's report on President Bush's National Guard service.

Although they're considered valuable outlets for marketers-especially PR practitioners—to monitor, Lloyd Trufelman, president of Trylon Communications, says blogs will eventually just be integrated into the media mix, rather than remain a stand-alone entity.

"Now blogging is becoming very simple and very pedestrian," he says. "I don't know how many of these blogs will exist as viable economic (entities). If a blog is going to exist as a commercial enterprise, it's going to have to track to the same economic rules that govern all other forms of media."

Mark Weiner, CEO of Delahaye, agrees that the excitement over blogs will settle down, although incidents where blogs break mainstream news will cause periodic spikes in interest. But for the most part, blogs' influence over a large segment of the population appears to be limited.

"We see that, except for a small handful of influential, opinion-leading blogs, for the most part bloggers are people who have an interest in something and are speaking to (those) people who share that interest," Weiner says.

Going forward, PR practitioners need to be mindful of the blog's place in a client's communication strategy, says Ray Kerins, EVP and managing director of corporate communications and media relations at GCI Group. "Every client is not appropriate to have blogs," he says.

### Celebrity Weeklies

Celebrity news and gossip have been part of the American media landscape since the days of Hedda Hopper and Walter Winchell. And *People* magazine, the modern founder of celebrity-based journalism, has been a bestseller at the newsstand for more than 30 years, selling more than 1 million copies weekly. Yet the past few years have seen the introduction of a new crop of celebrity magazines, especially weeklies, including *In Touch, Life & Style,* a retooled *Us Weekly* and *Star*, and British import *OK!*

Recent figures from the Audit Bureau of Circulations show a remarkable increase in circulation, newsstand sales, and subscriptions for these types of magazines for the first half of this year. Michael Schiferl, SVP and director of media relations for Weber Shandwick, says that part of the fascination with such magazines is that they provide an escape. And their success is due to the fact that they cut across a lot of demographics, he adds.

However, while the public appetite for celebrity news is not likely to disappear altogether, the recent rise of coverage, and the publications that provide it, is bound to plateau. "People will get sick of it," notes Kerins, "and turn more toward lifestyle news. (But) it'll never go away completely."

The trend in celebrity news is linked to one toward feature-driven content in general, says Schiferl. He cites the Chicago Tribune, which now includes a celebrity gossip column in its front section, as an example. And *The Wall Street Journal Weekend Edition's* Pursuits section adds to the publication's growing feature component.

Steve Cohn, editor of the *Media Industry Newsletter*, says such adjustments will continue as newspapers and newsmagazines try to attract new readers or keep ones they might be otherwise losing to other media outlets.

**Transparency**

It is no secret that traditional media have suffered in credibility and reputation over the past few years. While promises by public editors and apologies by editors-in chief for publications' transgressions have become far too common, some outlets are now considering other ways to regain readers' trust.

Kerins says media companies are more likely to utilize outside PR firms than in previous years.

"You're seeing a much greater convergence of public relations in the news media," he says.

For many media organizations, transparency is a growing trend, says Sam Whitmore, editor of Sam Whitmore's Media Survey, a website that offers analysis of the industry.

"I think media are trying to figure out a good way to involve readers and listeners in their processes without necessarily handing over the keys," he says.

*Business Week* recently began to offer weekly podcasts about the cover story for that week's issue. The podcasts include interviews with Business Week reporters and editors to offer insight into the story behind the cover story. And in May, *The New York Times* released an internal panel's recommendations on improving credibility with its readers, including blogs, a speakers bureau, and the posting of reporter's notes on its website.

"(Media outlets are) pretty much trying to be a little bit more intimate and less haughty because the media have always distanced themselves in some ways," Whitmore says, adding that letters to the editor were previously the only way readers could get in touch with media outlets. "You're going to see a lot of media companies and titles experiment with this sort of thing."

Indeed, after its black eye stemming from its inaccurate report on President Bush's National Guard service, CBS launched its Public Eye blog. Its "fundamental mission," according to the site, is to "bring transparency to the editorial operations of CBS News—transparency that is unprecedented for broadcast and online journalism."

## Hispanic Media

Look at any newsstand in the US and notice a display of the segmentation of American media: publications aimed at mothers, surfers, golfers, teenagers, health nuts, and celebrity-news junkies, to name just a few.

But across all forms of media, those with a Hispanic focus appear to be growing at a faster pace.

Peter Wengryn, CEO of VMS, says the monitoring company has noticed the trend in the TV content it tracks.

"We have seen an increase in Hispanic stations in the past three to four years," he says. "I see that as a fast-growing segment of the media."

Kerins describes the Hispanic market as a "booming" one. "You cannot look in any top 10 major city and not find a daily Hispanic newspaper," he says. "Any corporation that does not take advantage is missing the boat."

Roxana Lissa, president of RL Public Relations, says that the Hispanic market's largest area of growth has been in print. "We have seen tremendous growth and tremendous opportunities in that area," she says.

The sports category in particular has been very open to Hispanic-targeted publications, including *Sports Illustrated Espa–ol* and ESPN DeporŽts.

Other forms of media, including broadcast and radio, will continue to grow, Lissa says, as Univision and Clear Channel expand their presence. Also, many companies outside the US will try to enter the market, such as Mexico-based TV Azteca and Spanish media company Grupo Prisa.

While the internet is growing in its influence among Hispanics, Lissa says, it has a low penetration in the market compared to other forms of media.

"It will take a few more years to develop to the level of the general market," she says. For marketers of all types, the growth of such media signals an opportunity. "To be able to understand the cultural sensitivity and harness the power of this segment of the news is a winning proposition," says Kerins.

### Listing Business Woes for Newspapers

With a host of circulation scandals, a series of layoffs at some of its largest companies, and indications that readership is down, the newspaper industry has seen better days. The New York Times Co. and Knight Ridder were the latest to announce layoffs, a significant amount of which will be in editorial operations.

Colby Atwood, VP of media research firm Borrell Associates, says the newspaper industry is in the midst of a long period of transition that will take 10 to 15 years. Such a transition will result in more consolidations and reductions in work forces, as the industry adjusts to playing a smaller role in news distribution and advertising, he adds.

Because smaller workforces will undoubtedly affect a newspaper's ability to gather news, Atwood says, newspapers will have to focus on the news that is most relevant to their readers.

Weiner predicts that newspapers that have had circulation scandals will likely come to terms with their advertisers to survive. "There is such a huge vested interest on the part of the advertiser, as well as the media owner, that they're in it together, " the says.

Atwood agrees that papers will survive, but maintains there will be changes. "In general, newspapers will have to shrink to maintain profitability," he says, adding that they will likely become smaller and more sharply focussed.

## Explaining Digitalization of Print Media

When *The New York Times* announced in August that it would merge the operations of its digital and print news, it signified the latest step in the evaporating line between print and online content. Trylon Communication's Trufelman says that such an evolution will likely impact newspapers the most.

"There will be more of an impact on newspapers in (the next) two to five years than has happened in the past 100," he says. "Online news is going to impact the traditional newspaper much quicker and faster."

While online content has served as an adjunct to print for many years now, Trufelman believes that in the future the inverse will be true. Aaron Kwittken, CEO of Euro RSCG Magnet, points to *Forbes'* recent decision to offer its entire magazine online. MPG's Lanzano predicts that print publications will provide deeper analysis and more editorials than their online counterparts. This is comparable to the way newsweeklies like *Time* and *Newsweek* have already coped with the news-breaking qualities of online news sites.

But while chants of "print is dead" have been prevalent since the dawn of TV and radio, Lanzano says, print publications will always survive. "People like to feel, touch, hold (print publications); it's not going to go away," he says. "They just have to (find) their niche."

## Undertaking Media Consolidation

The model of one media entity owning outlets across multiple platforms is one that is not new to the industry. And it's likely to be something that will continue in the future. Conglomerates like Gannett, Clear Channel, and Time Warner hold a large stake in many forms of communication that Americans use on a daily basis.

Kerins says the trend of media conglomerates is one that shows no signs of slowing down. "Unless (the government) legislates it and regulates it, you'll never see a reversal," he says. "If anything, it's going to continue to drive in the same direction."

But Trufelman says that society has a way of getting past the negative effects of such media consolidations. He points to the rampant consolidation in radio, which resulted in standardized radio stations. Such a climate created a need for the current phenomenon of satellite radio, which was made possible by technology, he says.

"In an absence of government regulation on media industry consolidation, the only (form of) checks and balances is technology because it impacts the marketplace," he says. Such developments could follow in other forms of media, such as print and radio.

### Understanding Source Agnostic/Disintermediation

The merging of technology and the 24-hour news cycle has only increased the amount of news available to consumers. And some believe that the abundance of information will only decrease the importance of traditional media.

Magnet's Kwittken says the average consumer doesn't care where he gets his information. "Media credibility is at an all-time low," he adds. "People are less concerned about source and more concerned about content."

In such an environment, Kwittken says, wire services, including newswires, are going to be much more important going forward. "The average consumer...can no longer discern the difference between the press release and press story, especially on the web," he says.

In fact, with many wires distributing releases to sites like Yahoo News, many PR pros report that some clients consider such placement an actual media hit. Weiner says that the blurring of lines between what is journalistic coverage and what's not presents an opportunity for PR practitioners. "When a regular consumer can read a Business Wire story as if it's news from a bona fide objective journal, that's actually a short-term victory for the PR person," he says.

Kwittken says consumers are still concerned with authenticity of information, but will not rely on traditional media as much in the future.

### Further Refining Media Measurement

The issue of media measurement has always been a tricky one: How relevant is the impressions figure when referring to print placements? Are Nielsen ratings really measuring a good cross-section of the population? Will there be an equivalent to Arbitron ratings in satellite radio?

"There have to be new metrics," says Lanzano, adding that there has been some discussion of measuring engagement, as well, although no one has cracked the code. "We're all grappling with this right now."

Although Nielsen has faced its share of opposition from media companies with its new Local People Meters, Weiner says that traditional audience measurement companies will never go away. "You have a 200-year-old juggernaut that represents hundreds and hundreds of billions of dollars in spending each year that would have to be derailed to come up with a new system," he points out. "What we'll see is incremental adjustments."

Issues with Nielsen in particular, he says, have been around for decades and are not likely to cause a major overhaul. "There's just too much momentum in the current method to cause a revolution like that," he says. "They improve the Nielsen services to adjust to (the current media environment)."

## PUBLIC RELATIONS: MANAGEMENT AND PRACTICES

An effective PR can be carried out only if the organisational set-up of PR is defined. The main points which have to be kept in mind while organising PR departments are:

(*a*) the place of PR department in the total organisational structure of the company;

(*b*) how much has to be spent for a PR department by the organisation.

PR is relatively a new management discipline. Even big companies have PR departments which themselves have no clear terms of reference of Public Relations Officers and about the functions of the PR Department. More of them perform miscellaneous functions which cannot be assigned to any other specific department and are dumped on the PR department. Notwithstanding the fact that a PR department is expected to perform a wide variety of functions, it is necessary in the interest of efficient functioning of the department that the areas of operations be clearly defined.

### Reconsidering Management Function of PR

A new era of professional management has unhered in business, industry, trade, commerce and in other vocations replacing the age-old system of management by the owners, proprietors, promoters, partners etc. Development of industries and service organisations coupled with growth in population and education have revolutionised the management function. The phenomenon of having persons of professional calibre to run certain sections or departments has produced good results. In the modern environment and society-dimensions widened and have become so complex that systematic management base on scientific principles can only solve the emerging problems.

Professional management is growing in all its branches and discipline. PR is one of such branch of management science and profession. In the management sciences, behavioural attitude and opinion is given more importance for smooth running of the organisation. In this context, professionally managed organisations and industries lay more stress on effective functions of the publications to smoothen human behaviour and create favourable opinion in every sphere of activity.

The management is concerned with the attitude and opinion of the publics. It is the function of the management to see that PR department is properly functioning to achieve the objectives laid down by the Board of Management.

Public opinion and attitude is directly concerned with the management and management must carry out all the functions by taking proper decisions. In a large organisation it is not possible for the management personnel to handle this complex and tedious work. Hence, the needed powers/authority are delegated to PR departments.

PR is a management function because it is directly under the Board of Management or Board of Directors supervision. The PR department head is answerable to the management at the top and not other departments. An appraisal has to be made to the Board of Management at regular intervals about the organisational activities, profit, sales, production or financial matters, accounts etc, in regular periods. Likewise, the PR departmental head is appointed by the Board of Management or the Managing Director on their behalf. The head of department is made responsible to carry out the works as directed and he has to report the result of his departmental affairs and actions to the Board of Management. For facilitating this activity, the necessary details of all the departments are sent to the PR department.

All activities of the PR department, whether good or bad, inferior or superior, directed or non-directed, intentional or unintentional will affect organisation's credibility, goodwill or image, profitability and productivity in proportion to how the related functions are carried out. If not properly planned, it may lead to an irrepairable loss. That is why, the management must take care and interest in directing the affair of the PR department.

It is unwise to have the entire responsibility in the hands of PR department personnel. The PR departmental head should be made a member of the management team and has to be invited to attend the departmental meetings, decision-making meetings and be allowed to take part in the discussions.

PR being a management function, calls for expertise and skill coupled with knowledge and experience to handle complex situations. PR programmes can also be effectively implemented by PR consultants who are experts in functions of diversified nature such as organising conferences, exhibitions, preparing speeches, publicity material, company literature, direct mailings etc. Management is thus relieved of the burden of supervising and controlling the public relations activities.

In many cases, advertising agencies handling the accounts of business and industrial firms may have their own facility of handling PR. But this combined facility of services—advertising and PR has not proved effective. Their functions vary widely in the sense that advertising is selling goods where PR is to make publics of the organisation identify the company's images through the process of creating public awareness.

PR is thus a management function. The business community must understand the view of PR in their day-to-day activities. Its value is intrinsic and rewarding in the long run.

## Listing Functions of a PR Department

(*a*) Monitor the changes in the socio-economic environment and keep top management informed of them particularly of such developments as are likely to have an impact on the organisation either immediately or in the long run.

(*b*) Study the attitudes of different publics with which the organisation is concerned and report to the management any significant shifts in these attitudes.

(*c*) Advise management of any policy changes that may be necessary consequent upon changes in the socio-economic environment or changes in public attitudes.

(*d*) Maintain a constant flow of communication to the public relevant to the organisation to convey to them the management's policies and decisions by choosing the appropriate media that will combine optimum effectiveness at the minimum cost.

(*e*) In the sphere of internal communication ensure that the channels of communication from the top downward and from the bottom upward and laterally or horizontally remain open.

(*f*) Advise management of social service projects and programmes that will enable the company to contribute to the fulfilment of its social responsibilities and help execute such programmes.

(*g*) Where use is made of agencies or freelance artists/ journalists, maintain contact with them and act as a link between them and the department or units.

Only by clearly defining terms of reference, it will be possible to ensure that periohereal functions such as organising hospitability for visitors or executing miscellaneous errands for top management do not clash with the main function of the PR department.

Some PR departments also perform the work or sales promotion and product publicity besides PR proper functions. These are done for reasons of economy and also the basic skills involved in performing the two types of functions are similar. However, sales publicity or sales promotion can only be successfully performed by a PR department with its good understanding of the marketing objectives in addition to the knowledge and experience of the specific markets that are relevant to the organisation.

### Understanding the Job Nature

A PR staff is responsible for planning PR activities, producing communications media and aiding and advising line executives in carrying out their other public relations responsibilities. It has administrative responsibilities, coordinates and unifies functions, eliminates duplication of activities, ensures a well-balanced programme and provides for specialised skills essential in the production of communication materials. Most PR positions involve one or more of the following functions.

### Incorporating Programme

This involves analysing problems and opportunities, defining goals and the publics (or groups of people whose support of understanding is needed) and recommending and planning activities. It may include budgeting and the assignment of responsibilities to the appropriate people, including non-public relations personnel. Quite often, an organisation's president or executive director is often a key figure in PR activities.

### Analysing Relationships

Successful PR people develop skill in personally gathering information from management, from colleagues in their organisations and from external sources. Continually evaluating what they learn, they formulate recommendations and gain approval for them from their managements. Many PR functions require working with and sometimes through other functions, including personnel, legal and marketing staff. The pracitioner should be persuasive with others. PR people also represent their organisations, i.e., they are representatives to a trade or professional association. But in all their relationship with others—including people in industry groups, regulatory agencies and government, educational institutions and the general public—PR personnel are at work on behalf of their organisations.

#### *Writing and Editing*

Since PR person is often trying to reach large groups of people, the tool most often used is the printed word. Examples of its use are found in reports, news releases, booklets, speeches, film scripts, trade magazine articles, product information and technical material, employee publications, newsletters, shareholder reports and other management communications directed to both organisation personnel and external groups. A sound, clear style of writing which effectively communicates, is virtually a must for public relations work.

#### *Information*

Setting up channels of dissemination of material to appropriate newspaper, broadcast, general and trade publication editors and contact with them with a view toward enlisting their interest in publishing an organisation's news and features. A PR man has to have a wide knowledge of how newspapers and media operate, the areas of specialisation of publications and the interests of individual editors. Competition is the order of the day with the editors and broadcasters having a limited amount of space and time at their disposal. It is necessary for the PR man to get the right editor of the right publication with right story at the right time. Although ideas are accepted on the basis of news and other readership value, an ability to develop relationships of mutual respect and cooperation with the press can be useful to the practioner and the newsman as well.

### *Production*

Brochures, special reports, films and multimedia programmes are important ways of communications. The PR practioner need not be an expert in art, layout, typography and photography, but background knowledge of the techniques of preparation is needed for the intelligent planning and supervision of their use.

### *Special Events*

News conferences, convention exhibits, trade fairs and exhibitions, special showings, new facility and anniversary celebrations, contest and award programmes, open houses town and special meetings make up to gain the attention and acceptance of groups of people. They involve careful planning and coordination, attention to detail and preparation of special booklets, publicity and reports.

### *Speeches*

PR job requires skills in face-to-face communication, finding appropriate platforms, preparing speeches for others and himself delivering speeches. The person who can effectively address individuals and groups will enjoy an advantage over those who facility of expression is limited.

### *Research and Evaluation*

The first activity to be undertaken by a PR practioner is always fact gathering. This can be highly personal through interviews, review of library materials and informal conversations. It can also involve the use of survey techniques and firms specialising in designing and conducting opinion research. After a programme is completed a PR practioner should study its results and evaluate the programme's implementation and effectiveness. By and large the management expects research and evaluation from their PR advisers.

### PRO Reporting Authority/Executive

PR is a corporate function. It involves the two-way interpretation—external world to the top management and vice versa. It therefore follows that a PRO should directly report the Chief Executive of the organisation. Where PRO is responsible for product publicity and sales promotion, he will have to work in close cooperation with the product managers and will have to be guided by them so as to ensure that advertising and promotional activities are geared to the marketing objectives of the organisation.

### Considering Size of the PR Department

The size of a PR department will depend not only on the size of the company and the size of its budget, but also on the choice of the execution of PR programmes departmentally or through agency/agencies. Most organisations prefer to have a small staff and to take the assistance of one or more agencies in executing its programmes. This ensures not only economy but also keeps open before the organisation the best available talent for a particular job. Certain organisations, however which have very large budgets prefer to execute all their projects departmentally and maintain an elaborate set-up beginning from artists and studio to photographers, darkroom, copy writers etc. Some others start a house agency to execute programmes.

### Understanding Line Relationship of Staff of PR Department

As mentioned above, there need not be a said pattern of structure of a PR department for all organisations. Depending upon the size of the department, the organisation may design its own PR department to facilitate its day-to-day practices.

### Placing PR in Corporate Organisation

PR is the responsibility of all managers at every level of authority from top to the bottom of an organisation. A PR department is an administrative group that aids the managers of all departments in carrying out their PR functions. It has not line authority but exists to assist, advise and stimulate line operating executives and employees as to their PR responsibilities and stimulate them to increase public acceptance of the organisation and its policies and products.

### Making Division of Functions of a PR Staff

A PR department is organised by dividing the functions to be carried out by the members of the staff according to media of communication, publics, a combination of media and publics, geographical areas and products. Media of communication provides for sections to specialise in news service, advertising films, exhibitions, periodicals, radio and television. Some departments are organised according to publics with sections for employee, shareholders, community and government relations. The structure of PR departments is not standardised as mentioned earlier, but their design is affected by the size and number of publics served, funds available and objectives of PR programme.

### Undertaking Budgeting PR Programme

PR department spend money visibly and pay returns invisibly. The allocation of funds to PR departments is always looked at with grim attitude. A PR budget is a forecase of PR expenses that are incurred in the administration of a PR programmes. It is a financial plan for PR which establishes definite cost objectives for each of the elements in a programme, controls expenses and prevents waste by making plans conform to expense limitation.

A PR budget should be a combination of the anticipated expenses of each section of the department. The budget should be a flexible one to make adjustments for current developments that may necessitate expansion or contraction of the original programme and budget. The two basic considerations in preparing a PR budget are the activities planned for the PR programme and the costs involved in executing it.

An annual PR plan is developed by the PR departmental head in consultation with the other heads of departments involved in the programme. The annual plan describes objectives, specific activities and media of communication needed to improve relations with employees, community, shareholders, suppliers, dealers and other publics.

The plan may include special project such as an anniversary celebration or changing the corporate name, the cost of which is included in this budget.

The second consideration in determining a PR budget is establishing the cost of carrying out each element of the projected PR plan. Cost estimates should be made of administrative costs. In addition, the direct cost in programmes should be budgeted. These costs are for research and opinion survey, PR advertising, motion pictures, radio and television time, displays and exhibits, special events, periodicals, booklets and other media of communication.

## PUBLIC AND MEDIA RELATIONS: AN OVERVIEW

Public relations includes ongoing activities to ensure the organization has a strong public image. Public relations activities include helping the public to understand the organization and its products. Similar to effective advertising and promotions, effective public relations often depends on designing and implementing a well-designed public relations plan. The plan often includes description of what you want to convey to whom, how you plan to convey it, who is responsible for various activities and by when, and how much money is budgeted to fund these activities. Similar to advertising and promotions, a media plan and calendar can be very useful, which specifies what media methods that are used and when.

Often, public relations are conducted through the media, that is, newspapers, television, magazines, etc. Publicity is mention in the media. Organizations usually have little control over the message in the media, at least, not as much as they do in advertising. Regarding publicity, reporters and writers decide what will be said.

Regarding public relations, consider: What groups of stakeholders do we want to appeal to and how? What impressions do you want each of your stakeholder to have? What communications media do they see or prefer the most? Consider advertising, collaborations, annual reports, networking, TV, radio, newsletters, classifieds, displays/signs, posters, word of mouth, direct mail, special events, brochures, neighbourhood newsletters, etc. What media is most practical for you to use in terms of access and affordability? What messages are most appealing to each stakeholder group?

# 4

# Trends in PR, Advertising and Media Interviews

## ANALYSING RECENT TRENDS IN PUBLIC RELATIONS MANAGEMENT IN INDIA

To enable to understand this in detail an attempt has been made to outline impact of globalisation on the functioning of different organization in India; explain the concept of "integrated communications approach" in an organization; describe the effect of new economic policy and growing privatisation on the PR profession in India; draw the features of how PR has been made into a task-management function; enumerate how the new communication media could be employed to achieve the PR goals; analyse the impact of information technology on the greater access to the PR profession; discuss the role of accountability and cost-effectiveness in the PR functioning; delineate the rise in consumerism and its effect on PR; state the reasons why even non-commercial organizations are getting the PR counselling; and account for the increased tempo and growth in the PR field.

In the earlier chapter, we had an overview of the evolution and growth of the PR movement in India, particularly before and after Independence. Of particular relevance is the study of the PR units in the government, through the Ministry of Information and Broadcasting and its media units.

Further, we also dealt with the concomitant growth of the professional PR organizations and their impact on the growing professionalism. In terms of the PR practice, we have also discussed the importance of training and research in PR, particularly for evolving research methodologies suitable to the Indian socio-politics and economic conditions.

In view of the perspectives gained, it is worthwhile to project the PR profession into the 21 century, and try to visualise the emerging trends in the PR in India. You would realise that the restructuring of our economic policy has resulted in greater liberalisation and privatisation. What are the challenges posed by these changes to the PR profession in India? What are the effects of the so-called trend towards "globalisation" on areas, like business, trade, commerce, industry, and other fields, like education, science and technology, agriculture, health and environment? With increasing global competition, the emphasis is on the faster productivity with strict quality control. Would PR be able to cope with this? If so, would PR be called upon to perform, this task-management function also? This assumes importance in view of the trend of consumerism sweeping the country. We shall discuss the nature of the consumer movement in the country, and what role PR could play to supplement the efforts of the organization to meet the high consumer standards.

These new-found tasks and expectations would make heavy demands on the expertise of the PR profession. We shall, therefore, explain to you how PR can meet these tasks by using new tactical tools and strategies based on the latest technology available.

All this has increased the scope of research and evaluation in PR, more so because of the discipline's greater accountability. The major trend in the PR research abroad comprises elaborate surveys, opinion polls, social audits and tracking studies. We shall examine the efforts being made towards more-in-depth research and evaluation in the Indian PR scene.

Finally, an analyse have been made to the future prospects and trends in PR, particularly the demand for competent people who could handle the PR tasks either within the organization or outside with their specialised services.

Change is taking place all-around us especially in Marketing, Advertising and Public Relations, the professions we are concerned with directly. Public Relations in India, is witnessing its own special changes. Some significant, some challenging, some so radical that the evolving of new systems has become imperative.

The PR professionals, today, are no longer the "gin and tonic brigade" they were considered to be in the past. Gone are the days when 'winging and dining' was the main function of a PRO in an organization. It has been possible to overcome this misconception only through proven performance.

In India, the PR practice is generally associated with Press Relations and Institutional or Corporate Advertising, although, it is much more than that. The professional organizations and managements are making efforts to expand the scope of the public relations field for the PR professionals.

Before we proceed to assess the emerging trends in PR we should understand the environment of PR in modern organization, and what is expected of it. Let us put these facts in a nutshell.

(*a*) There is an on-going shift from an agrarian society towards a greater industrial society.
(*b*) There is also a visible trend in business management and ownership patterns. Business are no longer only family owned. More and more businesses are not being professionally managed.
(*c*) There is a need to have international communication, and, hence, the need to understand alien cultures in the context of global competition.
(*d*) Social issues like the Human Rights which demand equal treatments, have come up before the world fora.
(*e*) The greater education has made the general public less to tolerant of authoritarianism, and led to increased expectations.
(*f*) There has been a growth of public opinion power and the action-oriented public participates in matters of public interest, e.g., concern for environment.

In this present PR environment, the scope of the PR functioning is almost unlimited and it is not possible to summarize. However , the important PR tasks are: informing people, or instructing them in how to do things or behave in a particular way; enforcing or helping shape new attitudes under varying circumstances; maintaining loyalty of stockholders (customers, shareholders, employees and the key publics) towards the company or organization; neutralising public opinion on important controversial issues, winning over people who are hostile or opposed to the organization and influencing people to change their behaviour to ways conducive to the organization, which is the most difficult, but most rewarding function of PR.

One thing, that PR cannot do for long, is to maintain good reputation for an organization that does not perform in a deserving manner. Thus, good PR means truth as it is clearly and effectively communicated/understood by critical supporting publics/ audiences/target groups. Superficial communication that seeks to hide or distort reality is poor PR.

## Considering the Present Trends in Public Relations

The mega trends taking place in the Indian PR profession today are the PRO is emerging as a new professional; PR as a discipline is becoming more "Strategic"; PR is playing an important role in "Consumerism"; Accountability is becoming a key factor; Use of research and evaluation to validate the PR efforts is gaining ground; New tactical weapons and tools are being introduced and adopted; Technology is making a major impact on the PR practice, and Change in nomenclature to "Corporate PR".

Public Relations as a profession, and the Public Relation Officer (PRO) in it, are undergoing changes in response to the changing external environment. The practice of PR is today being accepted as a management tool, which is getting to be more professional in its 'delivery of goods', by adopting sound principles of managing PR and ethical conduct with greater accountability for its action.

The PRO today, is not just an expert communicator, but also an adviser to his management and organisation. In the changing external of the PR profession, the Public Relations Officers need to know and understand the changes taking place in the county's economic, political, social and cultural spheres, which directly affect an organization's operations. The PR professionals have to be in the forefront. Understanding and interpreting events around them is now crucial, so that they could satisfy those, who come to them for information and advice. The PR people need to know what the existing conditions are, and what could be influenced by the PR and communications.

The development of the PR consultancies in India is a further step in the direction of professionalisation of PR and PR people. In India, at one time it was only Consilium which existed as an independent PR agency. Today, we have Roger Pereira Communications, Good Relations, Spectra, among the known ones, started by some well-known advertising and PR professionals.

A parallel development to this was when big advertising agencies started setting up their own PR divisions to cater to the growing demand for PR. D & M, Trikayua, Mudra HTA are some of the agencies which have fullfledged PR outfits as part of their organizations. In the past, the PR services and advice at the ad agencies for their clients were rendered free of cost. Now, because PR has become a specialised function, the ad agencies have professional specialists working for them, they are charging the clients for the specialist PR services provided.

**Understanding Strategic Public Relations**

PR is becoming a highly specialist and "Strategic" discipline today. It is being termed as "Communications with a mission." This description of PR stems out of its new advisory role. To be successful, it has, therefore, to be highly target-group-oriented.

Conventionally, PR has been basically an image-building (or boosting) activity, through corporate advertising campaigns and public service communications on the external front, and house journals and brochures on the internal PR front. Today, however, the PR activities are greatly objective-oriented and target-group-oriented. Making these more strategic in nature, PR is an on-going dialogue between the organization and its target groups. It is no longer a white-washing department, nor a sales aid. Examples of this strategic shift in PR are seen in some specific activities of organizations, internally and externally.

Among Indian organisations, or companies, the internal communications had always been given less importance as compared to the external communications. The need and importance of the internal communications is today being accepted more and more widely in the professionals companies. In the course of the last few years or so, certain social and business influences have acted upon organizations from both within and without, calling for a more thiough and balanced approach to communications. An organization consists of individuals and groups of people whose work relates to the work of other individuals and groups, as well as the organization as a whole. Therefore, a healthy policy in terms of purpose, planning, and control is necessary to achieve corporate objectives. Internal communications play an important and decisive part in this policy.

Internal communications might have either a formal or informal character. Good PR managers, as well as organizations, keep their communication skills shining and sharp, and use them constantly in a planned manner for all-round effectiveness and productivity.

The PR professionals are getting to use the media persons (journalists) more and more to influence the public opinion. That way, they are getting better and better to influence the "Press opinion." Their contact with the press, in particular, and the other media people as well, as more personal and individual. This contact is supported with organized activities like Press Conferences and convincing handouts/releases.

The journalists, on their part, are imbued with an investigative spirit. Therefore, the expect greater intellectual inputs, including direct contact with the managements. Gin and tonic is no longer sufficient motivation for them. Therefore, the PR people have to cater to their demands, and give them due respect as professional colleagues.

With the recent liberalisation of the Indian economy, the government relations have assumed a new dimension. Merely knowing ministers and elected representatives are not adequate today. Lobbying, in the Western sense, is getting to be important. The PR people might not be directly involved in the lobbying process as yet, but their professional support is getting to be essential. The 'Liaison' people in India are going to be demanding PR inputs to make their impact on the ministers and elected representatives. This is going to be more so in the future, and the PR professionals would have to prepare themselves to meet the challenges of the situation.

The PR people have to be thoroughly knowledgeable about the organization and the environment around them. They must be armed with facts, rationales, and arguments in dealing with their shareholders, the financial community, as well as their employees at various levels. There are umpteen situation where their professional involvement is necessary and proves beneficial. Be it dilution of equity, share issues, announcement of a company's financial results, strikes and labour problems, or even anniversary celebrations, the PR persons have to adapt and gear themselves to meet the situation and implement what is required to achieve the desired objectives, quickly and effectively.

Human Resource Development (HRD) is a function of the personnel department. As organizations grow, the need for trained professionals also increases. Therefore, HRD is becoming vital. PR can also play a helpful role in the HRD function through effective communication of messages to employees about the corporate philosophy and culture. PR can greatly contributed to HRD in evolving a conducive work culture within the organization. It can also enable the employees to project the right image of the company to the external publics. PR's role in this is going to increases steadily in the coming years. The PR persons should do well by motivating all employees, and getting them involved in the organization. PR has tremendous potential to contribute to HRD.

The Crisis Management is a new phenomenon, which could be said to be an outcome of industrialisation and technology development. Until recently, most companies were geared for smooth sailing and good times, in terms of PR and corporate image. These failed to be able to safeguard and protect their image in times of problems and crisis. However, there is a sea-change taking place today in the handling and management of crisis, particularly after the Bhopal tragedy. Organizations have pre-planned rehearsed activities, and trained terms to handle any potential crisis situations.

There were many instances of the successful handling of crisis by the Indian Airlines at the time of a place crash and of the ONGC at the time of the fire on their oil well. As a result of their being prepared and taking timely PR action, the sailing, for these companies, was less traumatic. Even Harshad Mehta opted for the PR help at the time of his personal crisis to win the sympathy of the people, and to project that it was he who being victimised. The message that seems to emerge out of this was: "Be prepared. Be honest." Tackle the situation boldly and squarely.

## Analysing Relationship between Public Relations and Consumerism

There are many PR activities, which are genuinely concerned with the well-being of the population, and which are divorced from the ordinary commercial implications. The responsibility for the shifting from the Government on to corporations. This is happening in India as well and is resulting in various non-commercial organizations, for example, universities, police, municipal corporations, trade and industry associations and so on, recruiting their own PR advisers.

The first impact of 'consumerism' was felt in the USA, but soon spread to other parts of the world. Side by side with the growth of interest in consumerism, there has been a considerable increase in 'protests'. It has become fashionable for individuals and groups, aggrieved by events, or proposed developments, to organize themselves in order to protest as effectively as possible. Their protests range from peaceful protests to violent agitations and vandalism. The PR people, today, have to hand such development carefully and effectively, or else it could create major problems for the organization.

Not so long ago, top management's in India—Chairmen and Managing Directors—were accountable only to the shareholders, employees their unions. Now we have seen the emergence of consumerist groups and pro-environment lobbies, which are demanding that industry take cognizance of public interest in a wide range of areas, from profits at the expense of the consumers to issues like community development, pollution, etc. This is forcing the managements to justify their actions to their stockholders, and this social responsibility is being passed down to the PRO.

It is for this reason that a public relations department is today also termed as a public affairs department. It is expected to handle the commercial PR as well as the economic and social issues, competently. It is, thus, a "Public face of the organization, as well as the voice in community."

Management in modern society is accountable not only to the groups which traditionally control it, but also to the public at large. The concept of accountability to the general public is applicable to both the public sector and private enterprises alike. Business are subject to pressures from the government, parliament and legislatures, various statutory authorities, financial institutions, trade unions, trade and professional organizations, and from a variety of external groups. No organization, whether public or private, service or commercial, could afford to ignore these pressures. It is in this context that organisations need to be "Accountable." When the question of accountability of the organization comes up, PR could not absolve itself of its own responsibility to project the organization as a "socially responsible" one.

Thus, "accountability" has become a key factor in the functioning of PR. The present trend is for organizations to have a checklist of demands, needs, aspirations, fears and threats of their internal and external publics. They then examine their performance against this checklist, and review it at regular intervals. This is primarily to compare whether the organization is living up to the expectations of its publics. The PR professional is expected to provide feedback from these publics to the management, and devise means to project an image of accountability. What people are looking for in an organization today is a combination of professionalism and humanity, for this is what gains respect for an organization in modern society.

While learning how PR could help in project the organization as accountable at the bar of public opinion, we must also examine the corollary to it. This refers to the accountability of the PR department to the organization. The PR department has to justify the investment made in it by the organization through fruitful performance. This trend is slowly gaining ground and the PR professionals are now able to, if not quantity, at least present a cost-effective image through their performance. In future, there might emerge a way for quantifying PR's role as a key factor in the overall performance of the organization. This is an area in which research and evaluation in PR, could play a crucial role.

The general resource crunch and inflation in the media costs has resulted in another trend. Cost effectiveness is the buzz word. Validating of the PR efforts has become crucial. Establishing of benchmarks and evaluation of the PR efforts is being demanded by the managements. The PR persons could not escape this responsibility.

Research is beginning to play a vital role in planning and then demonstrating effectiveness of the PR strategies, and justifying the costs put behind them. The days of "shooting from the hip" are gone. These are the days of the responsible PR practices. There are more primary and secondary, quantitative and qualitative surveys being undertaken by the professional PR people in organizations. Broad, elaborate opinion polls, audits, and tracking studies have become a norm to provide the PR benchmarks. This trend is visible in India as well.

There are two kinds of research, which help in ascertaining the impact of the PR effort in the creation of a favourable image of the organization. These are motivation research and effectiveness surveys. Motivation research seeks to discover, through in-depth interviews, with a representative sample of the organization's publics, which kind of PR effort has motivated the company towards a favourable image of the organization.

Effectiveness, surveys are used to measure the impact on public opinion made by an organization's PR activities. One of the most precise measurements of the change resulting from the impact of communication on the public opinion is a "before-and-after" study of the attitudes of the publics. Prior to the start of the campaign, a representative sample of the organization's publics is interviewed to determine their attitudes and the extent of the public's knowledge of the organization. After the conclusion of the PR campaign, the same sample is interviewed to see if there has been any change in their opinions as a result of the PR messages. These surveys are used to measure the response to the PR messages by its anniversary celebrations lock-outs, strikes, etc.

## Understanding New Tactical Weapons and Tools of PR

As the PR practice continues to become more strategic, its relationship and interaction with other communications related disciplines grows closer, and provides some very appropriate and strong tactical weapons to communicate with the target groups.

Obviously PR and advertising joining together to achieve common goals in the present arena. Although advertising has always been one of the key strategic tools in PR, yet advertising and PR were always considered as two separate functions, and not to be mixed. Advertising was seen as a part of marketing, and PR a part of communications. Today, there are many instances where advertising and PR work together. Corporate advertising is one major example where PR and advertising always from a communications team. Another area is 'sponsorships.' PR and advertising go hand in hand. The Reliance World Cup Cricket Tournament is a classic example of this. The benefits of the integrated approach and its results, in terms of the impact and migrade to the company, are well-known. The dividing line between the product advertising and institutional advertising is blurring. It is a systematic relationships—quality product contributing to company's image and company's reputation leading to ready acceptance of its products.

Further still, the 'one stop-shopping' concept among marketing companies, i.e., hiring of an ad agency and its PR consultancy is another development which supplements and promotes this concept of joining forces for results.

The spurt in the variety and availability of a range of common communication media, like the television, home video, computer networks, facsimile, E-mail, etc., has brought about a change in the tools used traditionally for the PR communication, which has placed reliance on the press and related print media. Many of these new technology tools could be employed effectively. However, it still needs skill to choose the most appropriate tool for a particular job to draw upon the talent and knowledge for using it for impact and success. In a way, the PR person could be likened to a master craftsman.

The radical changes in technology has made tremendous impact on every field every walks of life including PR. The two areas in which the impact is quite noticeable are establishing of data-bases and global communications and instant communication.

With the computer becoming so much a part of our lives, data-base systems and software have become very important for business activities and these are becoming indispensable in the PR field as well. To personalise communications, the PR outfits abroad are not building data files on target groups, individuals, groups and companies. These are establishing target group 'pyramids' and 'matrices', whereby the target groups are identified by importance and by activities. This is going to be very much a part of the day-to-day PR work in India too, as one needs to closely monitor the moves of one's competitors also.

It is said that a whisper in a board room, today, could be front-page news worldwide in less than 10 seconds. The telecommunication technology has given access to a whole new range of existing opportunities. And instant global communications are increasingly recognized by both the users and receivers. Desk-top publishing, fax, newspapers, computer graphics and animation, video conferences, cellular phones and even photo-telephones are other new ethnological developments, which are making communications speedier and more effective. As a consequence, PR will be more result-oriented in the coming years.

## Corporate PR

Corporate public relations is a planned and coordinated activity which works towards projecting the image of an organisation to the public as well as to its employees. It presents the total picture of the organisation, its multifarious activities and the planning, coordination, analysis and synthesis of its many divisions.

A noted public relation scholar, classifies the central idea of corporate public relations as "It is a distinctive management function which helps establish and maintain mutual lines of communication, understanding, acceptance and cooperation between an organisation and its publics; involves the management of problems of issues; helps the management to keep itself informed on and be responsive to public opinion; defines and emphasizes the responsibility, of the organisation to keep abreast of and effectively utilize services as an early working system to help anticipate trends, and uses research and sound, ethical communication as its principal tools."

With the advent of globalisation and the need for organizations to reach out to its publics beyond national boundaries, big organizations, of both public and private sectors, have evolved a new concept called corporate PR. This concept envisages the inter-linking of corporate policy, corporate performance and communication, with the PR chief having the same status as the head of any other key management function. Whether it is the public sector National Mineral Development Corporation (NMDC) of the Oil and Natural Gas Commission (ONGC) or the private sector Hindustan Lever Ltd. (HLL) or Godrej, all these organizations have adopted PR as a corporate policy. Their PR chiefs handle top policy matters, whether the detergent soaps. Only rarely does the chief executive enter the picture. This has lent a high degree of credibility to the PR profession in India. Managements now agree that when it comes to the question of facing the press and its barrage of investigative questions, there could be no better choice other than the professional PRO to effectively place the organizations' view-point before the media. This trend is bound to increase the status of PR in India, and opens up new opportunities for the budding PR professionals.

In order to satisfy customer needs and fulfil its corporate mission, an organisation establishes and maintains relationships with their employees, customers, shareholders, media, general public as well as government and business organizations. These relationships are characterized by varying degrees of interaction and interdependence.

Corporate public relations aims to build overall acceptance of the corporation and its produces. The function involves two approaches—a defensive approach in the face of hostility or attack by clearing misconceptions and an advocacy approach for generating goodwill and enhancing reputation.

It is important to know some of the barriers of the functioning of a corporate organisation because public relations function is classified as a staff function and a management function. We, therefore take a brief look at the organisational structure of a corporation and also delve into some corporate concepts like corporate objectives, corporate goals, corporate planning corporate accountability, corporate results, corporate image, etc.

This will enable you to grasp the essence of corporate public relations. Whether, the public relation functions are carried out entirely by the internal public relations department or with the help of external consultants, the strategies, techniques and methods of building corporate image reaming the same.

A corporate body or an organisation may be defined as an apex body, with control over multiple units and diverse activities. It is usual engaged in business operations which may be service or production oriented. It lays down specific objectives and goals and ensures investment returns. Every corporation, whether big or small, has certain missions, objectives and goals which it strives to achieve. These corporate entities are central to its existence. They project the purpose of the organisation to the public and also motivate the employees to help the organisation achieve its targets.

Corporate missions are in-depth ideologies and precepts of the organisation, laid down its Articles of Association or its promotional preamble. These percepts give broad direction and outline to the philosophy of the organisation.

For instance, the mission of "Indian Oil Corporation" is to achieve international standards of excellence in all its operations with concern for customer satisfaction; to create a modern technology base for self-reliance, growth and development of business; to contribute to the national economy by providing adequate return on investment and by setting high standards of leadership and productivity; to foster a culture of participation, and to help enrich quality of life of the community and preserve ecological balance and national heritage.

*Corporate objectives* are a broad framework of guidelines provided to each of its operations to achieve efficient and effective performance. They spell out long- and short-term plant projects and programmes; define roles and responsibilities of each division; and indicate parameters of growth in keeping with its socially responsible reputation.

The corporate objectives of National Thermal Power Corporations (NTPC) are to establish thermal power capacity within a prescribed time schedule, cost and reliability level; to operate its power stations at base load with maximum efficiently and plant reliability; to build in-house facilities for self-reliance in respect of technical expertise, skilled manpower and latest technology; to manage financial operations of the company and to generate adequate returns; to develop a well knit personnel policy and a culture which motivates employees to contribute their best towards achievement of organisational objectives, and to function as a responsible undertaking bearing in mind its commitment to the society.

*Corporate goals* are specific tasks to be accomplished by a defined group of persons or individuals within a stipulated time frame. These are designed to meet targets of production, marketing, supply and distribution or similar targets of rendering services. They also clearly indicate the role and responsibilities of groups in achieving corporate goals, so as to enable one to measure effectiveness of the organisation.

Each corporation is a different entry per se. For example, some organizations are engaged in production and manufacturing; marketing or supply and distribution whereas others specialize in financial and service sectors. BHEL (Bharat Heavy Electricals Ltd.), TISCO (Steel Production); ONGC and Oil India Ltd., (Oil Production) etc., are examples of production-oriented organizations. Hindustan Lever Ltd. (Consumer durables); PCL, MODI XEROX (Computer Software), etc., are marketing companies. IDBI, ICCI (for financial aid) Travel and Tourism agencies; Hotels, Consultancy firms, etc., are examples of service sectors.

All these companies have a common corporate goal. They respond to the needs of their vast clientele by efficiently producing quality goods in a cost-effective manner. They have also to establish a vast marketing network for rendering prompt customers service, which reaches out to remote and inaccessible areas.

Entrepreneurship is a quality of business management which reflects the organisation's capability to explore new avenues: ability to take calculated risks; utilize the existing opportunities gainfully; practice modern and participative management, it includes business acumen to sustain competition; securing its due market share by adopting strategies and dynamics selling; prudent investment ensuring adequate financial returns; skilled and committed workforce and concern for environment. A desire to be socially accepted is also one of the important factors that reflects the quality of entrepreneurship.

No organisation is a monolithic structure where individuals behave alike. In fact, corporations consist of different departments with different functions.

A typical large scale organisation is governed by a Board of Directors consisting of Chairman and a number of other functionaries in-charge of different department. The division of responsibility helps the staff to concentrate on specific areas of work and contribute to the organisation's overall efficiency. An ardent supporter of such scientific division of work was Clearance Randall, an expert in the field of management, who said; "To know who is to do what and to establish authority within an institution are the basic principles of good administration...

A corporation may not only have multi-division but also a multiple chain of companies, like "The Thapar Group of Industries" which have "Ballarpur Industries" (Specializing in paper and glass water) "Crompton Greaves" (Market leader in transformer, electric fans and motors), and "Greaves Cotton" (Specializing in pumps). Owners of a number of paper mills, the Thapars are also diversifying into non-traditional areas like a Rs. 300-400 crore project in Goa. "Thapar Du Pont" (Nylon), Rs. 42 crore aquaculture project in Andhra Pradesh and Rs. 80 crore project in Pondicherry to make Green Glass for export. Besides this, Thapars have couple of overseas ventures like a "Glass factory" in Nigeria, a "Palm Oil Factory" in Malaysia and "Coasted Paper Plant" in Indonesia.

After having explained what a corporation is, its missions, goals and objectives, let us discuss, the most important asset of every organisation that is—the people who work for the Corporation. "Employees form the backbone of every organisation." Therefore, every organisation must. develop a "Strategic Vision" and incorporate Human Resources Development in its Corporate Mission.

Human Resource Development is essential for the growth and development of an organisation. The HRD system rests on the pillar of open communication trust and concern. An organisation has to create an open communication system, which will build confidence and mutual trust. Such a communication network enables free exchange of views and thoughts between employees and Management. It also helps to impart technical and administrative training. Thus, through the HRD sub-systems, employees are motivated to work with a team spirit to achieve common goals and objectives.

HRD depends on the leadership of the top management. An effective Human Resource Development programme includes monetary compensation, job privileges, suitable work environment and recreational facilities.

For example, Indian Oil Corporation Ltd. (IOC) is one such organisation which continuously upgrades facilities like holiday homes housing colonies, schools, hospitals. It also provides schemes for saving and accident benefit. Awards, bonus, incentives are provided with the objective of facilitating greater employee participation and cooperation for the overall progress of the company.

The physical and financial results of a corporation are annually brought out in the form of manuals, annul reports or balance sheets.

Physical results of a company are an assessment of the utilization of products manufactured by it, and whether the company is achieving the planned targets.

Physical results are in the form of a Balance Sheet which tells us what a company owns and owes i.e., the profits, losses liabilities, assets and shareholders equity. Financial results bring forth the strength and weaknesses of the company and help determine what steps the company ought to take, so as to make maximum profits.

However, allowances must be made for the unexpected. Hence, assumptions and preplanned programmes have to be made in the form of long-term or short-term plans, so that profits and losses can be easily measured.

## Understanding Corporate Planning and Image

Corporate planning is a vital and systematic method of scientific management. It is a methodical way of running an organisation.

This covers commitment to every decision, its implementation and performance standards. Through corporate planning, the organisation is able to define what it is trying to achieve. However, corporate planning, by no means, ensures that the corporation will not be affected by any crisis situation. In fact, it provides for such contingencies and incorporates disaster management plans as well. Corporate planning is an effective and innovative way of controlling the operation of a business organisation.

Corporate planning means: it is the "Route map" which plans, directs and controls the operations of an enterprise; it is an instrument of communication which helps coordinate various activities; it lays down. long-range profit targets and motivates employees with a sense of purpose, encouraging them to achieve organisational aims and objectives; and leads to better decision-making and accelerates the pace of growth and profits.

Planning may be broadly classified into three categories, viz; (1) project planning, which covers particulars of capital investment, production and marketing operation, (2) operational planning, which draws the plan of an established area of an organisation and (3) strategic planning, which lays out specific strategies and programmes by which the company intends to achieve its objectives.

Corporate image is the sum total of the perceptions and impressions carried by various publics, about the quality of a products efficiency and services and the behaviour of the organisation towards the community at large.

This image of an organisation largely depends on the way it is regarded by its competitors, shareholders, customers, general public and its employees; the confidence reposed in it, by its employees and customers and reliability of products and services, and its future plans.

The corporate image also depends on flexibility of an organisation to adapt to the changing environment; coordinated working of the various divisions and chains of a company, and, above all, its openness to communicate with public, employees and potential customers.

The Press, Electronics, Institutional advertising, Publicity, Internal communications, House journals, External communication, Speeches and Special events are the major channels used for projecting the corporate image of an organisation.

Logo can be described as a symbol chosen as an insignia of an organisation, which identifies the organisation in all the operations. From the sign of Mercedes to the immediately recognizable signature that "Cadbury's uses, logos are identified by everyone. It is used increasingly by corporations as a means of creating the corporate image which represents the collective pride of the organisation.

Apart from projecting the image, logos may also symbolize the nature of the work of any organisation. For example, Airlines or Travel houses have logo-signs moving from left to right giving an impression of motion. Diversified corporations use a variety of symbols, ranging from primitive to ornate symbols. In short, logos are a graphic representation of thought and belief of identity and personality and of image building.

David Berlo, a great thinker and management expert, once pointed out that, when two or more people are mutually dependent on one another, they have to find a way to relate their behaviour and their goals. Social systems are the consequence of man's need to relate his behaviour to the behaviour of the others to accomplish his goals. When a corporation's perception of public's expectation and the public's perception of a corporation's performance begin to match, it leads to mutual understanding.

Corporate behaviour can be defined as social obligation, social responsibility or social responsiveness which includes behaving according to a code of ethics; being responsible for every adverse or favourable action within an organisation; adopting new technology for protecting the environment and evaluating any possible side effects of corporate actions, well in advance; compensating victims of pollution and other corporate related activities; adapting to future changes; using public relation methods, to upgrade its public image; assuring public that its corporate practices meet social norms; communication with government organisation and assisting them in enforcing existing laws; projecting an honest image of the organisation by providing factual information and contributing to welfare schemes thus enhancing the organisation's image as being socially responsible. Organizations continuously adjust their relationships and behaviour with public in response to the ever-changing social environment.

A successful organisation must be constantly revising its policies and programmes to stay turned to the demands of a changing society. The most important method of bridging the gap between the public demand and corporate performance is "accountability." The value of accountability lies in its application to all the activities of an organisation, oriented towards the welfare of the society, which is its basic mission. It is even more important than corporate responsibility.

Corporate accountability implies a system of checks and balances. The management plans are tested, debated and provided with a sound guidance from the board of directors. This system is followed regularly if there is a select quality of people and a well coordinated information system. This enables the directors to perceive directions and outline priorities for the corporation to meet its goal.

All these factors, discussed above, contribute to the overall success of any organisation and reflects its distinct culture. Concluding this unit, we will explain to you briefly about corporate culture and emerging trends of corporations.

A Corporate culture is an important aspect of an organisation which is identified by its management's style of functioning, budget, priorities, and attitudes towards its employees or customers. Corporate culture is not affected by the organisation's profits and losses, but only by leadership to the top level management team, technological advances and market conditions.

A vital ingredient of a good corporate culture is the human resource development programmes, which is a long-term investment. Human resource programme brings forth a participative work culture and easy adoption to even changing environment. The employee must be involved in discussions with management about the work culture the company requires and the possibilities of creating an ideal culture. The public relation person has a significant part to play in nurturing and in the communication of corporate culture.

Public opinion arises from the interaction of individuals with their immediate social environment. Scoot Cutlip says, "The power of public opinion must be faced, understood and dealt with. It provides the psychological environment in which organizations, prosper or perish. It is to be noted that this social environment is forever changing due to changes in external factors, e.g., rise in educational level; changes in government policy; political fall outs; national tragedies, etc.

Relationships can change as a result of environmental change. An organisation's ability to adapt to the ever-changing circumstances depends on how sensitive it is, to its environment. In order to prosper and to develop, an organisation must continuously adjust and be responsive to recurring environment changes.

The corporate concept of Public Relations is to project its missions, ideology, and philosophy; to publicize its objectives and goals; to establish relations with its various publics, and to extend support for itself in the environment and be accepted.

Corporate Public Relation strategies can be broadly classified into —

(*i*) Defining corporate Public Relations objectives from annual and perspective plans;
(*ii*) Planning and implementing public relation projects for image building;
(*iii*) Communicating; and
(*iv*) Evaluating from feedback, research and analysis.

Based on this, Public Relations persons counsel management in decision-making. The first step involves defining the corporate objectives, which are a broad framework of guidelines provided for achieving efficient and effective performance. The second step is planning which involves decision-making on objectives or goals by Public Relations practitioners, setting and selecting strategies.

Planning includes: defining roles and missions; selecting objectives; determining the scope of the work to be performed and major result areas; preparing specific action plans to achieve the objectives; budgeting and implementing the programme and evaluating the results.

The process of planning also incorporates handling crisis situations. Regular training sessions for employees are essential. Training provides them with the basic knowledge of handling emergency cases. The media should also be kept informed and provided with factual details about any critical situation, if it arises.

The public and media understanding of an incident and how it is handled depends on the timeliness for employees are essential. Training provides them with the basic knowledge of handling emergency cases. The media also should be kept informed and provided with factual details about any critical situation if it arises.

The third and the crucial step of Public Relations activity, is communication, normal cousins has defined communication as:

"The most precious enterprise in the world... the ultimate art."

By communication we mean the transmission, reception and interpretation of information basic elements in communication are the sender or the source; the message and the receiver or the target public.

Effective communication requires efficiency of all there elements. A public relations communicator must have the ability to effectively transmit messages in a comprehensive manner to all its publics.

Communication is of two types; viz., Internal Communication and External Communication.

*Internal communication* is communicating within the organisation through the medium of house journals, newsletters, bulletin boards, pamphlets, memos, brochures, manuals, books, etc.

*External communication* is communication with the general public, customers, shareholders, competitors, through the mass media, direct mail or through group meetings.

One of the important steps in public relations process is 'evaluation', which teaches what happened and why it happened. It determines the methodology which was adopted by the public relations spokesman, to project the image of the organisation the adequacy of message content and structure the extent of media utilisation, its nature and suitability.

The target audience; and the effect the message has on the target audience and this step is also essential to review and modify (if necessary) the public relations activity oriented towards image building. Evaluation also helps to find out any discrepancies between programme planning and execution.

## Corporate Advertising and Media Relations

*Corporate advertising* as contrasted with product advertising is essentially for image building of an organisation. These advertisements carry "messages" about the total activities, with a unified or integral profile of the organisation. The opinion-makers, customers and other concerned public derive an image of the organisation largely through its advertisements. Such ads also project the behaviour and disposition of the organisation; its social responsibility and public accountability, as also its concern for environment. An organisation's support and patronage for promotion of fine arts, cultural heritage and sports is reflected as also the goodwill and reputation the organisation enjoys. Image building advertising is variously known as public relations advertising, corporate advertising, prestige advertising or institutional advertising.

An institutional advertising or prestige advertising are thematic and bring out capabilities and commitments of the organisation. These advertisements, through multi-media campaigns project the "corporate image" by which an organisation is ultimately rated and reckoned for its credibility and competence.

A series of "Themes" and "Key result areas", also the multiple roles and responsibilities of the organizations are identified from its mission, corporate perspective and annual plans. These are imaginatively illustrated, duly supported by a simple copy, highlighting the organisational profile.

An institutional advertisement may reflect the commitment or performance of the Corporation. Sometimes, it may seek to convey similarly image through its products also. Qualities like reliability, safety—may be reflected through product advertisement; for example, LML Vespas the picture of a little girl on a scooter with one bold line message, "A small argument in favour of choosing the safer scooter" thus using the angle of safety for promoting the image of LML Vespa.

Most organizations want the news about their organisation reported in a favourable manner, that will promote their objectives. Media in turn are dependent on the revenue generated by corporate advertising. This reflects their interdependence on each other.

*Media Relations* is an investment worth the efforts and has to be developed steadily and maintained ways: be honest accurate while dealing with the Press; provide them with interesting, timely and actual stories, thus gaining their confidence; never pressurize them to publish your story. Also remember not to complain about the treatment of your press releases; don't ask them to kill or suppress a particular story. Request them, if necessary, to delay its publication; stay within the boundaries of news interest and don't overload the media with many stories at a time and give them only relevant details stressing upon the vitalize issue are some of the ways to develop healthy media relationship.

In other words *good media relations* requires adherence to five basic elements viz; frank, fair, factual, fast and friendly.

The best way to give out your press release to all media is a Press Conference. A Press Conference is generally conducted for important and controversial matters such as labour disputes, policy announcements, industrial policy change or a technological breakthrough. All members, employees, officials of the organisation are briefed in a advance on the question that are likely to be asked by the Press. This facilitates the answers and places your organisation in a favourable light. Always remember to select a suitable time and convenient venue for the Press conference and invite the media well in advance. Prepare a press kit for their convenience which most contain a complete information manual of the organisation: a press release; introductory publication; copy and pencil or pen.

A Press release must be tailored for its medium news stories for newspapers, articles for industrial publication, conversational style releases for Radio, TV scripts with visuals for TV. An ideal release ought to be typed and—preferably hand delivered to the appropriate person; timely and precise and written in a journalistic style.

### Social Responsibility

John Kenneth Galbraith, one of the famous social thinker, feels that the society has yet to accept the dual role of business goals and social values of a business organisation. However, a business organisation should be aware of the impact on the society. An industry, such as chemical or engineering etc., may achieve high productivity, maximum profits and remarkable success, but at the same time their operations can cause environmental pollution, affecting the society and neighbouring areas thereby endangering human, animal and plant life. Thus, it becomes necessary for business organisations to conduct a social audit of their activities, to find out whether their activities are helpful to the society; whether their existence poses any threat or provides an opportunity to the community.

Business corporations must aim at securing social acceptance and earn goodwill by their philanthropic dispositions and also encompass certain, socially relevant principles, which include:

to carry out business operations compatible with the ethical standard of society; to work towards abating pollution and to never forget that their rights and interests are subservient to public welfare.

The doyen of Indian Industries, JRD Tata, had once said that "Let some of the time of industry managers, its engineers, doctors and specialists, be spread to help and advice the people village and to supervise new developments by cooperative effort between them and the company..."

You must know that corporate social responsibility is a part of the daily business activities of the organisations. More and more companies are now engaging in philanthropic missions and community based projects in their corporate mission.

Over the last 10 months "Escorts" has organised over 5,000 eye operations in 411 villages of Faridabad district. Similarly in 1979, "TATA" set-up a "Tata Rural Development Society" to involve programmes for people in areas 10 to 15 kms, away from Jamshedpur (which covers about 250 villages).

## RELATIONSHIP BETWEEN PUBLIC RELATIONS AND ADVERTISING

The application of public relations and the use of advertising are sometimes misunderstood, igniting a series of unanswered questions for companies needing to create awareness for themselves.

When do you use public relations? Why should you advertise? The best answer on both topics is, "It depends on what you're trying to accomplish." Use public relations and advertising (and marketing) together as well as separately when the situation calls for it.

Still confused? Don't fret. You're in good company.

### Message Control

A distinct difference between PR and advertising is their extent of message control. When, where and how an advertisement runs is quite controllable. Ad space purchased in the right format (i.e., broadcast, radio, print, online, sky writing, floating barge) means one has inherent control over what messages are communicated.

Conversely, while the process of creating messages through public relations is controllable, what occurs after the message has left the "nest" is often uncontrollable. The most common uncontrollable factor is whether the media view your information as newsworthy. In advertising there is no question whether your information will be publicized—if the check cleared, you're in.

I know what you're thinking. You want control of the message from beginning to end so you've decided that advertising is the way to go. Have you thought about the current shelf life of an advertisement? What about implied endorsement? Costs?

### Shelf Life: TV Commercials and the Press Release

Until recently, TV advertisements have had a shorter shelf life than a press release archived on the Internet. For now this is probably still true, but watch out. New Websites are coming online with nothing but commercial content that would make any ad executive smile. Corporations are also posting their commercials on corporate Websites to extend the shelf life of their ad dollars.

Obstacles to viewing archived commercials are many. The more common ones include slow Internet connections, lack of installed software for viewing, and unless there is an HTML description about the commercial for search engines to archive, add inability to find a commercial online to the list of obstacles. These barriers are coming down quickly as technology and computer training improves.

Archived press releases and news articles still rank high in terms of Internet longevity. Search engines can locate information (even in PDF format for some) long after the hype of a press release has waned. The major obstacle here is a person without access to the Internet.

### Implied Endorsement

No matter how interesting an advertisement might be, it is recognized as a self-serving communication. The only implication here is that someone paid to have a message filtered directly to a consumer. There is no third-party endorsement, no filter before it reaches you.

Public relations affords the credibility of indirect third-party endorsements. This means you are not paying to get advertising placed, but a publication is freely giving space to a story about your company. An endorsement such as this is a powerful tool in shaping public opinion.

Consumers today are far more cynical than previous generations, with only a small per cent saying they have a great deal of confidence in advertising messages. Anyone can buy visibility, however PR plays a critical role in sorting out the hype.

**Costs**

Advertising exposure is often proportional to the amount of money spent on the advertisement. Whether your ad sits on a billboard overlooking the highway or plays during prime time television, advertising will consume your budget faster than a well-positioned, well-written press release.

For small companies, public relations is the better method for direct and personal communication with a target audience. For larger companies with a sufficient budget, advertising along with public relations may be the right combination for success.

## ORGANISING A CORPORATE PUBLIC RELATIONS DEPARTMENT

There can be no rigid type of PR department; indeed, flexibility should be one of its chief characteristics. It needs to be ready to tackle any and every PR requirement and able to adapt itself to changing situations without much loss of momentum. There is nothing static about PR it is essentially a dynamic function both the character of the work it does and in its attitudes of mind towards the work. However, the character of this work differs from company to company. In some firms the emphasis is on employee relationship, whilst in others employee communications are divorced from PR and are the responsibility of the labour and personnel departments. It is, however, becoming increasingly evident in a large number of industrial companies that PR is being required as an aid to marketing, making possible improved communications with customers, suppliers, stockholders and the creation of favourable public image that is able to influence the attitudes of specific groups of people towards the company.

There are some companies that look up PR mainly as a means of contacting the press with the object of interpreting policy and communicating information about products and new developments; this is the narrow view.

Whilst some degree of specialisation is inevitable, the proper function of PR in an industrial concern is to help improve communications with all its contacts, including labour, customers, suppliers, stockholders, the press community neighbours and the public, and to provide management with advice and assistance on all matters which have a PR aspect.

The organisation or structure of a company PR department depends on the character as well as the volume of work and the policy of the Board towards PR i.e., whether the directors regard its functions as crucial to the well-being of the firm and encourage its management to give PR opportunities to improve and extend communications, or whether they look upon PR narrowly and rate the PR-man rather low in the hierarchy of the firm.

The pattern of industry changes year by year and there is a constant shift of emphasis so that whatever type of organisation is devised to cover the functions of PR there must at all times be a readiness to modify this to meet the new needs of management as they arise. And some of these needs may call for special skills.

For example, where employee relationship is a major responsibility of the PR department, as it might be in a large steel works or one of the nationalised industries, then personnel may have to be recruited with some experience in this field. The old idea that any competent journalist can do PR work is entirely wrong today and the person best equipped to communicate to employees should have had some experience in labour relations, as well as an ability to write and also to be able to staff and payroll. Similarly the new technologies and complexities of so many industries call for PR personnel with an academic or technological background so that they can talk the same language as the technologists, scientists and engineers. In other words, the communication problem has firsts to be solved at the PR end, if its personnel are to be able to communicate effectively with others.

## PR Responsibilities

The following breakdown covers most the PR functions likely to be carried out by an industrial concern:

### *Press Liaison*

Responsibility for all company relations with the Press; preparation and issuing of press releases and handouts, arrangement of press conferences, initiation and writing of articles for the press and the editing of material prepared by company staff, copywriting of prestige or institutional advertisements in collaboration with the advertising department; commissioning and supervising all photography required for PR arranging facility visits of the press to factories, laboratories, etc, arranging interviews of the press with among others, drawing up and keeping up-to-date press lists for different groups of publications, checking, filling and recording all press notices, circulating to top management selected press cuttings or summaries of press coverage.

Whilst the PR man himself would have the overall responsibility for press liaison, dictating policy and laying down procedure, he would delegate most of the day-to-day work to his press officer.

*Publications*

Internal responsibility for the planning and preparation of employee handbooks, works newspapers, staff magazines, staff bulletins, pay envelope inserts, posters and other publicity material.

*External*

- Annual reports.
- Recruitment publications.
- Publicity releases covering products, company policy Brochure, handbooks and other publications issued by the marketing departments.
- Company magazines and publications issued regularly to customers.

*Visual Aids*

Responsibility for the planning, direction and production of films, special displays, notice boards, charts, product exhibits, etc.

*Information*

Responsibility for answering general queries; supplying information of an educational nature to schools and colleges, arranging speakers from company staff to speak at clubs and organisations of various kinds; circulating to shareholders the publications prepared by the publicity section of PR.

*Control*

Responsibility for administration, preparation of the yearly budget and the actual running of the department.

***Research***

Responsibility for planning and organising opinion research amongst employees, customers, community neighbours, shareholders and members of the public so as to determine their reaction on company policies and to report the findings to top management.

Although the pattern of PR as outlined in this kind of organisation is excellent, covering as it does most of the major PR activities that one would except to be carried out in a large company, it should be possible to effect economics by streamlining some of the actions and to collaborate with other departments in certain operations for example, some of the work of the internal publication section might well be undertaken by personnel and labour departments. Similarly some of the work of the external publications section, notably that concerned with annual reports, could probably be passed over to the secretary's department. It might also be argued that the production of customer literature is primarily an advertising function and could best be done by the department.

A department organised on these lines would require a minimum staff of 10 including the manager or PR man, his assistant who would be the press officer, section heads and juniors. The head of the department's chief function would be planning and direction of operations, coordination of all PR activities, administration and, most important liaison with top management. In a large complex concern with a number of factories or manufacturing units or divisions, there might well arise a need to have PR advisers or liaison officers stationed at the various plants to give assistance and advice to local managements on handling PR matters, (including, of course, employee relationship), to maintain contact with the local press and to feedback to headquarters, i.e., the central PR departments, information about company activities and problems that have bearing or may influence future PR.

The minimum scale of operations for a medium sized company is indicated below:

*Publications and Visual Aid*

Responsibility for the planning, writing and publication of all types of company literature to be circulated to employees, customers, shareholders and so on. Production of firms displays notice boards, charts and special product exhibits needed for conferences and seminars.

*Press Liaison and Information*

Responsibility for all contacts with the press including the preparation and circulation of all press releases, handouts, organisation and running of press conferences, interviews and facility visits, supply of information of a general nature to all enquiries, including those from educational establishments contact where necessary, with suppliers, shareholders and others.

*Control and Research*

General administration including budgeting and carrying out of research.

For such an organisation, one well qualified PR man to run the show, two assistants and juniors should be just about sufficient, although it is agreed that they would be under some pressure to fulfil all requirements. The PR man would naturally assume direct personal responsibility for all press matters and information and his two assistants would look after the other two sections. A couple of really good secretaries would be needed to cope with day-to-day work, although for special exercises additional assistance would be needed.

*Close Liaison with Marketing Essential*

To be really effective, the PR man must be allowed to work on a large canvas and be free to recommend and to use the media of communication that he considers likely to be the best suited to the situation.

If PR is looked on by top management as essentially a marketing function then there must exist a very close liaison with the marketing departments. On the other hand, it would be fatal for PR to come under the control of marketing as this would rob it of all independence of thought and action, and PR thrives of freedom. The PR man must not be tied down to systems or regulations but able to switch methods and to change procedures so as to meet any new situation that arises, and marketing conditions are highly fluid. Ever uppermost in the mind of the PR man must be the likely effect on sales and the company image of every important decision that top management makes; how customers react to it; the effect of it on the competition, suppliers, shareholders, employees and the public. If PR work is always carried out in cooperation with marketing so that everyone connected with selling is aware of what is happening, then the maximum effect is likely to be achieved. It is when PR is carried out in isolation, as so often happens, that the results are so disappointing. Therefore before a major PR exercise is implemented it is vitally important to sell it to all branches of management to secure first their approval and interest and finally their cooperation.

*Staff and Qualifications*

While it is true that the ability to pass the examinations set by the Institute of Public Relations for its associates and members is an indication of the candidate's knowledge of the theory and practice of PR to be a successful practitioner requires a great deal more than this. It calls for the somewhat rare ability to think clearly and objectively and to be able to communicate information in a way that will create the maximum impact, using the most suitable media of communication. The PR man need to be experienced in dealing with people and able to secure the ready cooperation of all types, from the man on the shop floor to the Chairman of the firm. An extrovert, but one whose personality earns him the respect both of his colleagues inside the firm and the many contacts outside, he must have courage to express his opinions, even when they are unpopular, and be ready to make decisions and to accept the consequences if they prove to be wrong ones.

This is not the picture of a superman, but one who has graduated in the hard school of experience and achieved success in the profession because of his ability, personality and mature judgement. And most PR men, are either journalists or advertising men some have academic qualification, a few have technological backgrounds but the majority have gone into PR largely because of their natural aptitude for this kind of work.

Industry is becoming increasingly complex, the new technologies have a language all their own and even modern business procedures are not easy to understand. This means that those engaged in the actual operation of industrial PR must, if they themselves are to communicate effectively with their colleagues in the some scientific, technological or marketing experience.

This does not necessarily mean that the PR man himself needs to be a technologist or a scientist, although it would be helpful if he had some technical knowledge or background, but he would be well advised to recruit staff that is best suited to the particular type of business carried out by the firm. If, for instance, it produces electronic components and devices, a man with some knowledge of electrical engineering would be invaluable; similarly a company manufacturing plastics would ideally need someone who know his way around the tongue twisting polymers. Just as a PR consultancy recruits special skills to suit the client's accounts so too should the PR man in building up his department. Ideally it should be the press officer who has the technological background as he is the one who is called upon to translate the jargon of the chemist or the engineer into easily understood press notices and articles, and to be able to do this with any degree of competence calls for an ability to understand the language of the specialist. The press officer cannot be expected to be an expert, that is not his job, but he loses the respect of his colleagues in the firm unless he has a reasonable grasp of what they are talking about. There are some fortunate people who are blessed with technical appreciation. Although not technologists, engineers or scientists, they possess a smattering of knowledge on a variety of useful subjects and a great deal of common sense that enables them to follow a technical argument and to converse not unintelligently about technical subjects. Such men and women make invaluable PR assistants.

However, to sum up, the first essential is to study the pattern of business undertaken by the firm and then to try and recruit personnel with some experience or knowledge of the particular technologies that are involved, plus, of course, the ability to do their jobs as PR assistants.

### *Responsibilities to Board of Directors*

If PR is responsible to too many bosses the inevitable result is confusion, frustration and irritation, all of which sap the strength and destroy the effectiveness of the PR man's work whilst he should have ready access to all members of the Board of Directors, from the chairman downwards, his problem and queries receiving a high degree of priority, he should be responsible to one senior director, preferably a marketing director or the commercial or sales director. In some concerns, where there is a great emphasis on employee relationship, PR is the responsibility of the personnel director. This is not altogether a good move as it slants PR too much in one direction and encourages the view point that it is primarily a personnel activity. There are also objections to the responsibility for PR being in the hands of the managing director as he is usually so preoccupied with high finance and questions of company policy, and under such pressure from departmental managers that access to him proves difficult and quick decisions are not easy to secure.

It is important, for the smooth running of the PR department that the director in-charge is reasonably static because PR is a job that demands quick decisions and prompt action. There is always a sense of urgency about PR matters and some executives resent this, complaining that the PR man is constantly holding a pistol at their head. However, this urgency has to be accepted and top management must look upon it as part of the price to be paid for ensuring rapid communications. Their is, of course, a reluctance on the part of some directors to have anything to do with PR. They fear the repercussions in the board room when questions are asked about the advisability of making this or that statement to the Press. For this reason there is a tendency for directors to duck the really tricky questions and to refer decisions to the managing director or chairman. These tactics mean delays, failure to meet Press deadlines and the missing of opportunities, all of which result in loss of confidence in the PR man and general deterioration in his relations with the press and other media.

It is always an advantage if the director responsible for PR is also responsible for advertising and promotion and that is why the marketing director is the idea executive. He is able to ensure that responsibilities clearly defined, that collaboration is of a high order and that all PR activities are closely geared to marketing.

### The Free Enterprise

The task of nature countries is to bring a highly developed economy and government to maximum efficiency and equity in serving the needs of their people, it lies in the proposition that the function of government is to do for people what needs to be done that they cannot do at all for themselves, or do so well.

The difference between this view and the acceptance of nationalisation as a general principle is crucial. It is between government ownership or involvement as a transitional or limited device, and as a permanent and universal feature of a developed economy.

1. Free enterprise has a built-in stimulant to high production, production is limited only by consumer demand—and in modern times this has risen by the complementary process of the growth of high wages well distributed among the workers.
2. The enterprise system has a built-in stimulant to efficiency: the manager reduces costs, the more conscientiously he maintains machinery, the more prudently he uses raw materials and resources, the more profits we will make. Conversely, if he law in these respects, the relentless law of competitive survival will weed him out.
3. Free enterprise has a built-in stimulant to innovation: consumers are quick to reward the manufacturer of a new product or a better one, patent laws ensure handsome prizes to the ingenious and resourceful.
4. The enterprise system has a built-in stimulant to quality: The quota system has a built-in bias against quality. If your quota is 10,000 television sets, you will meet just as well with 10,000 passable TV sets as with 10,000 superbly built TV sets.

Even communist countries have recognised these inherent deficiencies, and are trying to inject private enterprise features.

The enterprise system has always stressed the objective of high productivity, holding that if everyone concentrates on increasing production, there will be more for all to share, and the standard of living of the worker will thus be raised.

Women grumbling to husband: "How can the government continually spend more than they get."

Husband: "That's because they've got confidence in us."

## Revisiting Public Relations

While mass media constitute the means, mass communication is the process through which people are approached. It is a scientific method around which a class of specialists has grown up in recent times who have developed mass communication into a fine art. This class, ordinarily identified as public relations men, is quite different from the persons who run and operate different media like the editorial and managerial staff of newspapers, the programme staff and the technicians of radio and television of the writers of books and pamphlets. The public relations staff are attached as specialists to the Government Departments, institutions or business houses whose objectives they try to put across to the people. They thus constitute, so to say, an intermediary between the institution and the people.

## Origin

The institute of public relations arose out of the phenomenal growth of industry in the Western countries in the nineteenth century and the 'public-be-damned' attitude of the industrialists which came in for strong criticism at the hands of social workers and political writers. The theory of laissez faire which held the field then in most of the advanced countries particularly helped this type of attitude. Business did not care for the people. Consequently, the public became intolerant of business. In course of time, pressure of public opinion compelled business magnates to try to present an acceptable front to the people about the industries which they were controlling. The institution of public relations arose out of this development. Practically all large industries and commercial institutions in the Western countries and many in our own country have public relations staff now, with specific functions and duties.

In the Government of India, the importance of public relations was realised even in the British days. With the emergence of freedom, the need became urgent as government took over a large number of nation-building programmes for which public cooperation in a significant measure was necessary. To explain the government's policies and programmes, to indicate to the people the area of cooperation in developmental activities and to keep people informed of the progress of planning and development, a body of specialists was required.

The institution of public relations has often been misunderstood, not without reason. Instead of considering the public relations staff as a part of an organisation and their function as scientific exposition of the merits and objectives of the institution, instances are not rare when public relations staff have been regarded as the personal appendages of the heads of institutions or Ministers. There are pliable and obliging public relations men, too, who have devoted their talent and energy to build up individuals or promote personal publicity. Almost every country has passed through this phase at some stage or the other so that honest public relations people sometimes got frustrated. Some PR men have sadly confessed in their memories that they "did work they detested for money they didn't earn to buy things they didn't need to impress people they didn't like!"

But this really is an aberration of public relations. Public relations at its best is a highly honourable profession. It has the dual role of explaining and interpreting truthfully the policies and programmes of an institution and secondly to keep the policy-makers informed of the people's reactions. It is wrong to expect that a public relations man will project half truth or untruth. Any employer who thinks that by employing public relations staff he can project before the people a false image of his institution or if public relations is to be successful, it must not compromise with truth.

**Listing Possibility of Misuse**

Wrong use of public relations has aroused criticism and, in some countries, even suggestions have been made that public relations practice should be made illegal except by registered practitioners. While too much importance should not be attached to this suggestion in the present Indian context when public relations is hardly extensive enough to constitute a problem, the suggestion underlines the delicate nature of the operation of public relations. The actual strength of public relations lies in its looseness, flexibility, its informal approach and the deft use of the contacts that a PRO is able to build up. It is thus 'a trouble-shooting profession' and in unscrupulous hands it can do harm. In developing countries, particularly in countries which have emerged into freedom after long periods of static existence under colonial rule and where the concept of democracy has not established its roots firmly, a public relations man who happens to be in the confidence of this Minister or department can exercise influence over the press and others mass media. This influence can be towards the good, in the national interest or, if the public relations offer so wishes, in the personal interest of the Minister, and ultimately in his own interest as by pleasing the minister he furthers his own objectives. But such practices cannot continue for long. As soon as the national press of country assumes its vigilant role, undue influence of the PRO ceases.

A public relation officer should be sufficiently competent to be welcomed into the policy-making level of the ministry of the institution which he has been called upon to serve. He should serve as a barometer of public opinion and keep the management informed of public relations. To discharge these functions effectively, the public relations officer should not merely be highly knowledgeable about his institution or his department but he should also be a man of character with respect for truth; he should have a progressive attitude, sincerity, unfailing courtesy, a sense of responsibility to the public and be fair in projecting the views of the institution or the government which he serves. These qualities, added to imagination and dynamism, can help significantly.

### The PRO's Job

The job of the PRO to the government is a specialised one. He is the visible and the immediate link between the government and the various media. It is he who received the first shock from the media and it is he who communicates the first reaction of the government to the various media. Therefore, it is essential that a public relations officer maintains a cool temper and does not get ruffled while dealing with controversial issues; that he does not try to bluff or assume an all-knowing air but is helpful in collecting information and providing it; and that he avoids red-tape and is not stand offish or evasive in his answer. The PRO should realise that any obstruction that he places in the way of a reporter in getting an answer to a legitimate question or a story will only make the reporter more curious and make him work harder in getting the information he is seeking. Stories collected through sources other than the official sources of the PRO are likely to contain inaccuracies which can only harm the cause of the institution when they appear in public. It should be possible for a PRO who has been able to establish an understanding with the press correspondents to convince them that they are not being obstructed and that there are justifiable reasons for withholding with the press correspondents to convince them that they are not being obstructed and that there are justifiable reasons for withholding information on certain matters in the national interest.

A PRO should not always take shelter in anonymity. If he has the confidence of his ministry or institution, he should be quotable. The PRO should not try to either misuse his position or exploit his friendship with the newspaper staff to gain personal benefits. Nor should he try to play the editional and the managerial staff of newspapers against one another. The judgement of a newspaper should be respected and direct complaints against the conduct of a press correspondent to his editor should be avoided as far as possible. If an error is of a minor nature, it is worthwhile ignoring it in the interest of good public relations. But if the error is major and positive harm is going to be caused by such erroneous publication, it should be contradicted. A still better course, depending on the circumstances, would be to give the correct news to the correspondent himself and it is more than likely that he would on his own make the necessary correction on his dispatch without even being asked to do so.

These are just a few hints that a good public relations men can keep in view. Basically, it is a problem of human relations. A helpful attitude, knowledge of one's own subject, ability to generate confidence on one's employer, sticking to the truth, balance in the presentation of controversial issues and fairness and impartiality in dealing with the correspondents are important traits of PRO'S character that are bound to go a long way in making him appreciated by his own ministry or the institution of which he is working as well as by the media people.

Finally, the government or the institution who maintains public relations men should treat them as integral part of the organisation, give them work and adequate responsibility, provide them with resources and also give them the credit that is due to them. Sometimes, heads of institutions invite outside public relations experts, ignoring their own people. This practice can be justified only for undertaking special campaigns of a temporary nature for which outside agencies may be specially qualified. Otherwise it is quite easy to make the public relations staff absolutely ineffective by simply ignoring them. It is hardly possible for any public relations man to prove by means of statistics and data the value of the contribution that he is making to his institution. He is not building a bridge or a factory that he can show something physical and tangible. He is selling ideas, dispelling misconceptions, correcting attitudes and approaches. The results of such efforts are not immediately measurable. The correct course for institutions which keep PROs is to select suitable persons and, having done so, take them into their inner counsels so that the PROs can be of real service to them.

**Planning a Public Relations Event**

The first thing to do is to decide whether the project will be worth the time it will take out of your life. The superiority of what you do will not come about by accident. It will rest on a solid base of preparatory work, and to this you must direct yourself. Planning an event takes into account the application of proper tools—telephone, memos, letters and interviews: the selection of workers, the systematic ordering of operations and sustained control of all that pertains to your project.

The word "project" is used because everything we do has in some degree the quality of something contemplated, devised, or projected. Some events are: meetings, conventions, displays (Scout and Guide displays, for example) concerts, festivals, field days, exhibitions parades, campaigns for funds and campaigning against pollution.

Here, in capsule form, are the ingredients for planning any of these projects: Decide precisely what form the event will take: establish the purpose the event is to serve; develop a sound organisation of capable people; inspire them with a sense of purpose; and maintain adequate control over the operation.

When you go before an audience to sell the idea of supporting your project spend ninety per cent of your time thinking of the people before you, and ten per cent on yourself.

**Selling an Idea**

Present your idea in terms of the experience of your audience. People a shrink from the mental effort of translating your idea into terms of their own thoughts. This technique reminds us that when a person goes fishing he chooses his bite according to the taste of the fish, not his own taste.

Predigest your plan and your ideas as completely as you can before exposing them to an audience, so that you speak with assurance. When you meet resistance, welcome it as giving you the opportunity to display the soundness of your ideas. Do not appear to rush things: people need time to null over and consider what you say.

Dramatise your presentation when it is possible if the nature of your project is suitable, present your plan accompanied by something visual-photographs, sketches a programme or a lost of events. Combine something new with what is already familiar to the people in your audience and show how they can make this new thing interesting and advantageous.

## Setting the Objectives

Every project must have a purpose; to make money, to construct something, to adorn, beautify or preserve something, to benefit a person, a group or a community.

When you are sketching the first broad outline of your project give imagination the right of way. This is the creative phase; judgement comes later. See that all who will be working on the project with you, and all those whose support you desire, get the big picture.

Your picture must have a point of interest. Every project needs a purpose, an objective. Of this be sure; you cannot lead a group toward goals you have not defined along paths you have not visualised. Without clearly stated objectives a project cannot possibly be effective and efficient.

## Planning the Event

A plan that hopes to succeed needs a minimum of detail, flexibility for adjustment and constant visibility. The method of its working out must show. This means that the leader needs to define the project in exact terms; breakdown the job into sub-jobs, each defined and limited, and make a count down chart starting now and ending on the date of completion.

When you have worked out your plan on paper, look at every part of it critically. It is workable? Are the steps to steep for the workers?

Making a list of things to be done is vital to your peace of mind. By knowing ahead of time that items are essential and what may be left out relieve your mind of the nagging thought that perhaps you are falling down on the job.

Write a list of five or six most important jobs and number one, the top priority item. Stick that you are working on the most necessary item.

Success of any event depends upon good organisation: disorder is an enemy to any sort of plan. At about every proposed action: is this the reasonable, most effective and most economic way to do this. Brief every person who will be working with you so that all will be pulling in the same direction. Imaging yourself writing a play: give your actors cures so that everyone knows when to come on stage and perform his part.

When setting-up committees or working groups make sure that they have definite, non-overlapping lines of responsibility. Just as you have to bear responsibility for carrying out the whole project successfully, there should be one person in every group responsible for that group's part of the work. This, as Oliver J. Greenway wrote tersely in Master-Planning the small company's future, will avoid buck-passing.

Most difficulties in meetings are not caused by the affair being discussed but by personality links in the people present. The most serious differences can be solved if we are willing to keep our egos out of the debate. It is necessary to show respect for other people's knowledge and opinions.

## Considering Timing and Control

A great deal of waste time and waste effort can be attributed to lack of proper and detailed instructions. Do not be backward about making clear to workers that what is to be done when, and who is responsible for doing it. Certain things are to be done by certain actors and you have to give stage directions. These when addressed to workers, are contained in action words: obtain, record, provide, check, receive, and forward.

You, as head planner, must pay attention to the calendar and the clock, because time is a most important ingredient in planning.

As the person in over-all control you must know day by day whether jobs are being handled in such a way that they will be completed in time to feed properly into other jobs. This knowledge puts you in position to push the right combinations of activities to keep the programme running smoothly on time.

This is where a count-down sheet comes in handly, work out calendar schedules for the individual jobs. Listing the joins with their start and finish times. Set down the dates on which sections of each group's job should be completed and check the list daily.

Only by such a system can you know with assurance that your objective will be reached on time. The list reveals where you need to put in a word to expedite performance.

A person accepting authority as a project leader must assume the responsibility that authority entails. You alone will be held accountable for final success. Guard against allowing yourself to become immersed in one aspect of the operation. Your good leadership of the total operation is the most essential element in the plan.

When you have people working to carry out your plan, expect the best but check frequently to see that you are getting it. An ideal working force would be one in which the leader found it unnecessary to check anything except and results, but few organisations are perfect.

Insist nicely but firmly on knowing the truth about group progress. When a group leader reports that his part of the job is 50 per cent completed, make sure that the "O" has not leaped in there on the wings of hope.

If your co-workers seem to be faltering, do no panic or subside into melancholy thought about your trouble. Food out what is causing the slowdown and act decisively to get things running smoothly.

You will learn quickly that being busy is not every thing. There is a vast difference between being busy and being fruitful. Some group leaders will give the impression of working hard, but they are not accomplishing. Persuade them to commit themselves to results. Having undertaken to do their job by a certain date they are in honour bound to deliver the goods.

If sweetness and persuasion fail to remedy the situation you have no alternative, in view of your obligations, except to say: "This is job that must be done on time if the project is to survive. Either do job or make room for someone who will."

The best way to get anybody to do anything is to make him want to do it, and it is therefore advantageous to give suggestions, not orders. Make the person feel happy about doing what you suggest.

If you have to prove a person at fault, do it adroitly that you give no offence. In certain situation you can say: "I don't blame you one bit for feeling as you do. If I were you I should undoubtedly feel just as you do. But there are other angels to consider.

### *A Few Guidelines*

Planning an event requires more old-fashioned brain power than it does banks on flashing computer planning is the only known method to make sure that you do not overlook vital details, and there is no other way in which you can provide a measure by which keep track of progress.

Here is a suggested drill suitable to the planning or any enterprise:

Fix the objective, plan the manner of reaching and set down the steps or levels of achievement to be reached at dated periods along the way. There are some steps involved:

*Assessment*: Gather data to show the present situation and the desirable goal.

*Strategic planning*: Determine the grand design of the project.

*Resource calculation*: What resources are there/where is the balance to come from.

*Tactical planning*: Decide how and by whom the job can be done best.

Recruit workers and get on with the first phase — Review. Make notes in your diary periodically and check progress against your planned schedule and then consider improvements in your plan.

### *Public Relations in Image Building*

"Image" is basically a mental representation or a conception. While an image may be clear in a person's mind, reasons he or she gives for holding such a view are often hazy, vague generalisation.

Public Relations is undoubtedly involved work but the building of an image: That is "Reputation Building: is not the exclusive preserve of any one communications skill or department.

### *The Image Processing People*

The practical way to project a clear persuasive corporate image beings by focussing it on the corporation itself. Each phase of a corporation's activity adds meaning to the picture in the public mind. Nothing is perfect, but management and public relations people may have to face up frankly to several internal problems before any face-lifting is effected.

Public Relations' image building programme needs to be developed in the light of each company's circumstances and business and has to basically cover the WHOs, the WHATs, the WHYs, the WHEREs and the WHENs of a company. Question has to be posed as to "who are you NOW and what is your present image? First, the character of the company has to be determined before you sensibly weigh the existing image.

Does the company have corporate objectives? If you can unearth them somewhere in the archives, they are probably out of date. Once you find them, can you truly challenge the status quo, you have to take out insurance against preparedness. Overconfidence spells out obsolescence. It is not enough to have well-manicured projections. It is important to determine the abstract values inherent in future growth.

Whether or not a corporate image is successfully changed depends, in the long run, upon the daily company wide effort to sustain the attitude of not achieving by heavy hand, gimmickry, far out advertising slogans or by corporate window dressing. This is the seed of a new reputation "Image Building." The job is not that of Public Relations executives alone, but it is his job to prime it. Image Building does not mean that it is an act of mere glorification where there is none:

"Image cannot be created out of nothing. It has to have a substance. Over 12 centuries ago a famous Latin philosopher, LUCRETIUS has aptly said: "Now then learn, how tenuous is the nature of an image."

Public Relations professionals are not "image building contractors!"

## Image Building for Corporate Health (Impression Management)

Impression management is an age-old concept but unfortunately many Indian organisations pay scant attention to this important and effective technique.

At the individual level, in everyday life, we are careful about how we present ourselves to others. By creating a good impression about our talents, integrity, work ethic and other traits we endeavour to build abundant goodwill that will help us in our advancement.

But such attempts to project a better image to the community are not even contemplated at the organisational level. The prevailing conditions of the economy which favour a buyer's market should definitely not make organisations obvious to the principles of good management of which impression management forms a subset.

**Effective Business Tool**

Impression management as an effective business tool is gaining increasing attention even in developed countries, where even successful organisations are particular about building customer goodwill through creation of an organisational culture attend to managing the projection of favourable impressions to the client systems and the public at large.

An organisation's personality and the very core of its philosophy are mirrored in the manner in which it reacts to the environment and interacts with and treats its clients. High professionalism, honesty and cheerful service to client systems and timely delivery of quality products are some of the aspects the society associates with a good organisation big or small. Projection of such an image should be the goal of all organisations.

There are many organisations in India which are noted for their impertinence, unethical behaviour, apathy and slovenliness, and insensitivity to consumer needs. A few episodes which the authors witnessed in just one week will illustrate the sorry state of organisational behaviour. These relate to a variety of organisational systems—manufacturing firm, retail firm, a hospital (eye clinic) considered 'reasonably well run' and a prestigious educational institution—all located in the metropolitan city of Madras.

A manufacturing firm of repute, in its zeal to procure more business from one of its valued clients in a mofussil area, was promising delivery dates for a sizable order, knowing fully well that it could not honour its commitment. The buyer was making disparate think calls everyday to ascertain the position and the company officials were giving false assurances starting that the goods had been already shipped. The misrepresentation was explained as necessary to protect the company's interests.

Judging from the numerous trunk calls put through by the client, one could safely presume that the impression management style of the organisation—from the short-term as well as long-term perspectives leaves much to be desired.

A well-known retail cloth store with several branches in the city seems to have given some thought to impression management. It provides ice-cold water even in these days of acute water scarcity.

The shop's layout and design are pleasing to the senses and good lighting and air circulation draw crowds to the shop.

Contrast this with the happy but rate experience of being served by the personnel with zeal where the shop assistant's aim is to clinch the sale with goodwill built through customer satisfaction come to think of it, how many of us have seen salespersons and other personnel receive and serve us with a smile? In the ultimate analysis it is the human touch and adherence to the goal of complete customer's satisfaction that will create a lasting impression. And impression management is a continuing management function like planning and organising.

**Many Irritants**

Now for the eye clinic manned by specialists comparable to some of the world's best. The newly constructed clinic is also reputed to have highly humanitarian values incorporated in its organisational philosophy and quite a few poor and needy receive treatment free of charge with the same care and concern as the rich fee paying patients get. These laudable services and the cleanliness of the hospital tend to project a favourable impression of the institution. But this good image is marred by several irritants in the system which frustrate the patients and their caretakers. The operations are performed ably and skillfully by top surgeons but the administrative details and management of the organisation with a high sense of values capable of projecting a flawless image to the public, if only it can monitor its administrative system, systematise its operations and communicate standard procedures through notices at various places. Imagine the reputation and public image this institution will create for itself by setting right such seemingly small but terribly vexatius issues as non-availability of milk, inaccessibility to telephones, and hold up of the elevator when electric supply is not out.

Finally, the authors would like to recount the experiences of a visiting professor of management from the United States at a premier educational institution in Madras. The incumbent an Indian wanted to have the experience of teaching university students in this country, so that she could decide whether or not to return to her homeland for food.

Even though she started corresponding at least 12 months before her arrival, apart from the written communication that she would be teaching at the insulation for a remember me has all act arrived of her designation or remuneration. In fact, she found that some of her papers were missing. And she could get an office of her own to plan her courses only after taking a firm stand with the authorities.

Earlier, she had made enquiries from U.S. to several institutions about a teaching assignment with them. Though they responded favourably their replies were not received before a third reminder was sent to each institution. Do educational systems have to irritate, frustrate and annoy scholars? Is this the way seats of higher learning promote cultural and educational exchanges between nations?

It may be true to a large extent that economic conditions being what they are in this country, people will take whatever they are offered and, however, they are treated. However, if not in the interests of social responsibility, at least from the selfish point of enhancing profits it is time that organisations began to realise the need to treat impression management as a fundamental function of the organisational system.

Impression management has only recently been recognised a potent management tool to create goodwill and attract a regular clientele. The time is ripe for Indian organisations to seek ways of projecting a favourable image through attentive and helpful service. They should train their personnel to serve and present themselves appropriately to the public they serve. A system of rewards and punishments should be developed to encourage desired behaviour and discourage undesirable behaviour and attitudes in the staff. Good impression creates goodwill which invariably results in high profits expansion and growth. Is there a less costly way of attaining these?

## PUBLIC RELATIONS AND MEDIA INTERVIEWS

It's perhaps every business person's worst nightmare: you return to your office from lunch and find Mike Wallace and a crew from "Sixty Minutes" waiting in the lobby. "We have only a few questions," intones the prosecutorial journalist as you are videotaped running down the hall and into your office, slamming the door in his face.

Not all media interviews need be as frightening. In fact, knowing how to get your message across to the media can do a lot to actually promote your business. The trick is to be prepared.

You must go into every media encounter with your own messages... two or three points that you want to get across regardless of the questions you're asked. What that message is depends a lot on who is reading/viewing/hearing the interview and when. You must tailor your messages for that audience in terminology they can easily understand.

Not all media were created equal. Print interviews, for example, are much harder than broadcast despite their lack of intimidating cameras and recorders. Print reporters take advantage of this seemingly conversational approach and can keep you chatting for hours... if you let them. You must set the guidelines for the interview: who will speak for your company, on what issues, where and when.

Radio interviews offer an opportunity to narrowly focus your message to a particular demographic or psychographic niche audience reached by the station you're on. On call-in shows you'll have plenty of time to deliver your messages... even from the comfort of your own home, as stations now can have guests by phone as well as callers.

Television is perhaps the most challenging of the media because of its brevity, complexity and reach. Even a lengthy interview may be distilled down to a "sound bite" of but a few seconds. But, with training, you'd be surprised at how much information can be conveyed in that limited time... and how well you can control what gets electronically quoted from your interview. Being a visual medium you'll want to keep viewers focussed on your message rather than your flashy attire, ineffective body language or shifty-eyed glances off-camera.

Here are a few media DO's and DON'Ts which I stress in my Media Training Workshops:

- Know what you want to get across in the interview. Build a bridge of words from the reporter's question to your messages... and say them several times during the interview.
- Don't be afraid to admit that you don't know the answer to a question but instead offer to find the answer and get back to the reporter before their deadline. Never respond to questions based on unfamiliar facts.
- Don't be rushed into answering. Don't feel obliged to fill "dead air" after a tricky question. Just pause, think... and then answer.

- Don't use professional jargon. Keep your message simple, but not condescending.
- Find out as much as you can about the reporter and his/her story before you agree to be interviewed. Have they covered your business and its issues before? Who else are they talking to for this story? Do you really want to be in that mix? You can always politely decline an interview. Nobody can force you to talk if you don't wish.
- On TV, always dress your part, projecting a cool, clean-cut professional image.
- Don't look into the camera. Instead, look at whomever is talking. Avoid the temptation to look at the monitor or acknowledge other distractions out of camera range. And remember: you are always potentially on camera, even if someone else is talking. TV Director's love "reaction shots" of your expression or body language when someone else is verbally skewering you.
- Project enthusiasm for your messages. That attitude is contagious. And if you're not excited about your message, the reporter and audience never will be.

Finally... don't wait for the media to come looking for you. Reach out to them with story ideas, professional commentary and fresh ideas. Call your local papers and radio/TV stations and introduce yourself to the reporter(s) covering your business. Briefly tell them about your work and offer to be "on call" to them should they need your expertise. And follow up with a note, a fact sheet and business card. You'll be amazed at their reaction as very few business professionals are so proactive.

With a little practice, these interviewing skills will become second nature. So the next time Mike Wallace is waiting to ambush you, instead of fear your reaction might be more like: "Sure Mike. I'd be glad to chat. In fact, I have a few questions for you!"

# 5

# PR Professionalism in Media and Journalism: Principles and Ethics

## INTRODUCTION

The nature of Public Relations, its scope and the process by which its activities are carried on along with the theoretical aspects of communication as the relevant concepts of advertising, publicity and propaganda had explained in the previous chapter. Public relations is the state of mutual understanding between an organisation or individual and any groups of person or organisations, and the extent quality of the reputation, that exists.

In this illustration we discuss the special importance of ensuring ethical standards in the practice of Public Relations because of its being a vital function involving public opinion. Certain misconceptions about Public Relations being a play or gimmick have brought some disrepute to this profession in its nascent stage because of a few unscrupulous persons. Today, it is a sophisticated and vital management function with its own code of ethics.

The role of Public Relations in society, its potential for good use as well as for abuse is to be examined in the code of ethics and how it was adapted in India.

Content of the relationships between the Code of Ethics and the development of professionalism in Public Relations. Public Relations has today helped evolving as an effective tool for motivation and management.

The generation of goodwill, understanding and image building are the chief objectives of Public Relations and this is achieved through varied communication strategies. This chapter also aims to explain to you, the use of mass media and other devices termed as 'tools' of communication. Some of the import and common Public Relations tools have been discussed and it will help you to relate the role of communication to Public Relations effort; list the various media that could be used for publicity; outline the advantages and limitations of each of these media; state the various ways in which media could be used for publicity; explain the importance of media relation and how to cultivate it; evaluate various tools of oral and written communication in an organisation; identify other selective· media like direct mail, house journal and understand these efficiency; describe the use of the promotional methods like institutional advertising, P.O.P. material exhibitions etc., outline the use of open days, special events and ways to organise it successfully; and summarise the use of all the tools and media for reaching various kinds of audience.

Freedom of expression in democratic societies, growth in communication technology, industrial growth and increasing public awareness, globalisation, etc., are some of the factors that have contributed to the need for professionalism in skilful mediation and information communication making it an essential service today. Thus, having established its essentiality and its persuasive and informative role, we will examine its impact on the society as a whole. Also, we consider some ethical and legal implications in Public Relations. We will discuss a few ways to minimize distortion and some ways of maintaining and sustaining high moral and ethical standards in the profession.

Finally, the concept of social responsibility of business and the need of Public Relations to relate private with public interest are discussed. The practice of social audit, to evaluate the extent to which various organisations are fulfilling their social obligations, will be explained briefly.

It provide you win a sense of direction, place in your hands a compass that will enable you to chart your course in the stormy seas of Public Relations practice.

Public relations is by no means a universal specific for every situation, by it is at least a concept of analysis, action and communication which can do a great deal to help.

Public Relations as it is known in Britain today first began to be generally recognized in the nineteen-thirties, although the phrase had been used long before in the United States and a few pioneers were operating many years earlier on both sides of the Atlantic. Not surprisingly, the thought that relations with the public mattered tended to mature first in those organizations where a major sectors of the general public could be identified as of commercial importance. Service corporations like London Transport and national promotional bodies like the Empire Marketing Board were, understandably, among the first to adopt public relations thinking and practices in Britain.

The functions of what would today be known as propaganda and psychological warfare were, of course, in use during the 1914-18 war and there developed the planned presentation of information, much of it ruthlessly doctored to meet the government's needs. After that war, the first information posts in ministries and government departments appeared.

The 1939-45 war suddenly enlarged the official need to inform more people in greater detail than ever, to relate the objective and progress of the nation's battle. For plain information and as we now know-for far-from-plain propaganda, the government developed machinery for issuing news, background information, and ideas through the press and radios posters and pamphlets, films and lecture tours, such as had never previously been known or needed. The informative and motive powers of radio were fully exploited for the first time during the war and the British-American public's devotion to spot-news coverage has continued more strongly still with television.

After the war, both in central and in local government, the information concept remained. Many of today's successful public relations men learned their craft in government departments or the larger local authorities, most of them having previously been newspapermen. From this point the realization of the potential values of public relations began to spread slowly into industry and commerce.

At first staff appointments were less common than the use of the services of a consultancy of advertising agency department, of which only a pioneering few had existed before the war. Now these developed at a mushroom rate, many of them with an inadequate appreciation of the nature and techniques of public relations of the nature and techniques of public relations and sometimes with little motive other than to provide a fashionable service to clients. The poor reputation of public relations people among journalists and businessmen that persists in some quarters today can be traced back to this period of uncontrolled and unthinking growth. A few charlatans and more than a few old-time publicists contributed during the late 'forties' and the 'fifties' to the confused reputation of public relations from which skilled and honest operations suffered and to some extent, suffer still.

### Reconsidering Ethics and Morality

Ethics is defined as "that branch of philosophy dealing with values relating to human conduct, with respect to rightness and wrongness of certain actions and to the goodness and badness of the motives and ends of such actions." By dictionary definitions ethics and morality are interchangeable Both are concerned with conduct that is right or wrong, according to the accepted standards or principles.

To elaborate further, it is the consequence of a conduct that determines ethicality e.g., when the consequences range from being harmless to being beneficial. We consider it ethical or right. If the results are harmful, it is considered wrong or unethical. However, the concept of right or wrong varies with time, place and situation. This evolve over a period of time and cannot be applied uniformly as they are relative concepts. Behaviour that is considered unethical by one society or a generation may be quite acceptable to another. However, ethical conduct remains of significance to the society ultimately.

The dividing line between civilised and primitive societies is that, in the former it is the rule of law that prevails as against the jungle law of survival of the fittest, in the latter. However, even in civilised societies the legacy of the past continues. Standards of professional conduct, as all ethical standards, have their genesis largely in the moral codes as expressed in various religious doctrines, for lending sanity to the civilized world. But with the spread of ideology whether Marxism, with its emphasis on centralised planning, or capitalism, which thrives on the concept of free enterprise, religious and moral codes have given way to mate realism and technological determinism. This, in turn, has led to corrosion of ethical and social values, which leads to newer forms of exploitation. The only way now open to correct the wrong is to inject strong doses of morality into our personal working lives and thereby into national life. Hence, there is a growing concern for ethical standards or codes of conduct. A reflection of this concern is the importance that the subject of human rights has been receiving of late.

Public relations, like most other forms of human activity, can be measured in moral terms. Indeed, it is highly desirable that it should be, since all communicators by the nature of their work are capable of influencing other and therefore having a responsibility to society to maintain decent ethical standards.

The ethical considerations of public relations are not easily decided. As the business is young in comparison with the established professions, there is as yet no universally acknowledged code of conduct and the case law that has accumulated is relatively slight.

Similarly, since public relations is not a fully organized or controlled business, and it is still possible for anyone to endeavour to step in practice, there is no disciplinary control outside the provisions of the law, apart from that covering members of the Institute of Public Relations, Public Relations Consultant's Association, National Union of Journalists and Institute of Journalists. Even the codes and disciplinary powers of these organizations are far removed from the strictly regulated and enforced standards of the legal, medical or architectural professions.

In effect, of course, there are other indirect controls which have a bearing on public relations practice. The rules and regulations governing advertising, the case law being built up by the Press Council, the pressures of the consumer organizations, the watchfulness of hundreds of groups representing particular interests, and, of course, the opinion of his colleagues and contacts in the communication business, all have their effect on the public relations man's attitudes and actions.

Endless ethical questions can be raised in an ordinary week's work in public relations, but most of them fall into four categories: social responsibility; relationship with the client or employer; relationship with the media of communication; and relationship with fellow public relations people.

Social responsibility, in addition to basic commercial honesty and fair dealing, is very much a matter of not engaging in practices which are contrary to the general good, and of not supporting or condoning such practices on the part of a client or employer.

For instance, if a process is to be installed in a factory and it becomes apparent that the noise level will be harmful to employees and constitute a major nuisance to the community, it would clearly be contrary to the public interest to deny or discount the hazard. The public relations man would be failing in his duty if he did not draw the attentions of the management to the social and human problems involved, encourage preventive and remedial measures, and do his best to explain to employees and other the necessity for the process and the mitigating action taken.

Responsibility for the process and its hazards lies with the management; responsibility for honest assessment of the problems created and for frank communication with those concerned lies with the public relations man.

A negative, but equally important, form of social responsibility is to avoid and prevent misrepresentation. This is far more complicated than not making exaggerated claims for products or services.

The choice of what type of product to make or service to offer, what to charge, and how to sell is management responsibility, although the public relations man can contribute to the marketing thinking preceding the decision. It is a public relations responsibility, often a matter of personal conscience, to be sure that the presentation of the product or service is honest and that not direct or indirect deception of the audience takes place. This does not mean that it is only possible to work for a Rolls Royce type of organization; there is nothing wrong in promoting a cheap ballpoint pen for what it is, although there would be in presenting it as a luxury product.

Misrepresentation can also take the form of suggesting incorrect or only partially true reasons for an organization's policies or deeds. For example, it would be unethical to suggest that a price reduction had been brought about by increased efficiency in production if it had been forced upon the manufacturer by failure to compete in the market place.

One of the most insidious forms of misrepresentation is the creation of 'front organisation.' For example, an organization might purport to be a research trust when in fact, it promotes a medical product or appear to be study group when in reality its purpose is political propaganda. Even when this type of organization is set - up with good intentions, its operation must involve deception and half-truths, if not worse.

Anything less than complete honesty in public relations work is bound to harm all those involved. In the communication business, falsehoods and deceptions seldom remain unrecognized for long and when they are discovered the trust which is essential among those who convey messages is damaged.

This trust is just an important in the public relations man's dealings with his client or employer. Confidence based upon frankness and honesty is necessary if a relationship is to be built up within which the full benefits of inward and outward communication can be enjoyed.

The public relations man must be happy that the clients or employer's affairs are decent, honest, and useful or, at the very least, harmless and innocent. On the other side, the public relations man must be trusted as a person of integrity. The client or employer must be sure that his affairs are regarded as matters of confidence and be secure in the knowledge that no detail of his business or item information is transmitted without explicit agreement.

Another aspect of confidence is that of loyalty. It is clearly not ethical to accept payment from or engage in work on behalf of any competing or potentially competing organization without the consent of one's client or employer. Consultation among all parties when such an issue arises is the only fair way to determine any conflict of loyalties.

Although a few people in public relations do not agree, it is generally held to be unethical and unprofessional to work on the basis that reward shall be related to specific achievement: for example, a fee of £X for Y column-inches of editorial coverage, or a fixed percentage of a sum to be raised for charity.

The public relations man's dealings with the various media of communication are usually critical, in more than they need his, and he therefore has to understand and play by their rules. At the same time, his activities are frequently regarded with scepticism and the man who offends against the unwritten laws is not readily forgiven.

The cynicism of the press, radio and television towards those who wish to give them information is a healthy safeguard which protects the public from deception and dishonesty; it should be welcomed rather than resented, even when it acts against the acceptance of entirely worthy approaches.

Corruption of the media of communication by misinformation. By the withholding of relevant information which can reasonably be held to be in the public interest, or by attempting to influence editorial judgement on the use or rejection of information is one of the most distasteful and damaging forms of unethical behaviour.

Immediately, however, problems of ethical judgement are raised. What is the dividing line between information that is in the public interest and facts which by normal commercial prudence, should be confidential? Is telling a journalist some additional background to a story over a friendly drink an attempt to influence his editorial judgement? Is a lunch for his news editor on a getting-to-know-you basis an endeavour to undermine his independence or merely an attempt to establish personal confidence? Is placing a series of advertisements in a trade paper to be interpreted as liable to affect the editor's view on the news value of store is about the advertiser?

The answers to questions like these mostly lie in the realm of common-sense. It is barely possible to lay down hard and fast rules, but the development of an objectives approach and a sensitivity to the attitudes of others can, with the growth of experience in communication and the help of mature advice, keep the public relations man on the straight and narrow path of unimpeachable behaviour.

The issue of human rights has indeed assumed such paramount importance in the world today that the United Nations which was set-up after the Second World War adopted a "Universal Declaration of Human Rights", and the character of the United Nations has affirmed its faith in these fundamental rights. A number of international conferences have subsequently been held to discuss how far these rights are being implemented. Human Rights Commission has constituted in India also to ensure that violations of these human rights do not take place in the country.

In fact, a code of ethics is an essential requirement for every profession. You will not doubt have heard of the "Hippocratic Oath" which all medical graduates are required to take. This is named after Hippocrates, a Greek physician, who was the first to free medicine from superstition and witch-craft or magic, and gave a scientific basis for the science and art of the treatment of diseases. It was this that laid the foundation for the emergence of the medical profession.

It is worth looking why a code of ethics and a code of conduct have been given a high priority by all professional Public Relations organisations. In the United States, where Public Relations first developed as a profession, a Code of Professional Standards was adopted as early as in 1954 and subsequently revised in 1959, 1963,

1977 to meet the requirements of the situation. The code of the Public Relations Society of America is given below. You will see from this code how it based itself on the fundamental human rights and on the value and dignity of the individual. Without such a code the profession could not have acquired the important place it has in the American Society.

**Public Relations Society of America,**
**Code of Professional Standards,**
**for the Practice of Public Relations,**
**Adopted and Effective from April 29, 1977.**

This code, adopted by the PRSA, Assembly, replaces a similar Code of Professional Standards for the practice of Public Relations previously in force since 1954 and strengthened by revisions in 1959.

### *The Process of Declaration of Principles*

Members of the Public Public Relations Society of America base their professional principles on the fundamental value and dignity of the individual, holding that the free exercise of human rights, especially freedom of speech, freedom of assembly and freedom of the press, is essential to the practice of Public Relations.

In serving the interests of the clients and employers, we dedicate ourselves to the goals of better communication, understanding and cooperation among the diverse individuals, groups and institutions of society.

### *We Pledge*

(*a*) To conduct ourselves professionally, with truth, accuracy, fairness and responsibility to the public;

(*b*) To improve our individual competence and advance the knowledge and proficiency of the profession through continuing research and education;

(*c*) And to adhere to the articles of the Code of Professional Standards for the Practice of Public Relations as adopted by the Governing Assembly of the Society.

### *Articles of the Code*

These articles have been adopted by the Public Relations Society of America to promote and maintain high standard of public service and ethical conduct among its members.

(*a*) A member shall deal fairly with clients or employers, past and present, with fellow practitioners and the general public.

(*b*) A member shall conduct his or her professional life in accordance with the public interest.

(*c*) A member shall adhere to truth and accuracy and to generally accepted standards of good taste.

(*d*) A member shall not represent conflicting or competing interests without the express consent of those involved, given after a full disclosure of the facts; nor place himself or herself in a position where the member's interest is to many be in conflict with a duty to a client, or others, without a full disclosure of such interests to all involved.

(*e*) A member shall safeguard the confidence of present and former clients as well as of these persons or entities who have disclosed confidences to a member in the context of communication relating to an anticipated professional relationship with such member and shall not accept retainers or employment which may involve the disclosure or use of these confidences to the disadvantage or prejudice of such clients or employers.

(*f*) A member shall not engage in any practice which tend to corrupt the integrity or channels of communication or the process of government.

(*g*) A member shall not intentionally communicate false or misleading information and is obligated to use care to avoid communication of false or misleading information.

(*h*) A member shall be prepared to identify publicly the name of the client or employer on whose behalf any public communication is made.

(*i*) A member shall not make use of any individual or organisation purporting to serve or represent an announced cause, or purporting to be independent or unbiased, but actually serving an undisclosed special or private interest of a member, client or employer.

(*j*) A member shall not intentionally injure the professional reputation or practice of an other practitioner.

However, if a member has evidence that another member has been guilty of unethical illegal or unfair practices, including those in violation of this Code, the member shall present the information promptly to the proper authorities of the Society for action in accordance with the procedure set forth in Article XII of the Bylaws.

(*k*) A member called as a witness in a proceeding for the enforcement of this Code shall bound to appear, unless excused for sufficient reason by the Judicial Panel.

(*l*) A member, in performing services for a client or employer, shall not accept fees, commissions or any other valuable consideration from anyone other than the client or employer, given after a full disclosure of the facts.

(*m*) A member shall not guarantee the achievement of specified results beyond the member's direct control.

(*n*) A member shall, as soon as possible, sever relations with any organization or individual if such relationship requires conduct contrary to the articles of this Code.

### The International Public Relations Association (IPRA)

The International Public Relations Association (IPRA) was set-up as a para-national organisation in May, 1955, to raise standards of Public Relations practice in various countries and improve the professional quality and efficiency of Public Relations practitioners. An early achievement of the organisation was the adoption of a "Code of Conduct" for the purpose of establishing standards of professional ethics and conduct in the field of Public Relations for all members of the association worldwide. The IPRA code of the conduct has served as a basis for the formulation of a number of codes for National Public Relations and societies.

Along with this an International Code of Ethics was adopted by the IPRA Council at its meeting in Athens held in 1965. Because of this fact, this code is often referred to as the Code of Athens. This constitutes IPRA's moral charter, and its principles have also been inspired by the United Nations Declaration of Human Rights.

The Code of Athens is also given under which will give you an idea of the moral standards that are expected to inspire the activities of the Public Relations practitioners every country.

### Code of Athens

*Considering* that all member countries of the United Nations have agreed to abide by its character which reaffirms its "faith in fundamental human rights, in the dignity and worth of the human person" and that having regard to the very nature of their profession, Public Relations practitioners in these countries should undertake to ascertain and observe the principles set out in the character.

*Considering* that from 'right' human beings have not only physical or material needs but also intellectual, moral and social needs, and that their rights are of real benefit to them only insofar as these needs are essentially met.

*Considering* that, in the course of their professional duties and depending on how these duties are performed. Public Relations practitioners can substantially help to meet these intellectual, moral and social needs.

And, lastly, *considering* that the use of techniques enabling them to come simultaneously into contact with millions of people gives Public Relations practitioners a power that has to be restrained by the observance of a strict moral code.

On all these grounds, the undersigned Public Relations Associations hereby declare that they accept, as their moral character, the principles of the following Code of Ethics, and that if, in the light of evidence submitted to the Society, a member of these associations should be found to have infringed this Code in the course of his personal duties, he will be deemed to be guilty of serious misconduct calling for an appropriate penalty.

Accordingly, each member of these Associations:

***Shall Endeavour***

1. To contribute to the achievement of the moral and cultural conditions enabling human beings to reach their full stature and enjoy the rights to which they are entitled under the "Universal Declaration of Human Rights";
2. To establish communication patterns and channels which, by fostering the free flow of essential information, will make each member of the society in which he lives feel that he is being kept informed and also give him an awareness of his own personal involvement and responsibility and of his solidarity with other members;
3. To bear in mind that, because of the relationship between the profession and the public, his conduct even in private — will have an impact on the way in which the profession as whole is appraised;

4. To respect, in the course of his profession duties, the moral principles and rules of the "Universal Declaration of Human Rights";
5. To pay due regard to, and uphold, human dignity and to recognise the right of each individual to judge for himself;
6. To establish the moral, psychological and intellectual conditions for dialogue in its true sense, and to recognise the right of the parties involved to state their case and express their views.

*Shall Undertake*

7. To conduct himself always and in all circumstances in such a manner as deserve and secure the confidence of those with whom he comes into contact;
8. To act, in all circumstances, in such a manner as to take account of the respective interests of the parted involved both the interests of the organisation which he serves and the interests of the publics concerned;
9. To carry out his duties with integrity, avoiding language likely to lead to ambiguity or misunderstanding and to maintain loyalty to his clients or employers, whether past or present.

*Shall Refrain From*

10. Subordinating the truth to other requirements;
11. Circulating information which is not based on established and ascertainable facts;
12. Taking part in any venture or undertaking which is unethical or dishonest or capable of impairing human dignity and integrity;
13. Using any "manipulative" methods or techniques designed to create sub-conscious motivations which the individual cannot control of his own free will and so cannot be held accountable for the action taken on them.

## Code of Ethics in India

In the early days in India there were people who masqueraded as Public Relations consultants but were in reality fixers and manipulators who indulged in unethical practices to get favourable decisions for their clients from the government or other authorities or to secure licences for them.

The first All India Conference of Public Relations Practitioners, therefore, found it necessary to formally adopt the International Code of Ethics to demarcate the genuine Public Relations practitioners from manipulators. This was an important step in development of professionalism in Public Relations in India.

Having adopted these Codes of Conduct and Ethics, Associations of Public Relations practitioners all over the world continuously monitor the activities of their members and deal with case of infringements of these codes. In India too one of the main functions of the Public Relations Society of India (PRSI) is to ensure that standards are maintained that the skill and efficiency of the Public Relations practitioners in the country are raised through training, education and research programmes.

The question of human rights and the observance of ethical standards is a matter of concern for humanity as a whole for all organisations and all professionals, be they accountants, bankers or doctors. It is even more so for a Public Relations professional as it deals with influencing public opinion. This is because the Public Relations Manager in any organisation is expected to function as its conscience-keeper.

The pressures that create ethical dilemmas in the government, business, universities, family relations, and all other spheres, also affect the field of Public Relations: emphasis on immediate gains and extreme monetary benefits; lowering of all standards resulting from overzealous desires to provide benefit to the backward classes, emphasis on materialism and desire for self-gratification, etc. Another factor is the doctrine of management by objective, with its emphasis on the end result becoming the overwhelming criterion in all decision-making.

The importance of ethics is as important to Public Relations as to any other profession. Those who are responsible for ensuring that the organisation they serve be value based, must necessarily observe strictly the principles of morality and ethics, themselves. Having established the need for ethics, we will now examine in detail where ethics comes into Public Relations activity and how it is handled.

Public Relations has now become a vital function affecting management decisions and influencing public opinion in every non-profit or profit making organisation. Almost forgotten now are the extravagant claims of those who spoke of public relations in the terminology of a new way of life, a philosophy, almost a religion. The merits of ensuring that mutual understanding is achieved by the skilled analysis of attitudes, the planning of programmes of action, and the carrying through of deliberate communication by a great variety of techniques, have won recognition in their own right. Public Relations passed through tumults phases before evolving as a profession and gaining universal status. Today PR is indispensable for any organisation because of the recognition of rights of expression and freedom of information; advance in telecommunication and transport; opening up of traditionally closed societies and increasing globalisation; governments employing public relation practice for staying in power and growth in business, amalgamations, collaborations, operating with subsidiaries, spreading across national boundaries and in different cultures.

### Listing the Unethical Practices in Public Relations

In the early growth stages of Public Relations there were quite a few people posing a Public Relations persons but working as press agents who indulged in puffery and other unethical practices to achieve their ends. This wrought considerable damage to the discipline and it has been difficult for Public Relations profession to outgrow such labels as 'white washing', 'sugar coating', 'fixing', 'propaganda' etc., even today.

The PR man in his relations with his colleagues, his competitors, and his employers, he is on surer ground. It is accepted that it is unethical to injure the reputation or practice of a fellow public relations man, to endeavour to supplant him with his client or employer, or to encroach upon his business in any way. This includes the soliciting of work by unfair means, such as misrepresenting another's ability or reputation, or implying that his work could be performed better or cheaper.

The common practice of agency and consultancy executives leaving their employer and taking with them certain accounts so that they may set-up a business of their own may be ethical dubious, although when agreement has been reached among all parties this procedure is quite proper.

There will always remain issues that cannot be decided by rule nor even by generally accepted practice. These must be a matter for the social, moral, and professional conscience of the individual. The responsibility of the public relations man is to remain alert at all times to the ethical aspects of his work, to act honestly and decently, to guard his loyalties and to respect the integrity of other. When all else fails, and his attitudes, advice, and opinions are not respected, his ultimate action must be to resign from the job.

It is a difficult task to describe what is ethical and what is unethical. It would be simpler to state it as a matter of choosing between the right and wrong options in keeping with conscience. Anything that causes dissonance in the mind brings about a feeling a guilt and dishonesty. And dishonest communication cannot be an aid to cementing relationship. Public are also not to be underestimated as fools. As Abraham Lincoln said, "You can fool some people all the time, and all of the people some of the time, but you cannot fool all the people all of the time."

Would you use your talents to promote some concept or cause that you believe to be wrong? A typical example is smiling which is a proven health hazard. In spite of this knowledge, is it right to publicise a cigarette? Dilemma situations like this are many wherein you are liable to get confused. Yet basically, it is important to have faith in the organisation or the cause that you are working for. Otherwise you cannot do a good job. You must be yourself convinced before trying to convince others. There are a number of acts that could be classified as unethical, ranging from suppressing of news to misleading the audience. It include: suppressing unfavourable news; misrepresenting facts; undercutting a competitor; purporting to serve a cause but actually serving some other interest; promising results that cannot be obtained and use of undesirable methods towards pressurising editors for carrying publicity material.

The above only shows that like in other professions, there is scope for abuse in Public Relations too. It is also often thought that wrong doing can be altered by effective Public Relations. This misconception also need to be done away with Public Relations recognises a long-term responsibility and seeks to persuade and to achieve mutual understanding by securing the willing acceptance of attitudes and ideas. It can succeed only when the basic policy is ethical, and the means used are truthful. In Public Relations, the ends can never justify the use of false, harmful or questionable means.

It is impossible to use Public Relations techniques to counter a weak case. We have instance of the Watergate scandal which rocked the entire world and which has large Public Relations staff of the President of the United States could do nothing about. Similarly, if a service industry like a public transport corporation is not running its buses properly or punctually, no Public Relations technique would help to brighten the image of that corporation in the eyes of the public—the communities. Or if a chemical factory's effluents were contaminating the environment, do you think a Public Relations gimmick would help in stemming the public outrage against it? For this reason, it is often stressed that good Public Relations, like charity, must start at home, and that denials never convince the doubting listeners. Public Relations, therefore, has not only to be practical and positive, but also be always ethical.

## Analysing the Impacts of Public Relation on Society

There are no suitable yardsticks by which Public Relations impacts can be measured. Publication of press releases may be a tangible sign but still it does not mean that it has been read by the target audience; it has been understood as desired by the source; it has brought about a change in the attitude of the receiver.

Besides, it is difficult to view the results of Public Relations activity in isolation. There may be other factors e.g., an increase in the sale of unsaturated oils could be related to the non.-availability of other brands of vanaspati rather than to the results of the campaign. Again, it is also not possible to bring about changes in attitudes by merely exposing the target audience repeatedly to ideas. We have examples of drug education programmes, anti-dowry or anti-liquor, anti-smoking campaigns, yet the malady lingers. This is because of these kinds of 'social engineering efforts' as they are called, require a lot of research into the communicator to be able to transmit the necessary messages into the minds of the audience to bring about a change in them.

At the same time, we are aware of the importance of skillful mediation and information communication role of Public Relations as an essential service to the society. This necessitates a closer scrutiny of what Public Relations does or achieves. We will begin by examining its dual role that of information and persuasion to see how far they are fulfilled by Public Relations.

When Ralph Waldo Emerson produced his aphorism about the world beating a path to your door if you made a better mousetrap, he was demonstrably correct in terms of a society where deliberate communication was virtually limited to religion, politics, education, and current affairs for most people the media of communication where newspapers, pamphlets and books, speeches and lectures, and most powerful of all-individual word-of-mouth report and comment.

The fame of a better mousetrap might lead to newspaper reports, read by a far smaller public than today's marker's reputation would be built and sustained by those who talked favourably about him. Small businesses operating in small communities where there was little demand upon people's mental time and receptive powers did not need to use the skills of the professional communicator for their messages to be acceptable and understandable.

Now there is rapid transport over any distance and instant communication around the world. The small business have taken their place as parts of large industries and the small communities are seen as part of one vast industrialized society. Television commercials assault the eye and ear in Bangkok as much as in Birmingham. Coloured magazine advertisements tempt readers in Helsinki and Hawaii, offering the same brands through the same selling techniques. The latest news from the remotest area is seen and read everywhere within hours and may be watched as it happens via telecommunications satellite.

The demands of every form of communication upon the time and receptive capacities of men and women in the advanced nations has increased enormously over the past twenty years, and is increasing still. At the same time, the media of communication have grown in number and complexity. Communication itself has become a twentieth century skill, or rather a group of skills with the attendant need for professionalism and the resolution of ethical problems.

This does not mean, however, that public relations is a new phenomenon. The first man who had a product to barter, the first leader with an idea to convey had an involvement in public relations: they needed to find their audiences and get their messages across effectively.

The tavern keeper who started the tradition of hanging a bush outside his door to indicate that he sold drink was engaged in advertising. The later tavern keeper who devise the phrase "good wine needs no bush" was alert to public relations, because he realized that, in his business, reputation was more important than merely making an announcement.

The demagogues of the past, from Tamburlaine to Hitler, crudely practice some of the techniques of public relations. They knew their audiences and what they card about, whether it was loot or nationalism, and they fired their imaginations by conveying to them dramatic concepts couched in colourful words. Their effectiveness derived much, of course, from the ruthlessness of their approach, careless of the effect on others, and the single-minded directness of their propaganda. They were not troubled over the morality of their actions; for them the end justified the means.

Today, society having learned something from the past, the terms of reference of communication have largely changed. The audience is better educated and more people are equipped and willing to make objective judgements on the messages they receive. At the same time, the forelock-touching meekness of previous centuries has long been left behind by the average western man and there is everywhere an impassioned belief in the right to be told what is going on and why. The objectives of those who communicate are constantly and rightly questioned; there is much healthy scepticism and the mealy-mounted can expect no mercy.

The checks and balances of what is known as "civilized society have brought about a situation in Public Relations Expert" Public Relations work by its very nature must have a high measure of ethical contents. Scott Cutlip of USA states that "A basic requirement for a profession is adherence to a set of professional norms and refers to the various codes of professional standards for Public Relations practice as examples of the efforts " to advance the ethics in this field.

## Reconsidering the Organisational Goals to Public Interest

In Public Relations the exercise of identifying the policies and programmes of an organisation with the public interest is of crucial importance. This has been made amply clear in Unit Indeed, among the various definitions 'of Public Relations quite a few, place the main emphasis on this aspect of Public Relations. As we have seen, the well-known American journal "Public Relation News", edited by Denny Griswold has emphasised that "Public Relations the management function which evaluates public attitudes, identifies the policies and procedures of an individual or an organisation with the public interest…."

Another American authority, Prof. Edward J. Robinson of Boston University also gives prominence to this aspect of Public Relations in his definition of Public Relations. According to him, "Public Relations as an applied social and behavioural science is that function which measures, evaluates and interprets the attitude of various relevant publics; assists management in defining objectives for increasing public understanding and acceptance of the organisation's products, plans, policies and personnel; equates these objectives with the interests, needs and goals of the various relevant publics; and develops, executes and evaluates a programme to earn public understanding and acceptance."

The aspect of public interest is so important that it not only a part of the definition of Public Relations but is given priority in the various codes of professional conduct adopted by different Public Relations Associations. For instance, the very first item in the code of Professional Conduct of the Institute of Public Relations of the U.K. states, "A member shall conduct his professional activities with respect for public interest." The Code of Professional Standards of the Public Relations Society of America (PRSA) states in its second article that "A member shall conduct his or professional life in accordance with the public interest."

Ethics practiced by the Public Relations persons vary widely as they too remain immune from the society they serve. Also, adoption of code of ethics is no guarantee that ethicality will prevail in all dealings. Codes can only provide guidance. There is no punishment for insolation of code, not is there any licensing of practitioners as this could mean infringement of a democratic right to freedom of occupation. Yet it is imperative for a Public Relations practitioner to be self-regulating as also be careful about the legal aspects of communication.

With the dissemination of knowledge the consumers and public have became aware of their rights and a Public Relations person may have to deal with pressure groups like trade unions, consumer protection groups, environment protection activities etc. A wrong act on the part of a PRCO because of ignorance of legal aspect can cause legal trouble for the company. Hence, it is better to be aware of legal considerations and work a legal team or seek advice in order to forestall litigation.

Messages should not be deceptive or unfair to the consumer. Misleading financial releases can be a deadly weapon and invite severe penalties as there are laws to protect the investor from unscrupulous traders with 'inside' knowledge.

Minimise credibility gaps by honest and accurate corporate communication; avoid false promise in news releases do not make exaggerated claims or promises about product, services or organisations; keep in mind increasing consumer litigation and use simple clear language instead of using phoney phrases; place greater emphasis on research to increase credibility maintain loyalty and commitment to your organisation, the society and to the system as a whole. Keep yourself upto date by constant reviewing and understand media process thoroughly and be scrupulously accurate are some of the guidelines to promote ethically in the professionalism of PR.

Changing social attitudes have since forced a new responsiveness and sense of responsibility in official and commercial like. The average man's belief that he is entitled to be told is gradually becoming matched by a sense of accountability that was largely missing from life and affairs as little as thirty years ago.

Governments are felt to be more directly accountable to the electorate, and MPs to their constituents. Boards of directors can no longer dispose the ordinary shareholders money without adequate explanation. Local authorities are unlocking the doors of their committees to press and public. Industrial concerns can expect a bitter reaction if they offend in some way against the communities around them. Each part of society is felt to be accountable to the rest for its policies and actions.

It is in this social climate that an appreciation of public relations as a management and advisory function has slowly been won, not by words but by the deeds of the professional communicators who have proved the value of their work in all walks of life. They have managed to make it plain that planned communication, ethically conducted from the base of a soundly consider policy, is a worthy and valuable activity.

There was a period, after the Industrial Revolution, when the captains of business and industry thought that their only responsibility was to make a profit. Following the Great Depression of the early 30s, public opinion became hostile to business and felt that it has behaved irresponsibly. A certain measure of state and social responsibility of business was born. It was accepted that part from its responsibility of making a profit and ensuring a fair return to its shareholders, every business organisation had a stake in the social environment and must make a contribution towards its continued existence and improvement. Now-a-days, almost all business organisations try to make some contribution to the public welfare outside the scope of their normal activities.

Following from the concept of social responsibility, there is a growing body of opinion that an organisation's social responsibility should be monitored and evaluated by an independent organisation. The list of areas in which a business organisation is now expected to make a contribution keeps growing, and is already quite a formidable one. To ensure that it is not found wanting in any of these areas, that its performance is in accordance with social expectations, many business organisations in the world subject themselves to a regular social audit, which is as stringent and as systematic as the audit to which their accounts are subjected. So far, there is no statutory obligation in any country with regard to social audit, but many organisations are submitting to such an audit voluntarily, and by doing so, brightening their image in the public eye. The areas that are generally covered in the social audit include : (*a*) safety, (*b*) employee welfare, (*c*) environmental pollution, (*d*) quality control and (*e*) community development.

It may be difficult for an organisation to fulfil all the expectations that society and various pressure groups have and at the same time fulfil its primary function of running a business at a reasonable profit. But it is necessary that it should examine its performance against an exhaustive check list and consider whether any modification in existing policies and procedures is called for. It is this examination which is being referred to as social audit. A social audit of this nature may be carried out by an outside agency or by an internal social audit group. Obviously, an outside agency would be able to give a more objective assessment, but even an internal audit would be useful, if the internal audit team is allowed to function freely.

## Revisiting the PR Methods

The growth of awareness of public relations and the increase in the number of practitioners has been phenomenal over the past twenty years. The recognition of the need for organized public relations activity has been equally remarkable.

No era of rapid growth is without its problems. Public relations practice has been no exception. It has been one of the major difficulties of practitioners to carve out their place in business life and society. Their own difficulty has been matched by that of the users of public relations services in trying to work out where the PR people fit in the structure of management.

In the process there have been many misunderstandings and misconceptions on both sides. Some of them still linger. In the early twenties of this century, when the first public relations consultancy was formed, it concentrated on publicity. Over the years the allied functions of promotion publicity, and organized public relations practice grew at uneven rates. If the growth were illustrated on a graph it would show a fairly recongnizable pattern. The different jobs met and parted steadily. They diverged wildly, overlapped frequently. Slowly they came closer and close together and began to run along parallel lines. Most public relations men are now agreed on where each part fits, even though they may disagree on matters of emphasis or method.

Since all public relations is concerned with human beings it is not surprising that the development of its practice have been over shadowed by human beings. Clever men, stupid men, sharp men, honest men, dishonest men and women—have all appeared on the public relations scene. Some have been larger than life. Some have crashed in a spectacular fashion. With the development of expose and in-depth journalism, the spotlight has been turned more than once on pressure groups. Inevitably this has sometimes included public relations men.

It is in the nature of public relations that it is difficult to explain exactly where it fits. This has left the door wide open for the intellectuals. At the same time, the techniques of communication and the need for it are constantly changing. Nobody who was in public relations practice twenty years ago doing the job the same way now as he did it then.

The first operators have had the twin tasks of learning the job while they did it and trying to create the conditions in which they could do it properly. They have had to work out for themselves and examine what relationship they should have or need to have with other in management. They have also had to present their needs in such a way that they could not be accused of merely seeking status. They have often not succeeded. Equally, when they have succeeded it has not always been for the right reasons. A man may have been able to walk his proper path along the corridors of power because he had luck, or because he married his employer's daughter, or because he choose his staff well. His ability to exercise judgement, to achieve the right public relations results for his employer by his sheer efficiency or professionalism, may never have entered in to it.

Basically speaking any organization—commercial or industrial undertaking, government, voluntary body—should consider the public relations consequences of any action it proposes to take. It does not matter whether those consequences are immediately beneficial or harmful, short-term or long-term, major or minor. It should always remember that there will be an effect of some sort on some part of its state of public relations. Any organization must retain the right to decide to ignore the consequences, provided it is clearly understood that ignoring then does not make them go away. If that premise is acceptable—and it must be—then it is also the duty of the organization to have available the best public relations advice it can afford. It goes without saying that, having go it, should use it.

There are two aspects of public relations advice in this context. One concerns the principles involved, the other the methods. It is in this dichotomy that public relations people have found one of their biggest problems.

Public relations men do not have the sole prerogative of ideas or ability to gauge human reactions. Many of them have believed that they do indeed have this prerogative and have become hidebound. They have also become presumptuous. For example, in the floating of a new issue of shares, a stock broker is just as capable of knowing likely reactions as a PRO; in most instances he will probably know much better. The public relations man can skills entitle him to a place at the decision-making table, but once there he is no marathon a man among his peers. It is because too many people in the past have tried to insist that theirs should be the sole deciding counsel that public relations has been exposed to many of the attacks upon it.

Once a decision has been taken the public relations man comes into his own. It becomes his job often, but not always, alone to communicate the decision, to interpret it, to maximize or minimize its impact. This is what he must be trained to do.

It is from this second part that the attitude of many public relations people has arisen. They are fond of explaining carefully that they are advocates. They add that it is their duty to communicate facts, opinions and decisions whether they agree with them or not. In this they are right. Of course, it is always open to them to resign of they disagree fundamentally with a decision.

Once the need to communicate has arisen, the public relations practitioner can begin to work with other people. And in so doing he must understand the ways they work and the rules by which they work. This is an area of human relationship which he must study carefully if he is to succeed. There are many simple examples of this. They have to do with the method chosen for communication.

If advertising is the method then he needs to understand how advertising works and how advertising men work. He may feel that the advertising schedule would include a magazine he known is read by the chairman's wife because this will please her. He must listen when the advertising man carefully explains that by doing this the public relations man firstly will not reach the people he wishes to influence and secondly will have to miss out a publication which is vital. The advertising man knows what he is talking about. The PRO may at the end of it all decide for a variety of reasons that the magazine must be included, but at least his decision will have been reached after hearing the facts.

If he communicates to shareholders, the public relations man must listen to the company secretary, who will explain the rules of the Stock Exchange. However, wrong either may think those rules, they must be observed.

The closing of a factory is a further example of the two-headed problem that is at the root of many of the difficulties both side users and practitioners—experience in setting the right place for public relations in management structure. The decision to close a factory is hard to make. It is dictated by many factors and can only be taken by the directors of a company after long, serious thought. Some of its effects will be obvious; some will not be seen until later. The directors most closely concerned in the reaching of the final decision will probably be the managing director, the financial director and the production director. The views of the sales director or marketing director will be sought. At some point, the views of the public relations expert—be he director or not should also be sought. It is not an essential prerequisite that he should be a member of the board. It is only essential that he should be brought in as early as possible.

There are many reasons why public relations people are not called in as early as they would like. Their professionalism could have been higher in the past. The readiness of directors to hear public relations advice could have come more quickly.

If the senior representative of public relations in a company is not a director, then he must work to one. If it is true that public relations is a management function then he must report to the chief executive, whether that is the chairman, the managing director, or another senior director. In practice, he will also almost certainly woke with other directors. There are many facets of a company's operations which involve public relations techniques and need public relations advice but which do not involve board decisions. It is a matter of debate what position the public relations man needs if he is to exercise his function properly and not become a slave to be pushed around by anybody. It is impossible to generalize on this question since it can only be related to the particular structure of the company in which he works.

A further consideration is that just as the function of public relations is to pass information both inwards and outwards, so the public relations man himself must be a bridge between the different islands that comprise a company. He must be equally acceptable—and for good reasons—to the directors and to the personnel on the factory floor or at the sales point. He must be impartial. He must never grind the axe of one side against another.

To understand all this it is necessary to consider briefly the structure of a normal commercial organization, whether it actually manufactures goods or provides a service.

The running of the company is in the hands of management, usually a board of directors. Not all board members necessarily work full-time in the company, but some will. The chairman may be the chairman of many companies, but in each, he will fulfil the same function of over all direction and of the ultimate responsibility to the shareholders. The broad day-to-day control of the company will be in the hands of a managing director. Around him will be specialist full-time directors covering finance, production, marketing, sales, export, research and development, personnel, and so on. They will draw the information which allows them to do their jobs from what is often called 'middle management' departmental heads who should be the directors of the future. These will include the public relations man, the advertising man, and a host of others.

This is not the place to argue whether the marketing director is more important in the scheme of things than the finance director, or the sales director, or the production director. It is important to record that the public relations officer faces one special difficulty. He becomes involved with all the directors, since every activity the company undertakes produces a public relations reaction. Thus the more senior he is the easier it is for him to put his point of view with some hope success. What he has to do is to earn whatever standing he gains.

Once again, it is almost impossible to make sensible generalizations. In a company making motor-cars and having a bad record of labour relations the most vital function of the public relations man for some years may be to concentrate on that aspect of the business. If, that is, so he will work extremely closely with the personnel director, but much less with the marketing director. In another company making say, plastic toys the important job may be to earn the goodwill of children. This will bring the public relations man into close contact with the marketing or sales director. It is merely a question of setting the right priorities and then adhering to them.

The public relations consultancy, large or small, is a slightly different situation. There is no genuine clash of interests between the consultant and the staff man; indeed, many staff men deliberately use consultants. The consultancy's resources in terms of people also give it flexibility in carrying out the work. Many companies use consultancies... "to obtain an independent outside view and a wider range of experience, skill and talent then would normally be available economically within a single organization.'

The Public Relations Consultants Associations (PRCA) grew out of the Institute of Public Relations and maintains close working links with it. Whereas institute memberships open only to individuals, PRCA membership is for firms. They must have been in business for a prescribed time and either provide comprehensive themselves or be in a position to recommend services from other firms. The Association publishes a code of practice, similar to that of the Institute, and a list of members with their clients. Not all consultancies belong to the PRCA.

Up to now, the comments have been dealing with what can properly be termed the 'creative' public relations practitioners. This means those who conceive programmes of activity, even if they may sometimes also implement them. However, there are many people in the whole field of public relations, who hold down what may be termed 'passive' jobs. This will include press officers, information officers, house magazine editors, assistant executives in public relations consultancies or agencies and others.

The distinction between 'creative' and 'passive' is not intended to cast a slur on the latter. A press officer is called upon to exercise his initiative and ingenuity in the implementation of a programme. He is expected to contribute as much as he can to the creation of that programme. In certain circumstances more his time may go into answering press queries than in trying to generate press interest in a subject. He is not given the responsibility for the total programme, but only for part of it. He is therefore working to general direction.

The organization and structure of a public relations department must be settled at the beginning. Its size is dictated by the scope of the job it is trying to undertake. The public relations needs and duties of a small company making cricket bats are clearly not comparable to those of a major civil engineering contractor. The cricket bat manufacturer would probably need only one man, or part of an executive in a consultancy. The contractor may need a number of specialists—mostly on the staff, but possibly also outside consultants—and someone to coordinate their work. This can lead to the growth of a large department.

Basically, there are three jobs to be done. One is the creation of a programme of activity, which carries with it the responsibility of ensuring that the programme is undertaken properly. This is followed by the job of disseminating information, as for the press or for internal use. The third job is the handling of print and other techniques.

As the practice of public relations becomes more professional, and the definition of its tasks more exact, it becomes less and less possible for a one-man department to do a proper job. An organization of any size should employ specialists and may well expect to have at least three people in its public relations department, who in turn will need a minimum of two secretaries. From that base the department will grow to whatever size is needed. In the process, one of the main tasks of the manager will be to see that the growth does out of hand.

Public Relations, as you know, is the "Art of creating mutual understanding between an organisation and its various-publics." "Public" in Public Relations parlance mean those group or groups of people whose opinion has a direct bearing on the functioning of an organisation. A typical organisation will have employees, shareholders, dealers, stockists, government, media and the public at large, as its "Publics." In fact, publics for different organisations will vary according to the nature of the organisation. To reach these "Publics", the Public Relations practitioner has to decide the media and the channels which will be most suitable. If an organisation has to disseminate information to a rural audience, where the literacy rate is negligible, what should be the best media which is cost effective? Newspapers obviously, will not be suitable, because the concerned target audience are unlettered. Then, what options does the Public Relations practitioner have? Depending on the availability of the budget, it can be radio, TV, interpersonal communication or traditional media. In order to make communication effective, you have to keep in view the message, the media and the audience.

Here we discuss the various media available to Public Relation professionals for reaching the varied target groups and their relative advantages or limitations. The choice of media will obviously depend on the audience, availability of funds and the time frame and the objectives of the message.

### Evaluating the Publicity Media

Media used for publicity are necessarily the mass media. Mass media as the name suggests are media which reach the mass spread over a vast area simultaneously. The Press, TV, Radio, Films and documentaries among others, comprise the publicity media. Mass media constitute a nation's public information system—a system in which the Public Relations practitioner play an important role by disseminating information. Let us examine the media options available to a Public Relations practitioner and how best they can use it for achieving the communication goals. Choice of publicity media will, however, depend on the needs of the organisation and aims of publicity, types of audience to be reached, the aims of publicity and the available budget.

## The Press

The Indian independence movement to attain the freedom from the British was noteworthy. The role of the Indian Press and its contribution in the country's freedom struggle were well-known. Press serves which reflects and moulds public opinion. In India the Press considered to be as a fundamental institution despite the factors of illiteracy and the advent of TV, newspapers continue to be the dominant medium which set the public agenda, disseminate information and shape public opinion.

The Press in India has grown in size, circulation and specialization at all levels—national, regional and local levels. Besides the business/financial dailies the national and local dailies too have regular columns on industry, trade, development etc. Thus, publicity through the Press is a popular and effective tool with maximum impact. The government, public and private sectors, and non-profit organisations use columns of newspapers to disseminate information to their publics.

There is a growing crop of specialised magazines catering to professional groups, business and industry. The explosion of magazines is seen even in regional languages for new audience with new interests. Besides the general circulation magazines and news magazines, there are periodicals catering to lucrative market of consumers, shareholders, tourism, textiles, women, computers, automobiles, etc. Magazines have become livelier, glossier and interpretative in content. Magazines are attractive in appearance, have excellent reproduction quality and can be kept for reference. They are read at leisure and have a longer lifespan. This makes magazine publicity a must for organisations who can reach selected audience through chosen periodicals.

The Public Relations, professionals, as the spokesperson of the organisation decides how and when the activities, policies for programmes of the organisation are to be projected to the public through the press. Information may be given to the Press in a variety of ways like press release, features, article backgrounders, etc.

It is important for you to remember as a Public Relations Officer (PRO) that information of your organisation has to compete with similar information emanating from various other organisations; so you must be carefully about the newsworthiness and timing of your news releases to ensure its publication.

News from organisations, also known as press releases, is the most common type of publicity. Organisations serve as source materials for media and hence they should provide such news and facts which will be of interest to the readers. Whether, the content has to do with planned activity like a major order bagged, or with spontaneous event like an accident.

While preparing a press release the PR professional must bear in mind certain tips like to indicate clearly the name organisation, address and telephone number along with the sender's name, designation, etc., give the date for the release; evaluate the contents should be newsworthy, error—free and written in a journalistic style and typed on one side of the sheet only; ensure it be brief and unambiguous; win a headline and it should be signed and it should be released well on time for publication.

A public relations person, having good rapport with the media and having sufficient persuasive skills, can recommend subjects for editorials by providing background material and suggesting possible lines of approach. A sufficient knowledge of the editorial policy helps to identify the most suitable medium. Newsworthy material on special events, anniversaries, landmarks, achieved, major policy changes or any controversial issues could serve as themes for editorials.

Columnists are always on the lookout for newsworthy material. At the same time, industry, trade and business houses often need publicity through feature articles to fulfil their marketing objectives. A feature of article thus becomes an ideal tool to talk about a common problem and suggest their product as the solution. These articles could be prepared by the public relations personnel or got done through a columnist by appropriate briefing.

This is yet another means that could be used by the public relation person to put forward the views of the organisation to inform people to correct a wrong impression. Since letters to the editor are a feedback from the public, those letters which make a forceful point, do get published without difficulty.

## Television

Television has great force and scope as a publicity medium—a medium which allows the use of the printed words, spoken word, pictures in motion, colour, music, animation and sound effects, all blended into one. With satellite communication having become a reality, the impact of TV is persuasive, worldwide and powerful. TV has come to be a dramatic and the most intimate mass medium. It has prestige value too, besides having an important role to play in our socio-economic development. Hence TV is an effective medium for developmental news also. Both, the Public Relations practitioners and the mass media depend on each other for news. Depending on the occasion the Public Relations practitioner can approach TV with a news release about his organisation and similarly a TV station representative can approach him for news. Public relations practitioners can make use of the medium by providing filmed news release to the TV stations. The news release will not be accepted, if it is too sales-oriented or resembles a paid commercial advertisement. The best approach will be to take a low profile approach in which the company presents facts of or information or educational nature. Non-profit organisations have better chances of publicising their activities over Doordarshan as they are non-commercial. With the arrival of cable television and growing competition among television companies, the publicist in India has unprecedent opportunities to cash in on. Industrial news, business programmes, development features, interviews, talks, discussions analytical programmes can all be used with great advantage besides the use of short telefilms, or sponsoring of popular programmes.

TV being a visual medium, it will pay dividends to make the news release or features, action-oriented and colourful for greater impact.

To decide a newsworthy subject and to identify a producer for the purpose are the two major tasks. TV stations accepts professional U-matic tapes and not unprofessional half-inch video tapes which are used in marriages, birthday parties, etc. Ideally, a TV news release should not exceed 90 seconds. The story should be arranged in an "inverted pyramid" style. The most important news should be arranged in the beginning and the less important in descending order so that the editor, with one look at the release picks up the important sequences. After the film footage is shot, the edited version will need voice cast, music, etc., which should also be carefully selected. You can send an edited film clip with a written script indicating the visual input in the film alongside, to enable the news reader to lend his/her voice over.

On special occasions, like a major landmark achieved by our company, or a crisis situation say a fire, or any disaster, the TV team may approach you for coverage. As a Public Relations practitioner, you must facilitate the coverage by providing them access to the place and supply background information about the occasion. Whenever, the coverage is after a crisis situation, the management's point of view should be included.

### Radio

Radio, like TV, can be effectively used in Public Relations. In India the radio covers more than 90 per cent of the population. It is a mobile medium with flexibility since no other medium can match. Radio is a mass medium, which possesses the qualities of a direct personal medium as it uses the spoken word and human voice for the most part to convey its message.

We were aware that news bulletins are broadcast over the radio at fixed intervals throughout the day. The Public Relations practitioners whether from the private or the public sector, can use radio as outlets for news about the company's performance and news developments etc. The All India Radio's code however does not permit to mention of the name of a private company in a news bulletin or news reel. News is selected for broadcast based on its newsworthiness to the listeners. A radio news release should be written in radio style so that it can be used by an announcer without much editing.

Besides news, the All India Radio has a number of programmes pertaining to current affairs, industry, panel discussions, etc., which can be appropriately utilised by the practitioners. In fact, AIR especially the local stations, look for development stories. Public relation personnel can serve as a news source for the broadcasting stations. Popular programmes can be sponsored by the company.

### Films

The shift in our dependence from words to picture, has made for the most profound changes in the way we think, learn and see the world. Film/documentaries make a powerful impact on the audience because of their audio-visual qualities. Films can be made on different formats like 35 mm, 16 mm and video. As a Public Relations professional we need not necessarily be expert film-makers, but we do need a working knowledge about the various aspects of film- making. This will facilitate decision-making, appreciating the inputs and providing guidelines to the producer.

Films as a Public Relations medium can be utilised in the following ways. They can be used for the internal or external public. IT could even be a documentary on the organisation. One could even sponsor a film for the Films Division under the Information & Broadcasting Ministry.

When a producer is hired, the public relations person is expected to provide guidelines on the aim of the film, content, length, presentation, background material and information about the target audience. Films could be used for training employees, educating consumers, development efforts for community relations or to build motivation among employees, or safety precautions, or company's achievements or ever for coverage of special occasions.

### Video

In the last decade or so, most of the films, except those for theatrical viewing, are being produced on the video format. The videotape has revolutionalised communication in the field of entertainment, information and education. Video equipment has the advantage of playing back the image and the sound immediately. It does not need processing as in the case of film. It is possible to reshoot on the same film, if the results are not satisfactory. Synchronised sound is possible with every video recorder and if necessary different, sounds tracks can be superimposed on a sound track, using a different language or dialect. Videotapes can be updated; in other words, a few shots can be replaced for updating the programme without disturbing the rest of the programme. Video also has the choice of computer backed special effects. When we compare the cost and time frame, video works out economical.

The video equipment is delicate and susceptible to moisture. The videotapes may get jammed or damaged with repeated use. As compared to film the videotape has a shorter life span. Videotapes are both professional and non-professional. The half-inch unprofessional equipment does not have much scope for editing.

The editing is done from tape-to-tape, but the special effects for dramatic effects. As film making is expensive, time-consuming and cumbersome, more and more Public Relations professionals use video films.

Besides the use of popular media, organisations may have to resort to other approaches to communication. While a local organisation may derive adequate satisfaction from using local media and the very simple and traditional media like bulletin boards, posters or even rural fairs/festivals, the more aggressive and large corporations like multinationals, have to use the more sophisticated technologies like E-Mail, Facsimile, teleconferencing etc, for exchange of information. Computing, data communication facilities and use of network linked through high-capacity multipurpose satellites in international system, affords worldwide access to specialised information.

Technological innovations have opened up a vast range of possibilities, each of which has immense potentials, depending on the situational needs.

## Oral Communications

Oral communication is used as a medium chiefly in employee communication for training them or informing them about the company's policies. It is also used in consumer, dealer, community and stockholder relation programmes. Oral communication may be carried on through meetings, telephone calls, public address system, panel discussions, counselling etc. Informed conversation between supervisors and subordinates also fall under this category. However, formal communication programmes are the responsibility of the public relation department. Oral communication is very effective, speedy, and with little expenses. However, it has limitations in that it may be forgotten quickly or partly understood as one cannot refer back to it. Let us examine some major tools of oral communication:

### *Meetings*

A meeting is the coming together of two or more persons. It could be just a meeting of two department heads, a small group meeting, committee meeting etc. Yet every meeting is arranged with some purpose e.g., to resolve conflicts, brief the employees, solve problems, obtain reactions to a new scheme etc.

Meetings are planned by sending notices containing the agenda, well in advance to members, to enable them to prepare for the meeting. All arrangements must be made for smooth conduct of the meeting. Listening is important and hence every participant must be given a chance to speak. The chairman must initiate, direct and control the discussion and facilitate reaching of conclusion.

### *Speeches*

Formal speeches are the quickest way of conveying information. Preparation of speeches and sometimes delivering the speech are jobs of the Public Relations department. Speakers must be trained and knowledgeable. The Public Relations department may also form a speakers bureau from among the volunteer speakers who are the executives of the company and possess competence on the relevant subject. The public relations department may help in research, speech writing and training of speakers.

The content of the speech must be newsworthy and of public interest. The timing and venue should be considered carefully. Any crisis message should be conveyed in a dignified and composed manner. Voice should be well modulate with sufficient pauses in between.

### Printed Literature

Every organisation, whether in business or service, whether commercial or non-profit making, needs publicity literature to promote its products, services or activities. These can take various forms like house journals, annual reports, brochures, catalogues, booklets, leaflets, direct mail etc. The objective of all these remain more less the same—to inform or persuade a target audience about a product, service or idea. We will now examine a few of these in detail to find out more about their mode of use.

In this chapter, we learnt that mass media reaches out to many people at the same time. It is difficult to know whether or not the target audience we wanted to reach out to really has read, seen or listened to a message. In selective media, in contrast, the target audience is identifiable. A house journal among others is a selective media and we can identify the audience.

There are two house journals viz. internal and external (1)The internal house journal is one of the important tools for effective employee communication. (2) The external house journals, however, aim at some segments of external 'publics' like dealers, shareholders, etc. A third type is a combination of both internal and external, meant for employees as well as external publics.

The primary objective of a house is to create a forum for exchange of thought and vision on various issues concerning an organisation and its employees. A house journal, if carefully produced, serves as an important link between a management and its various employees. With corporations becoming large, multi-dimensional and multi-locational, a house journal reaches employees belonging to different disciplines, cadres and interests, thus bridging the gap and creating a fellow-feeling among them.

Formats of house journals differ depending on management philosophy and availability of funds. Some may have a newspaper format and be just functional, while some others could have a booklet form with varying degrees of lavishness.

The Public Relations person in an organisation ideally would be the editor of the house journal. Before publishing the journal, decisions about its editorial policy/objects must be got approved from the management. A look at a house journal can reveal whether the organisation is an open or a closed one. A journal of a closed organisation tends to be a one-way channel of communication, putting the company's views to the employees. Such magazines are obsessed with coverage about top executives especially the Chief Executive Officer/Chairman/Managing Director of that company. An open company on the other hand ensures the editorial integrity of its publications and could have its employees contributing the news items and articles. The editor in this case will have the freedom to present stories according to the readers' interest. When the readers' letters are published, employees have a genuine opportunity to put forth their point of view, and the house journal, like any other reading material, competes for reader's time. Hence, if a journal is to meet its communication objectives, it must be attractive enough to compel attention and must be of interest to those who read it.

In order to bring out a successful house journal a very concerted effort in planning, organising, publishing and distribution has taken in to account.

*Planning*

The first is to develop a concept that best serves the company. Get management the format (i.e. the size whether to have tabloid format or a magazine format) and periodicity of the publication approved. This will, however, depend on the aims of the journal, target audience and availability of budget.

*Organising*

Once the PR professional have taken the approval of the management, the will have to organise staff to get going with the job. The more frequent the number of issues, the greater the need for more staff. It is advisable to develop a brand of freelancers/ correspondents from among our external "publics", if the house journal caters to them, however, have to take care to chose only those who have a flair for writing. A detailed schedule for collection/writing of stories, production, printing, mailing, etc, is to be worked out and adhered to strictly.

*Publishing*

The PR practitioners must inculcate the habit of planning several issues ahead in addition to the one being worked on at that time. Being an editor, we must travel as much as we can. We must be at the place where the action is so as to have first hand information about event. As the journal reflects the style of the editor, must strive to develop a 'personality' for our house journal.

*Distribution*

The purpose of a house journal is not served till it reaches the target audience. We must select the quickest and most economical means possible to get the journal into the hands of the readers. Some companies distribute the journal to their employees at their work-place, others mail it to their homes to ensure that it reaches the family members as well. In order to get feedback, it will be appropriate to include a questionnaire to elicit views about the articles which are liked most or disliked by the employees, and the reasons for that. This will help in improving the content.

With the advent of video technology, many progressive companies have come out with video magazines for employee communication. Cable TV network is used in their ownerships to reach out to the employees in their homes.

**Annual Reports**

Not long ago, Annual Reports were drab-looking journals without much thought about their presentation. Not any more, annual reports have come to be recognised as an important Public Relations tool for corporate communication. With more and more organisations going public, annual reports can serve as prestige publications to be sent to the shareholders and attract prospective investors. Although the Public Relations department of a company does not have a direct responsibility for preparing the balance sheet and the statements of accounts, it does advise the management on the overall approach of the report, the theme of the chairman's statement and on the format and presentation of the Report.

Apart from registered shareholders, there are other segments of the financial public, whose interests have to kept in view while providing information through the Annual Report. They are: the investing community in general, the potential shareholders who are on the lookout for investing in a suitable company; the banks, financial institutions, etc., the financial press; the business community in general.

As a Public Relations professional, we could seek the services of a professional advertising designing agency to handle the assignment. The profile of the company during the year under review can be projected in the Director's report. It could be made attractive and colourful with the use of glossy paper and graphic aids like bar charts, diagrams, pie charts and photographs of the development activities of the company.

Care should be taken to choose a right printer who has the expertise in printing Annual Reports. Bringing out Annual Reports is a statutory requirement. It is to be published before the Annual General Meeting. Hence, a strict time schedule must be worked out with the printer. In fact, most of the printers are busy printing Annual Reports of different companies at the same time hence, we must take care in selecting that printer who has the capacity to undertake the job and deliver the goods on time. An Annual Report needs planning to the minutes details. As the Annual Report contains Balance Sheets, we must be careful about proof reading to avoid errors. It is advisable to get the final proofs cleared from the Company Secretariat Department which has prepared the manuscript and the statement of accounts.

### *Photographs*

Photographs have tremendous potential to attract the attention and offer proofs of facts or events. Photographs, whether for purposes of news or for purposes of record e.g., inauguration of new premises, installation of machinery or hosting of a conference, provide a great creative opportunity to a public relations practitioner and serve as an important tool. They can also be used too illustrate house journals or other company literature.

Good skill, imagination and quality of prints are important to high quality photographs. Photographs may be taken by a staff photographer or a professional photographer may be commissioned. Unlike in news photographs, the photographs that are to be used for displaying purposes in a public relation programme, can be planned in detail well ahead. A creative industrial photographer can be briefed on your needs. You would have time to study different possibilities and choose the best. Dramatic use of light and shade can also make black and white photographs very arresting. Photographs must be kept catalogued for every reference and should be properly captioned when issued to the press.

### Brochures

A brochure is a multi-panel publication that covers information usually on specific subject. A brochure is also called a pamphlet, a flayer or a folder. A booklet has much the same purpose as a brochure except that it has more pages that may be stapled together rather than folded.

Organisations need brochures and booklets for a variety of reasons: to explain a new programme, process, a new building plant, or laboratory, to ask for donations, or to sell a product by describing its virtues. Such publications are reasonably inexpensive, relatively fast to produce, and are attractive to read, if prepared carefully. Although as a Public Relations person, one can have the services of a professional designer or a professional agency to go about the job, it is useful to know the basis so that one can guide the production.

The first step is to identify the aim to the brochure, or what problem it is going to solve and what information supposed to disseminate to the target audience. The copy or the text is the most important part of the brochure. It is not possible to write long copy because of the size of the brochure. We should identify the person who will write the copy. He can be from within the organisation or from the advertising agency. The copywriter must be given the right brief so that he can develop the text. Pictures, graphs, charts must also be selected carefully to go with the copy.

A brochure may have a fold configuration of four, six or eight panels. In deciding the number of folds, the ease in handling and reader's comprehension must be kept in mind: Reading should be smooth from one panel to another.

It has become acceptable in many companies that the public relations officer has the same standing as the advertising manager and that both work to the marketing or sales director. There are dangers in this, and there are countless variations on the theme.

To say that advertising is a tool of public relations is correct. To say that therefore the advertising manager should be sub-servient to the public relations manager is not correct. The same applies when the public relations officer or manager is on the same level as the marketing manager. They are all servants of the company in the same way as the directors are the servants of the owners. The argument is not affected even if the owners are also the working directions.

It is a common practise for one man to combine the jobs of public relations and advertising, with staff below him to carry out the day-to-day functions. Clearly there is nothing wrong in this, provided that the man in the job is properly qualified.

**Advertising**

Advertising is defined, as "any paid form of non-personal presentation and promotion of ideas, goods and services by an identified sponsor." It is called product advertising when it is used to promote sales of goods and services. In contrast to this, when space or time is brought for disseminating messages, aimed at creating a favourable public image of a company, it is called 'institutional' or corporate advertising. Public service advertising e.g. AIDS prevention, traffic safety, etc., which are aimed at public welfare also come under public relations advertising.

Public relations advertising can be a very effective tool in informing and educating the publics. The advertiser has full control over the timing and content of messages which can be communicated widely through the use of any medium. Public relations advertising aims at promoting favourable attitudes among the public for the organisation, so as to attract and maintain shareholders, build goodwill within the community to improve employee relations and morale, educate consumers, secure goodwill of dealers and suppliers, and keep the government informed. The themes used in public relations advertising will depend on the objectives of the campaign.

In the face of tough competition in the market place where similar products vie with one and other, it is necessary to promote the products of services continuously. Consumer durables and capital goods like suit cases, refrigerators, electronic goods, need a large number of support literature unlike small items like chocolates, candy bars or ice-creams. With the modern retailing techniques, products have to really sell themselves. This has led to aggressive publicity at the point of purchase or retail outlets. As a Public Relations person in charge of publicity we will have to decide on these kinds of promotional activities, including promotional literature, referred to as P.O.P. (point of purchase) material, because of its ability to influence purchase decisions, this is again an important tool that can be put to use. There have been a lot of innovations in this media. Some of the options can be: Stickers, posters, labels to serve as reminders; racks or bins for display of products, window display; identification on the pack; speciality gifts like calendars, diaries, pens, key chains, etc., and provision of any necessary leaflets, catalogues, etc., to assist customer's decision to buy.

### *Direct Mail*

Direct mail in some circumstances is the most powerful and certainly the most cost-effective Public Relations tool for disseminating of messages, announcements. It is also called a selective marketing technique. Direct mail is both a selective and a flexible medium. It is selective because it is addressed to only those people we want to reach. It is flexible because the number of letters we mail can be increased or reduced according to the situation. Besides, we are in full control of the content and timing of the message. Direct mail can be a friendly and personal medium of reaching out to a specific target audience, at a comparatively low cost.

Whatever is sent in a direct mail, a brochure, or a small sample of the product, it should be accompanied by a letter addressed to the recipient by his/her name, outlining benefits likely to be of interest specifically to that reader. The material has to be designed and copy written in such manner so as to create an instant rapport with the recipient.

### Press Conferences

Media relation from the most basic activity of public relations. Media relations, in fact, take a good part of the practitioner's working day and are exacting and demanding. Some of the tools for maintaining effective media relations include organising of press conferences, holding press briefings and arranging press visits or facility tours for the media men.

As a Public Relations practitioner, it is our sole responsibility to organise the press conferences. A press conference is generally used as the occasion for the release of news simultaneously to all media, provided the subject is newsworthy. This leads to an immediate question: when should we organise a press conference? The answer is—'as seldom as possible.' We should not fall to the temptation of calling a press conference, if the subject does not demand discussion between our organisation's spokesperson and the media. In such cases, a press release will sufficiently do the job. If, however our organisation has to announce a major policy change or speak about a labour-management rift, or launch a product which requires demonstration, the occasion demands a face-to-face dialogue and not a one-sided statement. This calls for a press conference.

Before holding a press conference it is highly essential to keep in mind some important points to make it rewarding. They are listed below.

(*a*) The decision about the spokesperson who will address the press conference. Remember, as public relations persons we need not address a press conference. Ideally, it should be done by the head of the organisation or a department.

(*b*) Prepare a press kit which must contain a press backgrounder, news release, pictures, literature about the organisation, a writing pad and a pen or a pencil.

(*c*) Make a list of invitees from the media carefully and decide a venue which is accessible to the media persons. Ensure arrangements for the transportation of media persons from a convenient place to the venue and return journey.

(*d*) Decide the timing, it should neither be too early or too late in the day. The conference should end at such a time, that the media persons are able to get back to their place and work for filing the story on time.

(*e*) Arrange hospitability of the media person preferably to their testes.

In fact, as a public relations officer, we should be in control of the press conference from start to finish. After the chief spokesperson and the media persons have taken their seats, we must give self-introduction and introduce the spokesperson who will be addressing them. After a brief address by the spokesperson on the subject-matter, the floor is opened to the media persons to ask questions. Set a time as to how long we would like the conference to continue. Depending on the occasion the ideal duration should be between 45 minutes to one hour.

Normally, after setting the conference in motion, we should take a seat and not interfere. At times, we may have to intercept to rescue the spokesperson who may have been cornered by a reporter's question. For good media relations, it is also important to establish a personal rapport with the media persons. It can't be achieved in a day but concerted efforts must be made in this regard. Press conferences should not be the only occasions when we meet the press. It serves our cause better if we have a friendly press.

Press briefings are different from press conferences in that they are informal and do not require elaborate arrangements. Press briefings can be both proactive and reactive. By proactive, it is meant, that certain clarifications or point of view is required to be given after a crisis situation. In this case, some media persons are invited for press briefings. In case of critical issues, besides an informal briefing given by the spokesperson, a written statement may also be handed over to avoid misquotation. In case of reactive press briefings, a press person seeks an audience with the chief spokesperson. In case of reactive press briefings, a press person seeks an audience with the chief spokesperson for seeking certain clarifications or to have his point of view, before filing the story.

### *Press Tours*

In press tours or facility visits much of the exercise is similar to organising a press conference. More elaborate arrangements are, however, required to be made as it may involve transporting the party to a long distance. The occasion could be a landmark achieved, commissioning a project or a crisis situation like an accident. Both occasions need careful planning and organisation. While inviting a reporter to join the press tour, it is always advisable to write to the editor or chief of the bureaus of different newspapers. In case of formal tours, sufficient notice must be given, because the concerned reporter may have to be spared for a number of days from the place of work.

As a Public Relations person, you would do well to give detailed considerations to the list of media men, their suitable travel arrangements, accommodation at site, briefing press party at site, background information and hospitality.

It is necessary that a responsible representative of the organisation accompanies the press party and personally supervises hospitality arrangements.

### Exhibitions

Exhibitions cover a very diverse series of events, ranging from major international trade fairs to small local activities organised by a community. Exhibition can be of a general nature of communication and help to increase the reputation and image of the company. It can become a meeting place for existing customers, potential customers and help to identify new sales area/outlets. New products can be launched. It also enables in assessing performance of the competitors in terms of product, service and presentation.

Exhibitions and fairs can also contribute towards generating inquires and booking orders. In face products can be exhibited and demonstrated in a relaxed atmosphere. The prospective customers are generally in 'buying mood'. Planning an exhibition should involve the considerations, viz., clear idea of what is to be achieved through the exhibition, a convenient and appropriate timing, a budget drawn up with allocations for each item, designing of the stand and preparation of other display devices like posters, photographs, animated flow diagrams, murals, sculptures, audio visual aids, etc., arrangements made for publicity, advertising, press conferences and preparation of literature for distribution, insurance, transport, lighting, hospitality, receiving of VIP visitors, allocation of duties, emergency precautions to be taken care of and visitors' inquiries answered fully and a visitors' book provided to help evaluation efforts.

Exhibitions are an expensive media. The costs include expenditure towards space, designing, construction of stalls, transport, delivery, hospitality, insurance, printed literature for distribution, advertising, etc. Hence, it is necessary to plan it well so that maximum benefit accrue from it.

Open house is an important tool to build rapport with the community/neighbourhood where the plants is located. It is also a widely employed way of building pride and morale among the employees and their families. The Public Relations departments organise visits for employees' families and community at large, to visit the plant to see the product manufacturing process and a tour of the company. There may be exhibits, films and other activities also. This is done on a few chosen days in a year which are referred to as 'open days.' The visiting public may also be provided with hospitality by plant owners.

It is important, however, to make suitable arrangements to receive visitors, answer questions and take them on a guided tour. This entails the provision of trained guides and also hospitality for the visitors.

It is usual in many industry-conducted tours to provide refreshments to visitors at the end of the tour. If, however, 'the factory is situated out of town, and it has taken a long time for the visitors to reach there, it is advisable to offer refreshments on arrival. Factories producing eatables, generally not only offer the visitor refreshments, but may also present gift packs, for example, chocolate factory or a biscuit factory can present their products which surely will be appreciated by the visitors and help in creating goodwill.

Delhi Milk Scheme, when it was set-up, organised open houses for school children. The children were treated with flavored milk on their visits. Similarly, Coca Cola organised such visits. The visitors were also gifted with bottle openers, trays with 'Coca Cola' logo painted on them as momentous. In fact, open houses and tours of the plant should be geared to serve a wide range of audiences, from employees, community members, press to elected representatives of parliament and legislative assemblies.

Special events are the most visible component of a community relations programme. The events, however, must be well chosen. The special events should reinforce key messages that we are trying to communicate to any target audience. The special events can range from participating in a community related activity e.g., a local festival, to sponsoring a national or international event. ITC one of the leading corporate sector organisations in India, organises music concerts every year known as "ITC Sangeet Sammelans." Besides providing a forum for upcoming artists, it honours veterans and famous artists. Free entry passes are distributed to community through their outlets. The programmes have become so popular that people look forward to this in advance.

In planning any special event, large or small, it is important to have a management structure that is ultimately responsible for the event, and to make timely decisions. The event itself needs publicity for better response from the target audience.

The operating costs of public relations programme will be much the same whether it is controlled from within a company or by an outside agency. The Institute of Public Relations has published a guidance paper on the subject entitled Fees and Methods of Charging. It makes the point, sometimes forgotten, that fees are the income of a consultant and expenditure is the cost of implementing an agreed programme. The latter is usually mainly a debit and credit transaction.

It is normal practice, although there are no definite rules on this, to charge operating expenses monthly in arrears. They will tend to fall into major and minor categories. The former can include research, market analyses, and similar surveys; advertising exhibitions, displays, and visual aids; the design, production, and distribution of printed materials, including house magazines; films and filmstrips; direct mail; the organization of speakers' programmes and special events. Minor cost can include travelling; entertainment, including press contact; toll and trunk calls and telegrams; press-cutting and monitoring services; photocopying or duplicating and special stationery.

The detailed items of major expenses are usually charged according to the customs of the particular trade, while minor expenses are charged at cost. For instance, advertising budgets include agency commissions, and printed material often includes a commission element.

If anything extra is added to an invoice to a client, especially when it is commission, the client should know and be able to see clearly how much has been put on.

At the same time, it is the responsibility of the public relations man, whether on the staff or outside, to supervise all work done and check the expenditure and invoices. This remains true even if a client has agreed to pay major invoices direct, such as for advertising.

It is normal practice for the agreed budget for a programme to be placed into categories, so that all involved can see show money is being spent and can maintain a regular check on the rate of expenditure. A fairly common list for predominantly minor expenses, with explanatory clauses, could read like this:

(*a*) *Travelling*: Travel within London is normally charged. Out-of-town travelling is charged, including subsistence and hotel accommodation.

(*b*) *Press contact:* When an account—the consultancy's term for a client—calls for regular meetings with the press the bills are charged.

(*c*) *Press releases:* When releases are regularly issued to a long list of papers in Britain, the postage, paper, envelopes, and handling are charged. The cost of special envelopes and postage for photographs is also charged.

(*d*) *Photography:* The cost of photographs and photographic sessions is charged, including the purchase or hire of special equipment or props, model fees, and any fees paid to specialist consultants.

(*e*) *Media monitoring:* The costs of press-cutting services, radio, television, transcripts and subscriptions to papers and periodicals are charged.

(*f*) *Special events:* When special functions are needed, the costs are charged.

(*g*) *Special stationery:* If it is decided that special stationery is needed, this is charge and may be subject to commission arrangements.

(*h*) *Temporary services:* It is sometimes necessary to call in temporary help—executive, secretarial or other—to deal with particular jobs. Costs incurred are charged.

(*i*) *Demonstrations:* Some accounts call for demonstrations and lectures. The costs incurred are charged.

(*j*) *Specialist consultants:* Routine advice from outside specialists is not charge, but for extensive work a special fee is calculated and agreed in advance.
(*k*) *Print:* Commission, normally, 15 per cent, may be added, subject to discussion.
(*l*) *Films and exhibitions:* Such work may be subject to a special additional fee.
(*m*) *Direct mail.* A commission may be charged in certain circumstances, subject to prior agreement.
(*n*) *Telephone calls, telex, telegrams:* Calls are normally metered and charged; messages are recorded and charged; photo-stats charged at an agreed rate.
(*o*) *Overseas assignments.* These may be subject to an additional fee, and out-of-pocket expense are charged in all instance.

Another simple example is press-cuttings. Whether papers are cut or a cuttings service is used, the public relations man may be required to circulate copies within his organization or to his client. The papers are relatively inexpensive in themselves, but added together over twelve months they can represent a sizeable chunk of the budget.

The point behind this—one which must always be kept in mind—is that he must always clearly be seen to be in contrail of the spending. In addition, it is vitally important that the public relations man should demonstrate clearly his integrity by never trying to hide costs or charge for something that was not a greed in advance. All it needs is care when making estimates to see that they are as accurate as is reasonably possible.

Naturally, a budget cannot cover every eventuality. It is for that reason that it should contain a reserve. However, this must be a reserve for unforeseen contingencies and not an excuse for floppy, uncontrolled forecasting.

Once the budget has been set it dictates the broad scope of work for twelve months. It should not be allowed completely to control the PR man, otherwise he will lost the initiative that is a part of his stock-in-trade.

Another task is to keep a running check on expenditure. It is easy to do this, either with a small notebook or a chart. The categories in which money is to be spent are listed and the accounts department provides up-to-date figures each month. There are two essential items of information: what specific jobs are in hand and what suppliers' invoices or petty cash have been paid or are due to be paid.

Naturally, it is never possible to tie up all the loose ends between the time a job is commissioned or handled and the time invoices either come in or are paid out. With a good system it should be possible to produce quickly adequate accurate figures at a moment's notice.

There are two further points. Hieroglyphics that only one person can understand should never be used; somebody else may need to refer to the figures. Secondly, many companies work on general financial systems of running estimates/quarterly estimates, annual estimates, five-year projections and the like.

The chart or book should show what is available in the budget and what has been spent up to any given point, plus expenditure that has been incurred even if not actually yet met. In this way the figures will be genuinely useful as a guide.

Many young people are afraid of figure work. They think it may turn them from being in public relations to being in accountancy. This is not so. It is the job of the accounts department to monitor or collect the money passing through an agency or department. It is the executive's job to see that he can explain why money has been spent and to ensure that, when it is his responsibility, it is not spent wildly. This is not accountancy or book-keeping; it is merely commercial common-sense.

## CAREERS IN PUBLIC RELATIONS: AN OVERVIEW

Public relations helps an organization and its publics adapt mutually to each other. Often, it is a term used to describe both, a way of looking at an organization's performance and a programme of activities.

The public relations function takes many forms in different organizations, including public information, investor relations, public affairs, corporate communications, employee relations, marketing or product publicity and consumer service or customer relations.

Basic to all public relations, however, is communicating. Well-planned, effectively handled communications are increasingly seen as essential to the success and even existence of organizations and causes in today's changing world. Every organization-government, business, labour, professional, trade, health, cultural, financial, recreational, educational and public service-depends on people. Their attitudes, attention, understanding, and motivation can be critical to the success or failure of an organization or idea.

Public relations, at its best, not only tells an organization's "story" to its publics, but also helps shape the organization and the way it performs. Through research, measurement and evaluation, public relations professionals determine the concerns and expectations of the organization's publics and explain them to management. A responsible and effective public relations programme is based on the understanding and support of its publics.

According to the Bureau of Labour Statistics, the number of people in public relations has been estimated to be as high as 98,000, and more than half of that number are women. The growth rate reflects increased recognition of the importance of communications and of professional competence in its planning and implementation. For example, it is rare today for medium or large-sized corporations not to have public relations staffs, consultants, or both. Increasingly, the person responsible for the public relations department of a major company is a corporate officer.

**Salaries**

Due to the growth of the public relations field, public relations practitioners tend to be well paid, although the range of compensation is broad. Earnings depend on such factors as the individuals' qualifications and experience, responsibilities of the position, financial strength of the organization, and the general state of the economy.

The average entry-level salary in public relations for a person with a baccalaureate degree is approximately $18,000-$22,000. Those with additional education or experience, as well as graduating members of the Public Relations Student Society of America, could qualify for higher salaries.

An account executive of a consulting firm can earn upwards of $35,000 as will a person with a comparable responsibility in a company's public relations department. A public relations director for a small to medium-sized organization may earn $35,000 to $40,000 while the range for the large corporation more likely would be $40,000 to $60,000.

Salaries from $75,000 to $150,000 are earned by a number of seasoned public relations executives, who often carry the title of vice-president.

Depending upon the profitability of public relations consulting firms, the incomes of their senior members may exceed those of public relations officials on the payrolls of corporations.

Various industries and companies tend to pay their employees higher or lower than others, and these characteristic compensation patterns generally apply to their public relations workers. Variations according to geographic location may also be found, with personnel located in the Northeast and Midwest regions tending to be higher paid.

**Public Relations Elements Counselling**

Providing advice to the management of an organization concerning policies, relationships and communications; in effect, "what to do."

**Research**

Determining attitudes and behaviours of publics and their causes in order to plan, implement and measure activities to influence or change the attitudes and behaviour.

**Media Relations**

Relating with communications media in seeking publicity or responding to their interest in an organization.

**Employee/Member Relations**

Responding to concerns and informing and motivating an organization's employees or members, its retirees and their families.

**Community Relations**

Continuing, planned and active participation with and within a community to maintain and enhance its environment to the benefit of both an organization and the community.

**Public Affairs**

Developing effective involvement in public policy, and helping an organization adapt to public expectations; a term also used by military services and some government agencies to describe their public relations activities.

**Government Affairs**

Relating directly with legislatures and regulatory agencies on behalf of an organization, usually as a central element of a public affairs programme; often called "lobbying."

**Issues Management**

Identifying and addressing issues of public interest in which an organization is, or should be, concerned.

**Financial Relations**

Creating and maintaining investor confidence and building positive relationships with the financial community; also called investor or shareholder relations.

**Industry Relations**

Relating with trade associations and other firms in an organization's industry.

**Development/Fund Raising**

Demonstrating the need for and encouraging an organization's members, friends, supporters and others to voluntarily contribute to support it.

**Multicultural Affairs**

Relating with individuals and groups in minorities.

**Special Events**

Stimulating an interest in a person, product or organization by means of a focussed "happening"; also, activities designed to enable an organization to listen to and interact with its publics.

**Marketing Communications**

Combination of activities designed to sell a product, service or idea, including advertising, collateral materials, publicity, promotion, packaging, point-of-sale display, trade shows and special events.

### Responsibilities of a Public Relations Professional

Most public relations positions involve one or more of these functions:

#### Programming

This involves analyzing problems and opportunities, defining goals, identifying the publics (or groups of people whose support or understanding is needed), and recommending and planning activities. It may include budgeting and assignment of responsibilities to the appropriate people, including non-public relations personnel. For example, an organization's president or CEO is often a key figure in public relations activities.

#### Cultivating Relationships

Successful public relations professionals develop skills in gathering information from management, colleagues in their organizations and external sources. Continually evaluating what they learn, practitioners formulate recommendations and gain approval for them from their managements. Many public relations activities require working with, and sometimes through, other organizational units such as personnel, legal and marketing staffs. The public relations professional who learns to be persuasive with others will be most effective.

#### Writing and Editing

Since the public relations professional is often trying to reach large groups of people, an important tool is the printed word. Examples of its use are found in reports, news releases, brochures, speeches, video, scripts, trade magazine articles, product information and technical materials, employee publications, newsletters, shareholder reports, and other management communications directed to both organization—personnel and external groups. A sound, clear style of writing is a must for public relations work.

#### Information

Establishing systems for the dissemination of material to appropriate newspaper, broadcast, general and trade publication editors, and communicating with them to enlist their interest in publishing an organization's news and features are regular public relations activities. This requires knowledge of how newspapers and other media operate, the areas of specialization publications, and the interest of individual editors. (Competition is keen for the attention of editors and broadcasters who have a limited amount of space and time at their disposal.) As a seasoned practitioner put it, "You have to get the right editor of the right publication with the right story at the right time."

Although ideas are accepted on the basis of news and other readership values, an ability to develop relationships of mutual respect and cooperation with the news media can be useful to both the practitioners and the media.

### Production

Various publications, special reports, videos and multimedia programmes are important ways of communicating. The public relations professional need not be an expert in art, layout, typography, and photography, but background knowledge of the techniques of preparation is needed for intelligent planning and supervision of their use.

### Special Events

News conferences, convention exhibits, new facility and anniversary celebrations, contest and award programmes, tours and special meetings are only a few of the special events used to gain attention and acceptance of groups of people. They involve careful planning and coordination, attention to detail, preparation of special booklets, publicity materials and reports.

### Speaking

Public relations work often requires skill in face-to-face communication—finding appropriate platforms, the preparation of speeches for others and the delivery of speeches. The person who can effectively address individuals and groups will enjoy an advantage over those whose facility of expression is limited to writing.

### Research and Evaluation

An important activity undertaken by public relations practitioners is fact-gathering. This can be highly personal, through interviews, review of library materials and informal conversations. It also can involve the use of survey techniques and firms specializing in designing and conducting opinion research.

After a programme is completed, the public relations professional studies its results and evaluates the programme's planning, implementation and effectiveness. More and more, managements expect research and evaluation from their public relations advisers or staffs.

## The Typical Day at Work

Public relations offices are busy places; work schedules are irregular and frequently interrupted. The junior employee may answer calls for information from the press and public, work on invitation lists and details for a press conference, escort visitors and clients, help with research, write brochures, deliver releases to editorial offices, and compile media distribution lists.

Employees will brief their management on upcoming meetings, help write reports, speeches, presentations and letters, research case histories, help produce displays and other audio-visual materials, proofread copy, select photographs for publication, arrange for holiday and other remembrances, conduct surveys and tabulate questionnaires, and work with letter shops and printers.

Public relations programmes operate against deadlines. Under such high-pressure conditions, nine-to-five schedules go out the window. Public relations executives are not tied to their desks for long periods. Meetings, community functions, business lunches, travel assignments, special speaking and writing commitments, and unscheduled work on "crisis" situations often mean long hours.

## Personal Qualifications and Preparation

Because public relations covers many kinds of tasks, there is no single set of "ideal" qualifications. Most people think of public relations executives as highly articulate and imaginative individuals. Yet, public relations executives themselves stress judgement as the most important single qualification needed in their field.

The public relations practitioner is a "counsellor whose advice and services are often sought when an organization faces the prospect of trouble. Therefore, it is important to develop the capacity to think analytically under pressure, to draw out necessary information, and to express persuasive practical solutions. Other qualities needed by the public relations work include:

Imagination for coping with present problems and anticipating future ones; Communication skills, with demonstrable competence in writing; Personal confidence, for successful face-to-face contacts with individuals and groups; Sensitivity to other people (simply to "like people" will not help a candidate get a job); both diplomacy and a more-than-ordinary ability to place oneself in the shoes of another are important in public relations work.

Organizing and planning ability, applied to oneself and others; as with many other occupations, managerial skills are invaluable for successfully climbing the public relations ladder.

### Academic Preparation

A college degree is essential and a basic grounding in the liberal arts is strongly recommended.

Though public relations is a relatively new field, many colleges and universities offer a public relations sequence or degree programme. In addition, there are more than 200 Public Relations Student Society of America chapters on college campuses nationwide.

Most public relations programmes are administered by journalism or mass communications schools or departments. The Accrediting Council on Education in Journalism and Mass Communications (ACEJMC) is the only agency authorized to accredit such schools or departments identified as "units." As a member of ACEJMC, the Public Relations Society of America participates in the Council's examination of units in which public relations is taught. Several of these institutions also offer the opportunity for graduate study in public relations.

Public relations programmes also are presented in other schools or departments, such as speech, liberal arts and business. In addition to coursework, the importance of gaining in-school experience through bona fide public relations internships or practicums is stressed. The most frequently recommended secondary or "minor" area of study for public relations students is business.

### Work Experience

Many of today's senior public relations professionals began their careers as journalists. For the majority with this background, public relations work represented a change of career objectives. A number of graduates still seek out journalism jobs, but as a specific stepping stone to public relations. With the growth of college training for public relations, it is possible that the importance of a journalism apprenticeship will diminish.

But, there remains something to be said about a journalism background. The experience gained in writing, personal contact and other aspects of work for metropolitan or smaller newspapers, general or trade magazines and broadcasting media is still deemed important by a majority of public relations employers.

To a far lesser extent, experience in general business, marketing, advertising and selling is considered useful for public relations work.

Sometimes work in specialized fields—such as finance, engineering, medicine and public or educational administration—can provide valuable background for a particular public relations position.

Outside activities—freelance writing, community organization work, election and fund campaigning, public speaking—are often looked upon favourably as supporting experience.

Internships with public relations counselling firms, corporate departments or non-profit organizations are extremely valuable for people still attending school. Professionally supervised, internships provide bona fide, hands-on public relations experience. The most valuable internships are those involving assignments of one or more of the following duties: writing, layout and editing for external or internal publications, promotional material, and brochures; news gathering; news release and feature writing; research and report writing; preparing local media lists; designing audio-visual presentations; helping to arrange or to take part in special events; and assisting in fundraising programmes. Graduates with one or more such internships have an edge in the entry-level job market.

## Finding Your First Job

No job is harder than finding a job, particularly your first. This is true of any field and certainly so of public relations. Success requires planning, preparation, energy and enthusiasm.

Research the field in which you have the greatest interest. Not only should you use library resources, but also find people who work in these fields, particularly those engaged in public relations activities.

Sometimes a journalist also can provide useful insights. The knowledge you acquire from all of these sources will confirm your interest in the field and will be evidence of your alertness and maturity.

### Resumes

One of the most important tools to landing your first job is your resume. It's the vehicle you use to market yourself to potential employers and it should distinguish you from all other candidates. A well-written resume is the key to securing an interview.

Your resume should be a one-page account of yourself, communicating your qualifications for a specific job. It should include your name, address, telephone/fax numbers, a statement of job objectives, your education, work experience—including pertinent internships or part-time work while at college—and extracurricular and volunteer activities, reported chronologically or in terms of the types of skills demonstrated or the work accomplished.

When writing your resume, always be persuasive and honest. Pay attention to the impression your resume makes by its layout and the way you express yourself. Remember to use action-oriented words, and check and recheck your resume, particularly for typographical errors.

### Interviews

It is important to prepare for interviews by learning as much as possible about the organization beforehand. For major business corporations, financial information may be available from the company's financial relations office.

Showing samples of your work is important, but keep in mind that they should represent your best efforts. Quality is more impressive than quantity.

If the interviewer does not choose to lead the discussion, be ready to take the initiative in describing your qualifications and what you believe you can accomplish on the job. Also, be aware of the fact that the quality of your questions about the company and the position can be as impressive and revealing of your potential as your background, particularly if your experience is limited.

Every candidate for a public relations position must remember that the number of persons hired for any particular opening is small compared to the number interviewed. Rejection is no cause to suppose believe that you will not qualify elsewhere. Consider your job hunt as a learning experience. Through perseverance you can win the opportunity to begin your public relations career.

# 6

# Guidelines and Approaches of PR in Media and Journalism

## INTRODUCTION

Public Relations professionals work within organisations, whether they work in internal or in external departments firms providing counsel and services. This chapter discusses the origins of the function, its responsibilities, its working relationships, and its implementation within organisations.

As a starting point, it is helpful to know some of the ways in which the function comes into being, and then evolves to accommodate special goals or needs. This makes it easier to understand why public relations practitioners and consultants may occupy positions or perform roles in or for particular organisations that seem unusual or incongruous.

For instance, the function is often activated when an employer discovers a need for better communications with employees. Perhaps an employee publication is desired in a small but growing organisation. An editor is appointed or hired by the personnel manager. Then the editor, being energetic and ambitious, is given or takes on the task of writing and issuing occasional news releases generated by material in the employee newsletter and to make the employee publication as a grand success.

One of the few safe generalisations on this subject is that an organisation's public reputation derives in substantial part from its senior officials. As those with administrative responsibility and authority act and speak, so go the interpretations and echoes created by the public relations function. Thus, public relations is inescapably tied, by nature and by necessity, to the management function.

In this context, long-term success in an organisation's public relations calls for the Commitment and participation by management; Competent public relations practitioners; Centralised policy making; Communication with both internal and external publics and Coordination of all efforts toward defined goals and objectives.

The first task, and a continuing one, is to earn and hold broad support for the public relations charter within the organisation. Unless support is earned, there will be conflict, not coordination and cooperation. Conflict soon begets friction and frustration. Support and understanding develop with time and on the basis of a track record of achievement.

Administrators determine basic goals; they manage by objectives and results, short range and long-term policies. Administrators set policies and they approve procedures for the guidance of everyone. In the process they decide, at least tentatively, on the scope and the place of all staff or line, office or field functions. In doing so, intentionally or not, they determine the relationship of each to the others.

A senior official relates this to public relations bluntly: "When it is all said and done, a public relations, office will; only be as useful to management as management wants it to be. If management thinks of the public relations operation in a small way, then it will occupy a small place in the scheme of things, and its contribution will be small. If management thinks it is important then it will occupy a prominent place, and its contribution will be significant."

## Analysing the Role of Staff

Public relations is a *staff* function, one of several that advise and support top official. Thus, practitioners need to understand the staff role.

The line-staff principle of management originated in the military but has been extended to most organisations of some extent. In industry, the product and profit-producing functions—engineering, production, and marketing—are *line functions. Staff functions* are those that advise and assist the executive—finance legal, personnel, and public relations. These functions become more and more necessary as organisations increase in size and complexity. Line executives have the authority and responsibility to see that the work gets done, but they need assistance in the form of plans, advice, and suggestions from staff executives. The job of the staff officer is to advice top officials and to support and assist the line officers.

Robert Sampson opines staff specialists need "a sense of organisation and operation; an understanding of people, there functions, their relationships; an acceptance of managers as full-scale managers; a humility about their contribution in their limited role; a desire to relate themselves helpfully and dynamically to the ongoing management process."

Management and staff have a right to expect certain things from each other. Management should expect the following from the public relations staff:

(*i*) Loyalty.
(*ii*) Help with the public relations aspects of decisions.
(*iii*) Skill in articulating principles and in enlarging understanding of the organisation.
(*iv*) Inspiration to help all members do their best cheerfully.
(*v*) Influence in restraining other members from saying or doing anything detrimental to the organisation's welfare.

*In turn, the staff should expect some from management viz;*

(*a*) Positive public relations leadership.
(*b*) Support of approved communications policy.
(*c*) A definite plan embracing all policies and programmes.
(*d*) A budget to do the job that needs to be done.
(E) Funds for adequate public opinion research and analysis.
(*f*) Reasonable availability for consultation and for public exposure.

Both have the right to expect of each other character and performance that will stand public scrutiny and fulfill the organisation's social responsibility. The difference between line and staff management in this relationship is important to remember. Line management determine the ground rules and sets the course. Public relations works within those rules and with others on matters having an impact on the organisation's relationships with others. Inside and outside. In those matter, both line and staff managers must participate. Once all points of view have been aired and debated, the resulting decisions may result from a consensus, or from choice made by line management. Final decisions are the province of senior line management.

As managing organisation relationships is an increasingly important function, some public relations practitioners have moved from staff support positions to line management. A few have become chief executive officers for major organisations, such as Martin Davis, chairman of Gulf & Western Industries, and George Weissman, chairman of Philip Morris. Henry Rogers observes, "The chief executive today realises that the public's attitude towards his company may have as much influence on the bottom line as the performance of his engineering, research, marketing and manufacturing executives. He realised that his public relations executive must be part of strategy meetings where important corporate decisions are made and help make those decisions. It is for some a short step to the next level—chairing those decision-making meetings. The same applies in associations, government agencies, and non-profit organisations.

**Undertaking Organisational Decision-Making**

The traditional and somewhat rigid distinction between line and staff managers giving orders versus giving advice—often does not accurately represent their roles when decisions are being made. The roles played by public relations specialists in organisations illustrate two staff roles with significant influence in organisation decision-making. Practitioners operations as expert prescribes often have power to choose among alternatives, with line management endorsing the recommendations, while holding veto power. In the problem-solving process facilitator role, practitioners work in collaboration with line managers to make decisions.

In organisations where public relations is seen as communication output only, the function becomes routine and highly structured. Practitioners working primarily as communication technicians in these setting deal primarily with what Simon calls "Programmed decision." Management of most organisations is dominated with programmed decisions order to free valuable time and money for in "non-programmed decision" that are "novel", unstructured and consequential. The difference may be that when public relations is part of programmed decisions it is viewed simply as a "means", whereas in the non-programmed decisions context the focus is on "ends." "Management by objectives" and "management by objectives and results" now dominate public relations programme planning and management as the function increasingly becomes concerned with impact and accountability.

Public relation's participation in organisational decision-making also depends in part on the extent to which practitioners are involved in organisational intelligence. In a survey of corporate public relations practitioners, Kraemer found those most actively engaged in various types of research—what she called "environmental monitoring"—were also the ones most involved in decision-making and planning activities.

The major determinant of public relation's role in organisation decision-making is the degree to which the function is viewed by line managers and practitioners as an integral part of the organisation's structure and process for adapting to change in the economic, political, social and technological environment.

The most common way to integrate the public relations function is to set-up a unit of specialists within the organisation—the public relations department. It may consists of only person or have a staff or several hundred. It may be concentrated in headquarters or scattered among many locations. The size, role, and place in the organisation varies from one organisation to the other.

## Listing the Advantages of PR Department

A staff practitioner has four factors working favourably for him or her in the department, namely: team membership; knowledge of the organisation; economy to the organisation; availability to associates.

*Team membership is a great advantage* : The confidence, trust, and support of colleagues that go with it tend to overcome or to relative into unimportance any antagonism toward the public relations function. At the same time, the close connection between the function, the department and the chief executive office of the organisation provides first-team membership rather than marginal membership. The price of admission is loyalty.

*Knowledge of the organisation* : Mean an intimate, participating knowledge that comes from being insides. The staff members know the relationships between individuals and their functions. They know the undercurrents of influence, the key people, the conservatives, the ones who put personal ambition and expedience ahead of the organisation's interests, the articulate and the tongue tied.

This kind of knowledge can be acquired by outsiders, but insiders are in a position to do most about it continuously. They can advise where needed, conciliate, and render services from within to induce attitudes and actions that will bring about harmonious relationships inside as well as outside.

*Economy to the organisation* : Economy can result simply from residence and integration in an organisation. For example, the department's bills for rent, heat, and light in a large organisation do not loom large. They are expressed generally as a part of an overall cost for many departments and offices or buildings. When the needs is long-term—and in most organisations it is—full-time, permanent staff are typically more cost-effective than hiring outside for counsel and services.

*Availability to associates* : Availability of staff practitioners has many facets. When thing's go wrong, practitioners are only a minute away from a face-to face meeting with delicate matters. If a senior executive defects in a huff, the president wants a public relations man or women on the spot who knows the background, understands the dangers of mishandling the news and has credibility and accessibility with the news media.

Availability means being on call for all departments, divisions, decentralised units. The staff can slip into and out of committees and meetings. They belong, they are handy for consultation. They have both acceptability and authority.

Availability to perform service functions involves practitioners in a broad range of activities. They may be asked to handle a tour for some foreign visitors who do not speak a common language, e.g. English. They may represent the organisation on a local civil-rights fund-raising committee. They may respond for the organisation on receipt of a citation. Or they may make the arrangements for the president's attendance at a charity social event.

### Mentioning the Handicaps of the PR Department

The advantages of team membership can, however, get in the way on occasion. The availability and loyalty can become possessive bear hugs. The practitioner risks loss of objectivity. In supporting and being supported, he or she tends to be absorbed and compromised by group views. There is also the danger of being co-opted becoming a "yes" man or women. Being a team player and helping others is one thing; having one's time diverted from goals, planning, and strategy to running errands for others is another. The practice can deteriorate into domination and subjectivity, resulting in loss of respect for the person and the function by colleagues and employer.

Practitioners walk a narrow line between rendering services that are valuable, helpful, appreciated, and rendering a subservience that is easily replaced. Walking this line successfully tends to sort out the potential staff executive from the person who cannot or will not attain executive status. Detractors like to describe this in oversimplified terms as "organisational politics," or "playing the political game." There is much more to it. The key is team play, but with retention of one's individuality and objectivity.

Availability has another down side—Practitioners may find themselves in the role of stand-ins for top executives who make commitments to serve on community organisation boards or committees, for example, but do not follow through. Such groups are seldom pleased to have the public relations practitioner instead of the Chief Executive Officer (CEO), but usually accept the switch as the price for the organisation's support and public use of the CEO's name as a member of team.

### Titles and Reporting Relationships

The positioning of departments and their titles in organisations very greatly. The 1983 O'Dwyer's Directory of Corporate Communications listing of department titles for the "Fortune 500" companies illustrates that "corporate communications" has replaced "public relations" as the most popular title in corporate settings. As of today corporate communications, "public relations," "public affairs," "corporate relations," and "public relations and advertising" are some of the tools and tactics in the corporate settings, though all these terms reflects the same meaningful.

There is no compelling reason to conclude that some other title will replace "public relations." To the contrary, "public relations" has survived almost ninety years in spite of the many attempts to find an alternative, as well as the occasional taint of malpractice by individual practitioners. Meantime, the news media and the lay public almost worldwide have come to understand the term and to use it to describe this function in organisations. That will not be changed simply by a different label.

Much more significant than the title of the department is the chain of command in communications policy decisions, and where the top public relations executive fits into the pecking order.

Organisation charts and job descriptions serve a useful purpose. They lay the groundwork for acceptance of the function throughout the organisation. The danger is that formal charts and job descriptions can be restrictive or, worse, can become shields behind which insecure people take refuge. Some practitioners become preoccupied with trying to change the charts and edit the job descriptions, as though these, with no other changes, would elevate their function.

One long-standing opponent of the organisation chart on principle was the late Clarence Randall, innovator in management approaches when he was head of Inland Steel. Once he stated that:

> to know who is to do what and to establish authority and responsibility within an institution are the basic first principles of a good administration, but this is a far cry from handing down immutable tablets of stone from the mountaintop.... It is not the preparation of the organisation chart that I condemn, but its abuse: this blowing up its significance to a point where guidance ceases and inhibition sets in.

Organisation charts are, at best, approximations, but they do clarify the role and relationships of various functions in general terms.

## Coordination with Other Department

Public relations staffers work most closely with marketing and the staff functions of personnel, industrial or employee relations, legal, human resources, finance and development. These functions intertwine and overlap in varying degrees, and sometimes the department finds itself in unavoidable conflict with another. Particular sources of internal friction are the departments of marketing, legal counsel, personnel, and human resource development. Such disputes are costly to all concerned, especially to the employer. Each function needs the support and cooperation of the others if it is to discharge its obligation effectively. But with the potential for conflict, practitioners should be aware, alert, and ready to mend fences.

## Marketing

Marketing is the function most often confused with public relations. As they are the major means of communication and outreach in most organisations, they must work in harmony. Conflict and the need for cooperation in companies usually arise over institutional advertising and product publicity. In non-profit organisation's, the main bone of contention is allocation of resources—budget and people—to raise funds, recruit members or reach publics with educational messages.

Confusion results from notions that advertising is the ultimate tool of marketing and publicity is the job of public relations. Advertising designed to establish, change, or maintain relationships with publics should, by its nature and objectives, be supervised by the public relations department. It will require the advertising department's expertise to produce and place the advertisements, but the outcome sought has more to do with public relations than with promoting goods and services. Conversely, publicity about products and services designed to increase sales or use is clearly part of the marketing function. Because public relations poise are typically more skilled at writing and placing publicity, they are enlisted to help with this aspect of the marketing effort.

Mobile Oil leads in the use of advertising for public relations purposes. Advertising and publicity produced by either public relations or marketing should be checked by the other to make sure efforts are coordinated. Backlash is an ever-present danger. The growth of articulate protest and consumer groups, investigative and consumer reporting, and government scrutiny all mandate public relations—marketing cooperations.

Competition and even conflict, between these two functions is understandable. Practitioners often complete on parallel career tracks for recognition, job advancement, and bigger budgets. In some organisations, marketing and public relations are combined in a single department with a single head to administer a coordinated effort. Most common, however, is a separate public relations department in a staff relationship to the chief executive officer, with marketing as part of line management.

## Legal Counsel

The conflict between public relations and legal counsel is an old one. In the days of the "muckrakers," corporate executives turned first to their lawyers to "fix things." Some still do Ivy Lee felt strongly pointed out this: "I have seen more situations which the public ought to understand, and which the public would sympathise with, spoiled by the intervention of the lawyer than in any other way. Whenever, a lawyer starts to talk to the public, he shuts out the light." Potential for conflict is demonstrated when one corporation counsel asserted, "The truly competent legal counsellor... should be expected to express his opinion not only on matters of factuality which have potential legal impact, but even on matters of good taste, logic, honesty, yes, even at times on the persuasiveness of your copy." Conversely, a seasoned practitioner could help make legal documents understandable to the layman. In doing so, he or she could save the organisation the "costs" of being misunderstood via obscure or needlessly harsh language in touchy situations. Cooperation between these two functions can protect the organisation legally while at the same time serving the public interest. It means the legal counsel can incorporate legal aspects with an increased value of information to the publics.

There are key areas in which the close coordination of legal and public relations counsel are beneficial to the employer: for instance, the area of labour contract negotiations and other legally based on explosive situations—an antitrust suit, a campus uprising, the threat of boycott, an accusation of discrimination, or a military court-martial. Additionally, there must be coordination on such matters as booklets explaining benefits to employees, announcement of new facilities, legality of advertising or publicity claims, and disclosure of financial information.

Close cooperation of legal and public relations counsel, once seen mainly in the business world, is now necessary in most organisations as they deal with an ever more complex environment, threats to health or safety, urban renewal, and the expanding scope of government. When parents go to court to protest grooming and dress regulations, or to block sex education in, the schools, the situation requires collaboration by the school board's legal and public relations counsellors. Similarly, such collaboration has long been required by the military in cases of publicised courts-martial, and more recently in antimissile protest.

**Understanding Personnel and Industrial Relations**

The relationships between public relations and personnel and industrial relations are many. The risk of friction is high. The fundamental problems concern whether communications in the community constitutes an extension of the employee relationship, and whether the employees are a "public," calling for public relations concepts of attitude measurement and communication. Compromise comes when practitioners and personnel specialists realise that internal relationships inevitably have their echoes externally.

In the past, clashes of career ambitions and careless statements of influential bystanders have fanned members of envy into open antagonism. One such example is the statement in a well-intentioned but overzealous commercial newsletter: "Indoctrinating the worker and equipping him to assume and discharge his citizenship responsibility intelligently are most assuredly phases of employee relations, an established area of PR." Control of employee communications is the most frequent bone of contention between these two functions.

The breakdown of specific tasks between the PR and personal and industrial relations showed that are often bounced from one function to the other.

Public relations showed dominance in annual reports; Open house, plant tours; News release on labour negotiations; Maintenance of biographical data on key employees.

Personnel dominant and industrial showed dominance in Suggestions systems; Bulletin boards; Reading racks; New-employee orientation; Exit interviews; Service awards; Recruitment programmes; Pay inserts; Christmas parties.

But in some other cases, Personnel considered dominant but public relations as advisory like: Employee attitude surveys; Employee meetings; Safety-promotion material.

In Employee publications, Employee newsletters; Liaison with civic bodies; Volunteers for local fund collection and Conducting career days felt a sort of responsibility split.

**Understanding Human Resources Development (HRD)**

Beginning in the late 1960s, organisations increased efforts to develop their major resource—people. Following a slow-growth period in the 1970s and early 1980s, the number of human resources development increased rapidly as the economy improved. Potential for confusion and conflict with the public relations function is apparent in the survey results of HRD activities. Among the list of primarily training-oriented tasks, appears "maintaining organisation relationships." Activities include various aspects of employee communication; writing reports, speeches, announcements, and articles for management; and communication with some government and community agencies. HRD specialists also counsel management on a wide range of employee and management issues closely related to the public relations function.

In corporate settings there is increased interest in this new staff function. Whereas, it is sometimes part of the personnel department, HRD departments have been established as separate staff functions. In one case noted by public relations practitioners, the public relations function was made subordinate to the HRD function resulting the designation of some top PR professionals.

As the number of HRD departments increases, public relations practitioners will have to take initiative to coordinate their programmes with HRD efforts to improve organisational relationships with employees, managers, and key outside groups.

### *Towards Better Coordination and Control of Conflict*

One means of increasing coordination and controlling conflicts is to form a communications or public relations committee, or consulting group, that includes the various overlapping or related functions. Formation of policy groups has advantages beyond removing conflicts. There is much to recommend in the occasional bringing together of the best minds available—all the specialists—to thrash out problems affecting the whole organisation.

A main consideration in the formation of such groups is to keep them small enough so they will not collapse of their own weight. Only those intimately concerned should be brought in, and only problems common to all participants in the group should be raised.

A number of the nation's major corporations, in an effort to eliminate overlap and conflict, have tried combining public relations and personnel functions into one department under one director or vice-president. Quaker Oats the public relations director advanced to senior vice-president, with law, public relations, personnel, and the corporate secretary's office under his wing. The conclusion was that public relations covers so many different area.

Most of those involved in this experiment agree that there is logic in combining these functions, at least in small companies and in plant operations away from corporate headquarters.

A large concern that has found having one department for public and industrial relations to be satisfactory is Texaco. Its former senior vice-president, Kerryn King, comments that, "There are any number of arrangements that can work satisfactorily.... In a company that has strong centralised labour negotiations and a high concentration of its employees, I believe it is better to have a separation of the two functions. On the other hand, where the centralised department furnishes primarily functional guidance to the operation departments of the parent company and its affiliates, there are advantages to be derived from the combination set-up."

**The Outside Counsell**

The 2,000 or more public relations counselling firms and agencies in the United States range widely in size and scope of service. Of the twenty largest firms, ten are subsidiaries of large advertising agencies—most acquired only recently as cash-rich advertising agencies.

Critics of this ownership arrangement believe that the firms lose their independence and clients lose the benefit of the counsellor's alternative view in communication planning. Those in firms owned by large advertising agencies point to greater cooperation between the marketing and public relations functions being served by the "full-service" team, better research provided by the more experienced by sophisticated research departments of advertising agencies, greater communication production resources and capabilities, and better management. No doubt the latter claim only strengthens the resolve of those in independent firms to remain autonomous.

Historically, advertising agencies have found it difficult to determine what public relations services to offer, how to effectively organise the function, and how to sustain it apart from marketing whence it derives its tonnage of dollar billings. N.W. Ayer pioneered in 1920, and Albert Frank-Guenther Law took the next step when it expanded its operations to offer a full-fledged public relations and publicity service. In the next few years J. Walter Thompson, Young and Rubicam, and Benton & Bowles followed suit. By the mid-1940s, seventy-five agencies were providing publicity service for clients, according to an Advertising Age survey. In 1953, Advertising age made another survey and concluded, "The role of the public relations department in the advertising agency is a strange one. Many topflight, multimillion dollar agencies still do not have one. Many of those that do regard it purely as a service function."

The attitude of many advertising agencies continues to be one of ambivalence. Wherever, public relations, advertising, and promotional services are all rendered, there is usually an effort to identify the firm as offering a "complete marketing service."

There is a discernible trend toward specialisation among public relations firms. The foremost area is media relations. After that come financial relations, community relations or civic affairs, legislative affairs or lobbying, marketing support, attitude surveys, political campaigns, and fund raising for purposes other than political campaigns. There is specialisation in agriculture, healthcare, religious affairs, sports, a and travel and tourism.

## Listing the Reasons for Retaining Outside Counsell

Chester Burger lists six reasons why organisations retain firms, even though some have internal departments:

(*a*) Management has not previously conducted a formal public relations programme and lacks experience in organising one.
(*b*) Headquarters may be located away from the communications and financial centers.
(*c*) A wide range of up-to-date contacts are maintained by a firm.
(*d*) An outside firm can provide services of experienced executives who would be unwilling to move to other cities or whose salaries could not be afforded by a single organisation.
(*e*) An organisation with its own public relations department may be in need of highly specialised services that it cannot afford on a permanent basis.
(*f*) Crucial matters of overall outside policy dictate a need for the independent judgement of an outsider.

There are ethical procedures by which counselling firms seek clients they feel they can help. Sometimes the client seeks the counselling firm. The client may have a nagging problem, a government regulation of offshore drilling has been for the oil industry. Or a client may perceive an opportunity to capitalise on a situation that requires quick response. Or there may be an emergency, as was the case when researchers announced that a widely used artificial sweetner causes health problems. The announcement created a great deal of media coverage and called for responses on both national and international scales.

In an emergency situation the counsel has no choice. There must be immediate effort to correct existing communications problems. Either later or simultaneously, the sources of the breakdown can be investigated and preventive measures for the future suggested.

But in normal circumstances the counsel will begin the service to a new client by exploring the health of the relationships between the client and those publics on whom the client depends. This is sometimes called a "public relations audit." The initial exploration might take months. When it is completed, one of three things can be expected to happen: (*a*) The counsellor tells the client that there is no problem or threat of harm in communication of a magnitude to require outside assistance; or (*b*) that the problems disclosed by the research are not in the counsellor's area of expertise; or (*c*) that there are problems that can be solved through the application of public relations techniques.

In the last case the counsel usually arranges to make a presentation outlining the central core of the difficulty; its current status in terms of harm to the organisation; related difficulties that must be considered; ultimate alternatives to be faced; desirable objectives; a long-range plan toward the objectives and an immediate programme of action involving anything pertinent, even if it involves the removal of a senior official, or an aggressive published response to an allegation.

Not all factors in a presentation are invariably exposed at one sitting. However, to establish a suitable working climate, the counsellor must obtain an agreement over the full range before the firm's talents can be committed sincerely to the tasks. The counsel submits progress reports, holds periodic meetings with key people in the client's organisation and coordinates the programme.

As the counsellor-client relationship matures, the shape of the client's enterprise may probably changes. Action and communication programmes are revamped, scrapped, or replaced. New ones are activated.

The counsellor usually functions in one of three ways with clients:

(*i*) Provides advice, leaving the execution of plans to others.
(*ii*) Provides advice and undertakes full execution of plans.
(*iii*) Provides advice and collaborates with the client's staff to execute the plans.

Counsellors rank variety of talents and skills as their greatest advantage, compared with internal staffing. Their objectivity, as relatively free agents untrammeled by the politics within an organisation, ranks second. The range of prior experience is third, the geographical scope of their operations fourth, and the ability to reinforce and upgrade a client's internal staff fifth.

A number of counsellors emphasise the flexibility of their staff and their operations as a prime advantage. In their shops, or no farther away than the telephone, are artists or models, copy editors, magazine-article writers or placement specialists, talk-show experts, lawyers and home economists. A client can say what is needed or wanted now, and an account executive can attend to the need immediately.

Flexibility is also tied to scope of operations and to range of experience. From an office in New York, Washington, or Chicago, the counsellor can serve clients in Figi, Canada and Colombo. If that becomes impractical, the counsellor can open branch offices in major population centers. Services can be exchanged with firms in other cities and countries. With new satellite communication technologies and frequent meetings made possible by efficient air travel, intimate contact can be maintained. In a few cases, practitioners from firms actually set-up shop on clients' premises.

Sometimes the counsellor's reputation is a major advantage. Outside "experts" can often introduce ideas that internal staffers have struggled unsuccessfully to place on the agenda. Knowing that the counsellor's reputation and subsequent referrals are on the line helps ensure performance.

In the course of any year a counsellor will be confronted with many different communications problems. Typical would be a strike, a protest movement on skyrocketing hospital costs, the introduction of a new product, prospective unwanted legislation, and the inauguration of a university president. The range of a successful counsellor's services is wide. In a sense, a public relations firm is a repository of living case histories. Each project adds to its fund of knowledge. Experience and versatility of staff make this synergy possible. The counsellor approaches each case bolstered by familiarity with the type of situation and knowledge of the success or failure that attended previous encounters.

## Listing the Handicaps of Counsellors

The rendering of a counselling service—and this applies to almost all consultants—with rare exception, meets with some opposition ranging from non-acceptance to antagonism. This is, at least in theory, the counsellor's most serious handicap. The resistance to outsiders is a natural human trait. The old guard resists change—the new idea, the new approach, the new look—as a threat to its security. This resistance is almost a certainty in organisations that have been static for years. Perhaps what they need most is a new look in public relations; but they put up resistance—probably plenty of it—and this is logical. That does not mean that a new idea is no good. Hostility comes naturally when drastic or sudden changes are proposed.

The counsellor, more often than not, is in—the position of having to suggest changes designed to improve relationships. And whether the changes involve policies, equipment, methods, or practices, the people originally responsible for them can be alienated by these suggestions. Their realm is being invaded; their judgement is being criticised. The offended ask, "What does this outsider know about our organisation... our way of doing things?"

Counsellors, however, do not rank this problem at the top. They overwhelmingly cite questions of cost as the chief bugaboo with clients. They list "threat to old guard and set ways" as the second most persistent handicap. Resistance to "outside" advice comes in third, and fourth is unforseen conflicts of personality or conviction.

Other problems expressed frequently by counsellors are a stubborn lack of understanding of public relations by clients, client inertia when it comes to doing what counsellors think ought to be done; and the unavailability of clients, presumably the decision-makers, at times when counsellors want decisions. This would suggest a problem of priorities.

Whatever, the first stumbling block—costs, threat to the status quo, resistance to change, or inertia—others can pile up. Insiders may attempt to discredit the counsellor. The anxieties of insiders and old-timers can be barriers. A finger of concern can be pointed at the cost of the proposed services or programme. A question can be raised as to guarantee of return on investment. Accusation can be made of the counsellor's superficial grasp of the organisation's unique problems—the local and historical angles to the problems, the sacred cows, the "things we never talk about." Under such circumstances it is uphill all the way for the counsellor.

The service of a counselling firm may be obtained for a specific project or for a continuing service, reviewable and renewable at intervals.

Fees for continuing services are usually established in one of four ways—A monthly retainer; A retainer plus monthly billing for actual staff time on an hourly basis or per diem basis; A base fee, billed monthly, to which are added increments for services performed beyond the retainer and Straight hourly charges.

Out-of-pocket expenses are generally billed at cost and are exclusive of the fee. There are wide variations in fees. Large counseling firms have charged exorbitant fees as counselling. At the other end of the scale, counselling firms may provide a minimal service, such as writing occasional news releases. Hourly fees for assistant account executives or other junior staff. The figures differ from city to city, but four elements are reflected in counselling fees and charges. They are the cost of the staff used on the project; executive time and supervision; overhead costs, and a reasonable profit for doing the work.

## Towards Integrating the Function

A significant indication that public relations is integrated and having an impact in an organisation appears when people begin to tell each other that candor in communication is the best policy and socially responsible actions are in the best interest of the organisation. This means that public relations consciousness is gaining ground and there is growing confidence in the staff.

With the appearance of this important symptom, the public relations group can actually apply more candor in communication and action wherever it may have been lacking. The various groups sharing in the organisation can be told more of what they want to know. Outsiders can be helped to get any kind of look into the organisation that they want.

The exposure to public gaze of a clean organisation, operating in the mutual interests of itself and its publics, does not mean that everything about the organisation should be blurted out. In business there are competitors to think of. In the military there are security considerations. In health institutions there are ethical qualifications. In government agencies there are political and regulatory factors. Every where there are legal pros and cons. Common-sense helps, but organisations must have in place staff and strategies for dealing with their social environments.

## CASE STUDY: DESIGNING WEBSITES AND GUIDELINES

Journalists often work under tight deadlines.

This statement may not seem like a brilliant new insight, but it leads directly to many of our guidelines for how to design corporate websites that are both usable for journalists and deliver the desired public relations impact. Most of the PR sections of sites we have studied failed to support journalists in their quest for facts, information, and points of contact that they can use when they write stories about companies or their products.

Websites must be painfully clear about what a company does and what products and services it offers. Websites for high-tech start-ups are notorious for presenting generic, buzzword—filled mission statements that could apply equally well to both their worst competitors and companies producing completely different products.

Websites must provide fast access to basic facts and figures, as well as a simple way to contact a live human being in the PR department. Journalists don't have time to wade through deep, complex navigation trees or sift factual wheat from marketing chaff. In particular, pages must present information in well-organized chunks that are easy to scan. Distracting animations and irrelevant stock photography of smiling people do not help journalists who are in a hurry to find facts.

If journalists cannot find what they are looking for on a website, it could impact whether they include information about that company in the story. Journalists repeatedly said that poor website usability could reduce or completely eliminate their press coverage of a company. For example, after having a difficult time using a site, one journalist said:

"... I would be reluctant to go back to the site. If I had a choice to write about something else, then I would write about something else."

Another journalist described what he'd do when he could not find a press contact, or any of the facts he needed for his story:

"Better not to write it than to get it wrong. I might avoid the subject altogether."

Many journalists are freelancers or work from home, typically using slow dial-up connections. Many have old computer equipment and do not feel an obsessive need to download all the latest software. Thus, non-standard data formats or cutting-edge technologies tend to clog their limited Internet connections and sometimes even crash their computers. It is wise to ensure that all your Web pages work on low-end home computers running several years' old software. We recommend that sites present all press information as simple, standard HTML, designed for minimal download times.

**Understanding Journalists' Information Needs**

The Web is one of the most important research tools for journalists. When asked how they would get basic information about a company, all the journalists in our study said that they would begin by doing some Web research. About half the journalists started by visiting the target company's website; the other half started by searching an outside service (mainly Google, but also traditional services like Dow Jones Interactive and Lexis-Nexis). This finding emphasizes the necessity for having a clean corporate website with a clearly labeled Press or PR section that can quickly provide answers for journalists. It also emphasizes the need to be well represented in external search services and databases, especially since the trend over time is that more journalists are relying on search engines (mainly Google at the time of this writing).

Journalists are not gullible, and they do not take a company's own word as truth. On the contrary, they almost all stressed that press releases are useful only to find out how a company is trying to position itself. We strongly recommend that a company's PR area have links to external sources, including press coverage, since articles from independent newspapers and magazines are often considered to be much more credible than the company's own press releases. We have seen similar findings in studies of prospective customers evaluating products on consumer—and business-oriented sites, so links to external press coverage will also help promote sales.

The top-five reasons journalists gave for visiting a company's website are:

- Find a PR contact (name and telephone number).
- Check basic facts about the company (spelling of an executive's name, his/her age, headquarters location, etc.).
- Discover the company's own spin on events.
- Check financial information.
- Download images to use as illustrations in stories.

This basic information must be easy to find and should be cleansed of the marketese and excessive verbiage that smother the facts on many sites.

### Evaluating Success Rate

In our usability study, thirty-two journalists attempted to use the press areas of eighteen websites to gather information for hypothetical story assignments. Among other tasks, the journalists tried to find basic information about each company's financials, management, commitment to social responsibility, and PR telephone number.

On average, journalists found the answer to each one of these simple questions 70 per cent of the time.

In some ways, a 70 per cent task success rate is a reasonably good outcome for a Web usability study. In a *study of 20 B2C e-commerce sites,* we measured an average success rate of 56 per cent for shopping tasks; success rates around 50-60 per cent are the norm in many Web usability studies.

There are two reasons that this study had a slightly higher success rate than other studies:

- Our test users were professional journalists; in other words, they are people who are highly skilled at ferreting out information.
- The information-finding tasks were very focussed and could often be answered by finding a single piece of information on the site. Broader questions like "Which product should I buy?" are typically more difficult to answer.

A website success rate of 70 per cent implies the site has a failure rate of 30 per cent, which is considered an unacceptably low quality level for more traditional products. It is astounding that we have become so accustomed to seeing difficult websites that we can consider a 30 per cent failure rate a reasonably positive outcome when it comes to usability.

To look at our results in another way, leaving 30 per cent of press inquiries unanswered would be considered a very poor performance for most traditional PR departments.

Luckily, the situation is improving. We conducted this research in two rounds. In the first study the success rate was only 68 per cent; by the time of the second study, the success rate had increased to 73 per cent.

Even better, our two rounds of testing revealed that the biggest improvement in success rate was for the most critical of the tasks: finding the PR contact's telephone number. Although a website can answer many basic questions and provide them great help, journalists still almost always want to talk to a person. In the first round, our test users found a PR telephone number only 55 per cent of the time, but by the second round, the success rate for this key task had reached 82 per cent.

Here are two quotes from journalists who had a particularly difficult time trying to find a PR contact and financial information:

> "I'm sure I saw an *E-mail us*, but I forget where it was. I never know if someone is reading the e-mail. It's not uncommon for me to have a deadline today, and I wouldn't use e-mail if I needed it today. I would go without a quote from Merck."

> "My momentary frustration, I like to think it will not spill over into my story. But it makes me wonder about the competence of the people in the company. You know journalists use the site. Makes me think someone is being evasive, or that they are incompetent."

The ability to find information on a PR site has a strong impact on the journalists' impression of the site and thus on the way they perceive the company. Sites where users have a high success rate are rated highly, and sites where they have a lower success rate are rated much lower, as shown in the correlation diagram in this report. The correlation between the success rate and subjective satisfaction is $r = .63$, which is a fairly strong outcome for a human factors experiment.

## Towards International Usability

All companies, except maybe the corner grocery store, need an international business strategy for their websites. This is true for a site's e-commerce offers, for customer service, for content strategy, and it's true for PR. Don't ignore international PR because you assume your overseas agencies are handling it. Even if they do a good job, your corporate website still plays a role in international PR, since journalists from all countries are likely to visit the site.

Usability for domestic users was not good, and it was a little worse for overseas users. Among our test users, we included journalists from both the United States and Europe, and we included both U.S. and European companies among the tested sites. Usability dropped slightly when a test had an international component, such as testing a European company with U.S. journalists or a U.S. company with European journalists.

We have seen more severe findings in much of our other usability research. In general, international usability is sorely neglected on the Web today. This is true despite the fact that it's called the World Wide Web and the even more important fact that any website will attract international users the moment it is placed on the Internet.

Providing a perfect site for international users can be difficult, but the most basic *guidelines for international usability* are reasonably simple. For example, we had cases where journalists thought that a list of press releases contained nothing but old news because of a violation of one of the most basic internationalization guidelines: Use proper date formats. When the top press release on a site was dated 10-03-2000, a European user naturally assumed that it had been released on the 10th of March and concluded that the site was stale. This test session was conducted in late 2000, and the press release was in fact dated October 3rd, something that would have been communicated better by spelling out the name of the month in the date.

## Design Guidelines

This report contains seventy-five design guidelines that, if followed, will improve the usability of a corporate website's PR area. Most of these guidelines may seem fairly obvious. Because the usability field aims to make user interfaces simple and easy to understand, our design guidelines are almost always grounded in common-sense. In the world of Web design, however, common-sense is not nearly common enough. For example, the eighteen sites we studied in this project complied with only 69 per cent of our advice about how to present press releases online.

To improve the usability of your website PR efforts, we recommend the following process:

First, conduct an internal audit. Take a hard look at your site relative to the design guidelines in this report. Count how many guidelines you systematically follow, how many you systematically violate, and how many you follow only sporadically. Assign fractional credit for partial compliance, using a rough estimate of how frequently a given guideline is followed or violated. Average your score across all the guidelines. Ideally, you should have about 90 per cent compliance. If your score is less than 75 per cent, your PR area probably has severe usability problems and is far from fulfilling its potential. If your score is lower than 50 per cent, you probably need an urgent redesign.

Second, take one more hard look at your online PR information and determine how well it supports the journalists' tasks and preferences described in this report. If journalists arrive at your homepage under extreme deadline pressure, will they get what they need? Impress on all your writers, designers, and other PR site staff how important it is to deliver concise answers to users' questions.

Third, consider conducting *your own usability testing*, using methods similar to those described at the end of this report. Ask reporters who cover your industry to test your site. This is guaranteed to reveal numerous opportunities for usability improvement.

We tested the PR sections of eighteen websites, including major multi-national companies, high-tech start-ups, and government agencies. Every site had significant usability problems. At some point in every single test session, journalists said that they would have to leave the site because it failed to deliver what they needed. Don't bet on your site being the first exception to this finding. Instead, use this report to help discover the usability issues with your site and fix them.

### Study Overview

The purpose of our research project was to learn which website designs are easy or difficult for journalists to use and why. We studied how journalists find information on the Web, and what impact site usability has on them.

This study was conducted in two stages. In the first stage we studied twenty journalists: fifteen based in New York City and five in Copenhagen, Denmark. In stage two, twelve journalists participated: two based in New York City, six based in Boston, and four based in London. Participants were given tasks to perform and were asked to think out loud as they worked.

We studied websites from eighteen companies of varied sizes and from different industries. Most sites were American companies, but some were European. The sites we tested were:

- BMW, www.bmw.com
- Deutsche Bank, http://group.deutsche-bank.de/ghp/index_e.htm
- Fidelity Investments, www.fidelity.com
- GlaxoSmithKline (pharmaceutical), www.gsk.com/index.htm
- Hemscott (financial), www.hemscott.net
- Merck (pharmaceutical), www.merck.com
- Nokia, www.nokia.com
- Pace Micro Technologies, Americas (digital home gateways), www.pacemicro.com
- Philip Morris, www.philipmorris.com
- Qwest Communications International, www.qwest.com
- SeeItFirst (interactive streaming media solutions and services), www.seeitfirst.com
- State of Maine, www.maine.gov
- Tellme (interactive voice portal), www.tellme.com
- Tyco (electronics and telecommunications), www.tyco.com
- United Colors of Benetton (retail clothing), www.benetton.com
- United States Patent Office www.uspto.gov
- Vivendi Universal (entertainment), www.vivendi-universal.com/vu2/en/_home/home.cfm
- Wal-Mart Stores, Inc., www.walmart.com

For more thorough information about methodology, users, and site selection, refer to the following sections of this report: About the Sites Studied, About Participants and Methodology.

By the time you read this, several of the websites will have updated their design. This is fine. In fact, we hope that all of the sites will remove all of the usability problems we found. The screenshots in the report and our comments refer to the designs that were in place during our user tests. The lessons learned are still valid and are still useful for other sites, even after the site where we observed a mistake has stopped making that mistake.

# Bibliography


A. O'Brein (1995). *Management Information Systems—A Managerial End Users Perspective*, New Delhi: Galgotia Publications Ltd.

A.M. McDonough (1963). *Information Economics and Management Systems*, New York, McGraw Hill, p. 5.

Aggerholm, Barbar (1993). *'UW to probe offensive images in computer network'*. Kitchener Waterloo Record Tuesday, 20 July: 1.

Baroudi, J., Olson, M.H. and Ives B. (1986). "An Empirical Study of the Impact of User Involvement of System Usage and Information Satisfaction," *Communications of ACM*, Vol. 29, pp. 232-238.

Chawla, N.L. (1982-83). "T.V. Networking Through INSAT-1B", *The Times of India*, Delhi, Oct. 20, 1983.

Clarke Caywood, (1997). *The Handbook of Strategic Public Relations and Integrated Communications*, McGraw Hill, New York, p. 23.

Darnton, Robert, (1982). *The Literary Underground of the Old Regime*, Cambridge, MA: Harvard University Press.

David Phillips 'Online Public Relations'.

Dean, "A Comparison of Decision Tables Against Conventional COBOL as a Programming Tool for Commercial Applications," *Software World*, Spring 1971.

Doll, D.R. (1977). Data Communications: Facilities, Network and Systems Design. New York: John Wiley and Sons.

Douglas, Mary (1982). *In the Active Voice*, London; RKP.

Duncanson, John and Pron, Nick, (1993). 'Computerised bulletin boards abuzz with Homolka trial details', *Toronto Star*, 31 July: A3.

Eapen, K.E. (1979). "The Cultural Content of SITE", *Journal of Communication*, Vol. 29 (4), Autumn, p. 112.

Eapen, K.E. and Thakur, B.S. (1989), *Journalism/Communication Alumni: Their Assessment of Professional Education*. A study sponsored by the University Grants Commission, New Delhi. Printed in Bangalore: The research findings referred to in this paper can be seen on pp. 53, 57- 60.

Edstrom, A. (1977). "User Influence and the Success of MIS Projects: A Contingency Approach," *Human Relations*, Vol. 30, No. 7 pp. 589-607.

Gallop, Jane, (1988). Thinking Through the Body. New York: Columbia University Press.

Globe and Mail (1993). 'Public's right to know gains here, loses there'. Globe and Mail, 2 December: Al.

Gooderham, Mary (1994). 'College drives sex titles off info highway'. *Globe and Mail*, 5 February: 1.

Greenberg, Alan and Hull, Ron, (1992). 'What is Usenet?'. *McGill University Computing Centre Newsletter*. May/June: 2-7.

H.A. Goddard, (1958). *Principles of Administration Applied to Nursing Service*, World Health Organisation, Geneva, p. 84.

Hafner, Katie and Markoff, John, (1991). *Cyberpunk: Outlaws and Hackers on the Computer Frontier*. London: Fourth Estate.

Harold Burson, *e pluribus unum—The Making of Burson-Marsteller*, (2004).

Hopper, Max.D. (1990). 'Rattling SABRE—New Ways to Compete on Information', *Harvard Business Review*, May-June 1990.

International Association of Business Communicators (IABC) Bookstore.

Ives, B. and Baroudi, J.J. (1983). "The Measurement of User Information Satisfaction" *Communications of ACM*, 10, 26, pp. 785-793.

J.E. Grunig and T. Hunt, (1984). *Managing Public Relations*, Thomson Learning.

Jacqmotte, Benoit and Broadhurst, Michael, (1993). 'Homolka newsgroup suspended', *McGill Tribune*, 16-22 November: 8.

Jim Macnamara's, (2005). *Public Relations Handbook (New Edition)*.

John Stauber and Sheldon Rampton, (1995). Toxic Sludge Is Good For You: Lies, Damn Lies and the Public Relations Industry.

Joshi, P.O. (1983). "Television, Culture and Communication", *Mainstream*, June 4, 1983, p. 20.

Joyce Nelson, (1989). *Sultans of Sleaze: Public Relations and the Media*, Between the lines.

Keith, Davis, (1972). *Human Behavior at Work*, New York: McGraw-Hill Book Co., p. 517.

Larry Tye, (1998). The Father of Spin: Edward L. Bernays and the Birth of Public Relations.

Mody, Bella (1979). "Programming for SITE", *Journal of Communication*, Vol. 29 (4), Autumn, p. 91.

Petrek, Melissa and St. Jude 1992. 'Putting It On The Line'. *Mondo 2000*, 6: 113-15.

*Public Relations Bookshop.*

Raymond, Eric, (1991). *The New Hacker's Dictionary.* Cambridge, MA: MIT Press.

Scott Cutlip, *The Unseen Power: Public Relations: A History.*

Singh, J.P. (1983). "Satellite Communications", *Communicator*, Vol. 18 (2), April 1983, p. 20.

Skornia, H.J. (1965). *Television and Society—An Inquest and Agenda for Improvement*, McGraw Hill Paperbacks.

Spigel, Lynn, (1992). *Make Room for TV: Television and the Family Ideal in Postwar America*, Chicago: University of Chicago Press.

Stephenson, Neal, (1993). 'Smiley's people'. *The New Republic*. 13 September: 26.

Stuart Ewen, *PR! A Social History of Spin.*

Young, T.R. and Swartzman, G. (1974). Public Opinion, Tradition and Information Half-life, *Intl. Jl. of General System*, Vol. 1, 259-261.

# Index